Semănătorul

The Journal of Ministry and Biblical Research
Volume 1, Number 1.

Emanuel University of Oradea, Romania

The Proceedings of the Bi-Annual International Theological Conference of the Department of Theology in Emanuel University of Oradea. The Conference Title was: "Hebrews in its Historical Context and Theological Significance."

Editors: Dr Hamilton Moore (QUB, Belfast); Dr Ilie Soritau and Dr Adrian Giorgiov (Emanuel University, Oradea).

Editorial Advisor: Dr Eunicia Ile (Emanuel Publishing House, Oradea).

WIPF & STOCK · Eugene, Oregon

Wipf and Stock Publishers
199 W 8th Ave, Suite 3
Eugene, OR 97401

Semanatorul (The Sower), Volume One, Number One
By Moore, Hamilton and Soritau, Ilie
Copyright©2018 Apostolos
ISBN 13: 978-1-5326-6958-3
Publication date 9/23/2018
Previously published by Apostolos, 2018

Contacting the Editorial Board

Universitatea Emanuel din Oradea
Str. Nufărului nr. 87
410597 Oradea, ROMÂNIA
Tel./Fax: +40 259.426.692
Email: contact@emanuel.ro

Facultatea de Teologie
Mirela Csaki, Secretară
Email: teologie@emanuel.ro
Tel.: +40 359.405.602

Dr Hamilton Moore (Editor)
Semănătorul (The Sower) the Emanuel Journal of Ministry and Biblical Research
Universitatea Emanuel din Oradea
Str. Nufărului nr. 87
410597 Oradea, ROMÂNIA
Email dr.hamilton.moore@gmail.com
Tel.: +40 781 259 1743

This first volume of Semănătorul (The Sower): The Journal of Ministry and Biblical Research, has been produced through the collaboration of Emanuel University Press, the Emanuel "Ethics and Society" Research Centre and distinguished colleagues from the Hungarian Baptist Academy. The publishing efforts were aided by Dr. Almási Tibor, Rector, Hungarian Baptist Academy.

The volume comprises the Proceedings of the International Theological Conference held by the Department of Theology on 6th May 2016 in Emanuel University of Oradea. The theme of the Conference was Hebrews: Its Historical Context and Theological Significance. For many scholars, Hebrews 13:22 gives some guidance concerning the nature of the epistle, "Bear with my word of exhortation, for I have written to you briefly." The suggestion is that the background may be a sermon, given on a certain occasion and then later adapted into letter form with the addition of personal comments at the end. But what of its readers? It is thought that the first readers were Hebrews and the camp of 13:13, ancient Judaism. They were Jews attracted to the Christian community and who had identified with it. But Christianity had none of the "ritual trappings" they had known, no altar, no priests, no sacrifices. They were meeting ridicule, opposition, imprisonment and being disowned and disinherited by their families (10:32). Some had coped well with this adversity, but others were looking back to the temple from where they had come (10:32–39). Was not Judaism God-ordained?

The author of Hebrews seeks to set before them the "better things" which have become theirs: a better priesthood, better sanctuary, better sacrifice, better covenant, true access to the very presence of the Most High (10:19–21). Also the "greater things," that is: Christ greater than angels, Moses, Joshua, and Aaron.

The Proceedings Papers in this Journal will touch upon some of the aspects of the situation outlined above. The significance of the opening verses of Hebrews for the whole epistle is outlined in the opening paper. Other papers focus on the themes endurance, pilgrimage, "echoes" in interpretation, a comparison of the epistle with Philo, the significance of "the time of reformation" for worship in Hebrews, a semiotic approach regarding Psalm 2 and the profile of the "Son," the concept of repentance and critique of the perspectives of George Milligan regarding the importance of the epistle.

Emanuel University continues to be a strong witness as a conservative university in all of Europe. It should be understood that the sources highlighted and the views presented in these papers remain those of the contributors themselves.

Hamilton Moore, Editor.

CONTENTS

THE EPISTLE TO THE HEBREWS: THE IMPORTANCE OF THE OPENING VERSES (1:1–4)..............7

by Maurice Dowling

THE CONCEPT OF ENDURANCE IN THE EPISTLE TO THE HEBREWS: KEY ELEMENTS AND THEIR RELATION TO CHRISTIAN EXPERIENCE 17

by Peter G. Firth

HEBREWS 13:15–16. THE NEW WORSHIP BY THE NEW PRIESTHOOD IN THE "TIME OF REFORMATION" 27

by Hamilton Moore

ECHOES AND INTERPRETATION IN HEBREWS....................................37

by George H. Guthrie

PILGRIMAGE IN THE BOOK OF HEBREWS 50

by István Borzási

PHILO OF ALEXANDRIA AND THE EPISTLE TO THE HEBREWS ON THE CONCEPT OF THE SPIRITUALIZATION OF THE CULT 67

by Aurelian Botica

THE USE OF THE PHRASE "YOU ARE MY SON." A SEMIOTIC APPROACH TO THE PROFILE OF THE SON IN HEBREWS 1:5a......................................93

by Calin Ioan Talos

WHEN OLD AND NEW COLLIDE: THE PERSPECTIVES OF GEORGE MILLIGAN ON THE RELEVANCE OF THE EPISTLE TO THE HEBREWS..........................105

by Ciprian Simuț

METANOIA IN HEBREWS: EXEGETICAL INSIGHTS 115

by Ovidiu Hanc

THE EPISTLE TO THE HEBREWS: THE IMPORTANCE OF THE OPENING VERSES (1:1–4)

MAURICE DOWLING[*]

ABSTRACT: The opening verses (Hebrews 1:1–4) form one sentence in Greek. The first four verses set out in a very condensed style the principal features of the Son's superiority and significance. We find here a series of seven statements setting out who the Son is and what he has achieved. These verses have been described as setting out the programme for the whole letter. While not being an "agenda" in the modern sense they certainly announce important themes to be developed in the epistle.

KEY WORDS: last days, son, heir, Royal Psalm, angels.

Hebrews 1:1–4 (NRSV)[1]

[1] Long ago God spoke to our ancestors in many and various ways by the prophets, [2] but in these last days he has spoken to us by a Son, whom he appointed heir of all things, through whom he also created the worlds. [3] He is the reflection of God's glory and the exact imprint of God's very being, and he sustains all things by his powerful word. When he had made purification for sins, he sat down at the right hand of the Majesty on high, [4] having become as much superior to angels as the name he has inherited is more excellent than theirs.

Heb 1:1–4 represents one sentence in Greek. The central point of the passage is that "God has spoken by a Son." The writer emphasizes the continuity between this "speaking" and God's message through "the prophets" – a shorthand way of referring to "the Old Testament." This continuity is one of the letter's major themes. The writer does not suggest that the Jewish faith and ritual were a false religion, he does not deny their God-given character, but he aims to demonstrate their provisional nature. The opening sentence indicates that what has been said in the past has its culmination and fulfilment in, and indeed has been superseded by, the revelation through God's Son. "In these last days" means much more than simply "recently." "Last days" is an OT phrase used to indicate a new stage in God's involvement in the history of his people and the writer adds "these" to emphasize that this new stage has been inaugurated through what God has done and revealed by the person and work of his Son.

English translations reflect the absence of the Greek definite article before "Son" by using the English indefinite, "a Son." However, the writer has a clear emphasis on the uniqueness of this Son and wishes to highlight the distinction between him and "the prophets." One of the letter's recurring themes is the superiority of the Son over (i) the angels, and (ii) anything relating to the old covenant. The first four verses set out in a very condensed style the principal features of the Son's superiority and significance, using a series of seven statements explaining who the Son is and what he has achieved. In a perspective which has been popular in Christian theology since the Middle Ages, the writer has introduced Christ as a prophet through whom God speaks; he now proceeds to show him to be the lord over the universe who reigns as king at God's right hand, and also the priest who effects the purification of God's people.

The Son's role in creation and providence is emphasized in phrases which resemble the teaching of passages such as John 1:1–3 and Col 1:15–18. Against the background of the OT teaching on the distinction between God and creation the writer is emphasizing that the Son belongs in the category

[*] MAURICE DOWLING (BA BD MTH PhD) Irish Baptist College, Moira, N. Ireland. Tutor in Old Testament, Historical Theology and Church History. Recognised Teacher of Queens University, Belfast and Chester University. Dr. Dowling went to be with the Lord on December 10th 2015. This summary of his introductory paper on Hebrews is published as a memorial to him.
[1] The translation used in this article is The New Revised Standard Version.

"creator" rather than "things created." The reference to "his powerful word" echoes the OT theme of the creative and active word and wisdom of God, which is now related specifically to God's Son. His being "appointed heir of all things" indicates his sovereignty over the universe – he is the one to whom all things belong by right – and the phrase echoes Ps 2:8, a Psalm which plays an important part in the writer's presentation of Christ. Ps 2, one of the "royal Psalms," depicts the king as being given lordship over the nations as his "inheritance" and "the ends of the earth" as his possession. The writer to the Hebrews links these ideas with Christ.

The high Christology of these verses is demonstrated by the very graphic statement that the Son is the "reflection ($\alpha\pi\alpha\upsilon\gamma\alpha\sigma\mu\alpha$, "radiance," only used here in the NT) of God's glory and the exact imprint of God's being." The basic thrust is that what God essentially is, is manifested in his Son. $\alpha\pi\alpha\upsilon\gamma\alpha\sigma\mu\alpha$ is used in the LXX of Wisdom 7:26, which says that Wisdom is "a reflection of eternal light, a spotless mirror of the working of God, and an image of his goodness." God's glory is an essential attribute of God, which cannot be communicated to a creature – Isa 42:8; 48:11. Christ <u>is</u> (and not simply reveals) the glory of God (cf. John 17:4 – where Christ speaks of sharing the glory of God). The "imprint of [God's] being" is an even stronger metaphor than $\epsilon\iota\kappa\bar{o}\nu$, "image" (Col 1:15).

Hebrews thinks in terms of an interweaving of creation and salvation (cf. 2:10) and the opening verses emphasize that the Son whose lordship and uniqueness have been presented was also the one who "made purification for sins." This is an obvious use of a theme from the Levitical system, a theme which will receive extensive coverage in the letter's later chapters. Having made this purification the writer introduces the idea of "Christ seated at the right hand of God," which was one of the earliest affirmations of Christianity, based on Jesus's use of Ps 110 in Matt 22:44; 26:64 (and parallels). The text is also quoted or alluded to in Acts 2:33f; 7:56; Rom 8:34. Ps 110 plays an important part in our writer's understanding of Christ, but he goes further than other NT usage by dwelling on the significance of Christ as "priest in the order of Melchizedek" (Ps 110:4). The phrase implies the doctrine of the Ascension and the Son's being "seated" is stressed in 10:12, in contrast with Aaronic priests who stood because their sacrificial service never came to an end.

The concluding clause of the introduction introduces the theme of the Son's superiority over angels, which will be developed at some length in the following verses (possibly aimed at some kind of excessive angelology known to the writer and readers). The use of "became" here suggests that the Son, through his priestly work and exaltation, has achieved, in the sense of having publicly demonstrated, a superiority over these rather mysterious, supernatural beings. The Son is "better" than the angels; "better" is one of the letter's key words – e.g. the focus on "a better hope," "better promises," "a better covenant," "better sacrifices," the blood which speaks of something "better" than Abel's. The Son's being "better" than angels is related to his "more excellent" name. This may refer to the status which he has as Son, and specifically in the context of the passage to his status as the Son at the right hand of the Father. It may also echo the distinctive references in 2 Sam 7 to the "name" which God promises to the royal line of David, by which the name of God itself will be honoured (2 Sam 7 was a passage of some significance for our writer).

The opening verses have been described as setting out the programme for the whole letter. While not being an "agenda" in the modern sense they certainly announce important themes to be developed.

THE LETTER TO THE HEBREWS

Chapter 1 The Son's superiority over angels

A.   Continuity between God's revelation through "the prophets" and his final word spoken through his Son (1:1–2a)

B.   Seven statements about the Son (1:2b–4)

   i.   whom God appointed heir of all things.
   ii.   through whom God made the universe.
   iii.   who is the *apaugasma* of the glory and the *charaktēr* of the being of God.
   iv.   who sustains all things by his word of power.
   v.   who provided purification for sins.
   vi.   who sat down at the right hand of the Majesty in heaven.
   vii.   who is superior to the angels in being and in "name."

C.   Seven OT quotations to make the author's point (1:5–13)

   i.   Ps 2:7
   ii.   2Sam 7:14
   iii.   Deut 32:43 (LXX); cf. Ps 97:7
   iv.   Ps 104:4
   v.   Ps 45:6f
   vi.   Ps 102:25ff
   vii.   Ps 110:1

Emphasizing: the Son's unique relationship to the Father; the Son's enthronement; the Son's superiority to angels; the Son's eternal reign and role in relation to the universe.

Chapter 2 The Son's humanity

A.   First of the "warning passages:" an *a fortiori* argument – "If the message spoken by angels was binding, then how much more…" (2:1–4).

B.   The privileged position of man (2:5–8).

   i.   argument based on Ps 8:4–6 – everything subject, but not yet subject, to him

C.   The Son also became lower than angels but is now crowned with glory and honour because of his suffering (2:9).

D.   The significance of the suffering of the Son (2:10–18).

Christ:

   i.   tastes death on our behalf –v. 9;
   ii.   brings us to glory – v. 10;
   iii.   is *archēgos* of our salvation – v. 10;
   iv.   makes us sons/children – vv. 10,13f;
   v.   makes us his brothers – v. 11f;
   vi.   sanctifies us – v. 11;
   vii.   partakes of our nature – v. 14;
   viii.   defeats the devil – v. 14;
   ix.   delivers us from fear – v. 15;

x.   comes to our aid – vv. 16 (?),18;

xi.   becomes our High Priest – v. 17;

xii.   makes possible mercy and forgiveness – v. 17.

E. The "angel theme" runs through the two chapters:

i.   the Son's superiority over the angels

ii.   heeding the "angelic word" superseded by heeding the Son's word

iii.   mankind made "a little lower than angels"

iv.   the Son becoming "a little lower than angels"

v.   divine purpose: to save mankind rather than angels

Chapter 3

A. The superiority of Jesus, "the apostle and high priest of our confession," over Moses, although both were "faithful" (3:1–6).

B. A warning against unbelief, based on Ps 95:7c-11 (3:7–19).

The significance of the wilderness wanderings, particularly the Massah ("testing") and Meribah ("quarrelling") incidents of Exod 17 and Num 20.

Chapter 4

A. A "rest" for the people of God (4:1–7).

i.   The significance of Ps 95 extended by reference to Gen 2.

B. An implied comparison – Joshua and Jesus, and the superiority of the latter (4:8–10).

ii.   The provisional nature of the "rest" provided through Joshua and the prospect of entering God's "rest."

C. Application and warning (4:11–13).

iii.   The significance of "the word of God"

D. Resumption of the theme of Jesus as our High Priest (4:14–16)

i.   He has "passed through the heavens."

ii.   continuing the theme of arriving at a destination (the "rest" theme)

iii.   anticipating the theme of Jesus as our "forerunner" (6:20)

iv.   He is the Son of God.

v.   He shares out nature.

vi.   We can approach God's throne with "confidence" (cf. 3:6; 10:19,35).

vii.   We should hold fast to our "confession" (cf. 3:1; also 10:23).

Chapter 5

A.   Jesus qualified to be High Priest (5:1–10).

i.   chosen from among men.

ii.   appointed by God: Ps 2:7; Ps 110:4.

iii.   Melchizedek.

B.   Spiritual immaturity of the readers (5:11–14).

Chapter 6

A.   Going on to maturity (6:1–3).

  i.   the "elementary teachings."

B.   Warning against falling away (6:4–8).

  i.   "It is impossible…."
  ii.   agricultural illustration.

C.   Confidence and exhortation (6:9–12).

D.   Confidence in God's promise (6:13–18).

  i.   example of God "swearing by himself."
  ii.   "two unchangeable things."
  iii.   hope and encouragement.

E.   Confidence related to Jesus (6:19–20).

  i.   Jesus has entered "the inner sanctuary" as our *prodromos*.
  ii.   He is there as High Priest for ever "in the order of Melchizedek."

Chapter 7 Melchizedek.

A.   Genesis 14 – Abraham's encounter with Melchizedek (7:1–4).

  i.   significance of "Melchizedek" and "king of Salem."
  ii.   significance of there being no mention of his genealogy, parents, birth or death.
  iii.   Melchizedek obviously superior since Abraham "the patriarch" gave him the spoils (and was blessed by Melchizedek – v. 7).

B.   Significance of Abraham being Levi's ancestor (7:5–10).

  i.   Levi's priestly descendants <u>collected</u> tithes and offerings from their fellow-Israelites (Num 18:21–28; Deut 18:1–4).
  ii.   Levi "in Abraham's loins" <u>paid</u> a tithe to Melchizedek.

C.   Melchizedek's significance (7:11–19).

  i.   symbolic of a priesthood superior to the Levitical/Aaronic and of the need for one.
  ii.   symbolic of "a different priest, in the likeness of Melchizedek" (v. 15), with a priesthood not dependant on tribal background or ancestry – "our Lord" was of the tribe of Judah – but exercised by virtue of "the power of an indestructible life" (v. 16).
  iii.   significance of Ps 110:4b – "a priest for ever."
  iv.   the imperfection of the Law (vv. 11,18f).
  v.   "a better hope."

D.   Jesus's priestly status and role (7:20–28).

  i.   priest by "divine oath"– Ps 110:4.
  ii.   unlike all other priests (v. 20f).
  iii.   the oath initiating "a better covenant" (v. 22).
  iv.   the oath coming after the Law (v. 28).
  v.   the oath appointing "the Son perfected for ever" (v. 28).

   vi.   guarantee/guarantor of a better covenant (cf. 8:6).

  vii.   a priesthood which is "not transferable" because he lives for ever (Ps 110:4).

 viii.   superiority over human priesthood (v. 26).

   ix.   complete salvation.

    x.   intercession.

   xi.   his unrepeatable self-offering (v. 27).

Chapter 8

A.   A series of contrasts (8:1–7)

    i.   earthly priests contrasted with our High Priest "who sat down at the right hand of the throne of the Majesty in the heavens" (v. 1; cf. 1:3)

   ii.   earthly sanctuary contrasted with "the true tabernacle set up by the Lord" (v. 2), the former being "a copy (*hypodeigma*) and shadow (*skia*) of the heavenly things" (v. 5a)

  iii.   ministry of the earthly priests contrasted with the "more excellent ministry" of Jesus (v. 6; cf. the "more excellent name" of 1:4)

  iv.   the "first" covenant contrasted with a "better covenant" – of which Jesus is "mediator" – established on "better promises" (v. 6f)

B.   Focus on the new covenant (8:8–13) – lengthy quotation from Jeremiah 31:31–34

    i.   The new covenant foretold by Jeremiah is set in contrast with the covenant Yahweh made with Israel when delivering them from Egypt.

   ii.   The new relationship would involve in particular

  iii.   implanting of God's law in people's hearts

  iv.   knowledge of God as a matter of personal experience

   v.   blotting out of sins

  vi.   By predicting the "new" (v. 13) covenant's inauguration Jeremiah in effect announced the obsolescence of the old order.

  vii.   Implication: if the covenant of Moses's day is antiquated then so is the Aaronic priesthood.

Chapter 9

A.   The earthly sanctuary (9:1–10)

    i.   details of "the Holy [Place]" and "the Holy of Holies"

   ii.   duties of the priests and especially the High Priest, who alone entered the inner sanctuary once a year and "not without blood" (v. 7)

  iii.   the sanctuary's provisional and prophetic character

  iv.   contrast between "the first [covenant]" (v. 1; cf. 8:13) and "the time of *diorthōsis*" (v. 10)

   v.   contrast between "the first tabernacle" and "the [true] Holy [Place]" into which the way was not yet open (v. 8), the former being a *parabolē* of "the time which has come" (v. 9)

  vi.   ineffectiveness as regards the conscience

B.   Christ's ministry as High Priest (9:11–15)

    i.   <u>coming</u> as High Priest "of the good things which <u>have become</u> [real]" (v. 11)

   ii.   going through "the greater and more perfect tabernacle" (v. 11), "the Holy [Place]" (v. 12)

  iii.   "offering himself unblemished to God" (v. 14)

  iv.   the significance of his self-offering

   v.   his blood more effective than that of animals

  vi.   achieving "eternal redemption" (v. 12) and "eternal inheritance" (v. 15)

  vii.   "the mediator of a new covenant" (v. 15)

viii. a ransom setting sinners free (v. 15)

C.   Christ's death and the new covenant (9:16–22)

   i.   human illustration – death is what makes a *diathēkē* effective
   ii. OT background – "even the first [covenant] was not effective without blood" (v. 18) – Exod 24:1–8
   iii. blood-shedding necessary for forgiveness (v. 22)

D.   Christ's death and the heavenly sanctuary (9:23–28)

   i.   contrast between purification of the earthly "copies" (*hypodeigmata*) and purification of "the heavenly [realities] by better sacrifices" (v. 23)
   ii. contrast between the earthly sanctuary (the *antitypos*) and the heavenly, "the true one," which Christ has entered (v. 24)
   iii. contrast between the repeated sacrifices made by the earthly High Priest and the unique sacrifice of Christ (v. 25f; cf. 10:10ff)
   iv. contrast between the earthly High Priest using blood "not his own" (v. 25) and Christ offering himself as a sacrifice (v. 26; cf. 7:27; 10:10,19)
   v.   eschatological significance – Christ will emerge from the heavenly sanctuary, but for a different reason than the earthly High Priest (v. 28).

Chapter 10

A.   Uniqueness of Christ's sacrifice (10:1–18)

   i.   general principle (10:1a; cf. 7:11,18f; 8:5; 9:9,23f): the Law has only a *skia* of the coming good [things] and not the "true form" (ESV, NRSV, *eikōn*) of the "realities" (*pragmata*, cf. 11:1)
   ii. inadequacy of repeated sacrifices (vv. 1b-4)
   iii. application of Ps 40:6–8 (vv. 5–10)
   iv. ministry of the OT priests contrasted with Christ's (vv. 11–14)
   v.   symmetry of vv. 1 and 11

v. 1	v. 11
The Law	Every priest stands
each year (cf. v. 3)	each day
by the same sacrifices	the same sacrifices
which they offer	offering
perpetually	repeatedly
can never	which can never
perfect those who draw near	remove sins

   vi. application of Ps 110 – contrast between "every priest stands" and "he sat down"

vii. contrast between the sacrifices which can never "make perfect" (v. 1; cf. 7:19; 9:9) and the "one sacrifice [by which] he has made perfect (cf. 11:40; 12:23) perpetually those who are being sanctified" (v. 14; cf. v. 10)

viii. application of Jer.31:33f (vv. 15–18)

B. Exhortation and warning (10:19–39)

i. summary (v. 19ff)
ii. entering the Holy [Place] now applied to us
iii. by his blood, through his body
iv. with boldness (cf. 3:6; 4:16; 10:35)
v. having a "great priest"
vi. exhortations (vv. 22–25)
vii. drawing near to God
viii. with sincerity, faith, hope
ix. having been cleansed (OT imagery)
x. mutual encouragement (v. 24f)
xi. warning (vv. 26–31)
xii. impersonal tone
xiii. OT echoes – dire consequences of rejecting the covenant
xiv. uniqueness of Christ's sacrifice and the dire consequences of rejecting it
xv. recollection (v. 32ff)
xvi. personal tone
xvii. persecution
xviii. assurance of "a better property and an abiding one"
xix. exhortation (vv. 35–38)
xx. boldness (cf. v. 19), perseverance, commitment
xxi. eschatological perspective – receiving what God has promised (cf. vv. 23,25)
xxii. use of Hab.2:3f
xxiii. summary (v. 39) – "We are not of shrinking (for destruction) but of faith (for possessing life)."

Chapter 12

A. Exhortation and warning (12:1–17)

i. basic theme: "Let us run with perseverance (patience, endurance) the race set out for us." (v. 1c)
ii. exhortations related to
iii. the "witnesses" (v. 1a)
iv. the need to deal with sin (v. 1b)
v. the example of Jesus (v. 2f)
vi. warning of possible persecution (v. 4)
vii. divine discipline (vv. 5–11) – use of Prov. 3:11f
viii. readers' weakness (v. 12f)
ix. need for peace and holiness (v. 14)
x. dangers of
xi. lacking God's grace
xii. defilement (echo of Deut 29:17f)
xiii. sexual immorality – example of Esau

B. Encouragement and exhortation based on the Sinai theophany (12:18–29)

i. extended contrast between Mt Sinai and Mt Zion: "you have not come...you have come" (vv. 18–24)
ii. use of Exod 19:10–25; 20:18–21; Deut 4:10–12; 5:22–26; (9:19?)
iii. contrast between earthly and heavenly realities
iv. glories of heaven (heavenly Jerusalem, city of the living God, judge of all; angels "in festival")
v. privileged people of God
vi. made possible by Jesus: major themes brought together in v. 24
vii. mediator of new covenant
viii. sprinkled blood
ix. eschatological perspectives (vv. 25–29)
x. warning *a fortiori* (v. 25)
xi. prospect of a shaking to come – Hg.2:6 (v. 26f)
xii. promise of receiving something which cannot be shaken (v. 27f)
xiii. final word of exhortation – Deut 4:24 (v. 28f)

Bibliography

Bruce, F. F. *The Epistle to the Hebrews.* Rev. Ed. Grand Rapids: Eerdmans, 1990.

Ellingworth, P. *The Epistle to the Hebrews: A Commentary on the Greek Text.* Carlilse: Paternoster, 1993.

Hay, D. *Glory at the Right Hand: Psalm 110 in Early Christianity.* Society of Biblical Literature, Atlanta, 1989.

Hurst, L. D. *The Epistle to the Hebrews: Its Background and Thought.* Cambridge: Cambridge University Press, 1990.

Kistemaker, S. J. *Hebrews.* Grand Rapids: Baker, 1984.

Lane, W. L. *Hebrews 1–8.* Word Biblical Commentary. Dallas: Word, 1991.

Lane, W. L. *Hebrews 9–13.* Word Biblical Commentary. Dallas: Word, 1991.

Lindars, B. *The Theology of the Letter to the Hebrews.* Cambridge: Cambridge University Press, 1991.

Articles

Davis, C. W. "Hebrews 6:4–6 from an Oral Critical Perspective." *Journal of the Evangelical Theological Society* 51/4 (December 2008).

Griffith, S. "The Epistle to the Hebrews in Modern Interpretation." *Review and Expositor* 102/2 (Spring 2005).

Guthrie, G. H. "Hebrews." Pages 919–995 in G. K. Beale and D. A. Carson, eds. *Commentary on the New Testament Use of the Old Testament.* Nottingham: Apollos IVP, 2007.

Johnsson, W. "The Pilgrimage Motif in the Book of Hebrews." *Journal of Biblical Literature* 97/2 (June 1978).

Lane, W. L. "Hebrews." in R. P. Martin and P. H. Davids, eds. *Dictionary of the Later New Testament and Its Developments.* Leicester: IVP, 1997.

Mathewson, D. "Reading Heb 6:4–6 in Light of the Old Testament." *Westminster Theological Journal* 61 (1999).

McCullough, J. C. "The Old Testament Quotations in Hebrews." *New Testament Studies* 26 (1980).

McCullough, J. C. "Hebrews in Recent Scholarship." Part 1. *Irish Biblical Studies* 16/2 (1994).

McCullough, J. C. "Hebrews in Recent Scholarship." Part 2. *Irish Biblical Studies* 16/3 (1994).

Young, N. "'Bearing his Reproach' (Heb 13:9–14)." *New Testament Studies* 48/2 (April 2002).

Unpublished

Diceanu, M. "The Distinctive Soteriology in the Epistle to the Hebrews." PhD Thesis QUB, 2007.

THE CONCEPT OF ENDURANCE IN THE EPISTLE TO THE HEBREWS: KEY ELEMENTS AND THEIR RELATION TO CHRISTIAN EXPERIENCE

PETER G. FIRTH[*]

Irish Baptist College

ABSTRACT: This paper explores the theme of endurance in Hebrews.[**] It identifies and examines four key elements critical to the author's concept of endurance before presenting some practical ways in which the author's teaching may be applied in the lives of Christians today. In addition to highlighting the importance of endurance in the lives of Christian believers (both then and now), the study shows that an integral component of the author's concept of endurance is the hope that believers have of one day entering fully into eternal realities which God has promised to them through Christ Jesus. The importance of Christology in engendering and developing endurance is explored, as well as the place and role of meaningful fellowship with other believers in nurturing it.

KEY WORDS: endurance, Christology, eternal, faith, community.

In 2010, author Laura Hillenbrand published, *Unbroken: A World War II Story of Survival, Resilience and Redemption.*[1] In it she tells the true story of Louis Zamperini. In 1936, Zamperini, aged nineteen, became an Olympic track athlete and competed for the USA at the Berlin Games. During World War II he became a bombardier in the American Air Force but was involved in a plane crash in the Pacific Ocean. He was one of only a few survivors and ended up drifting on a raft for forty-seven days over 200 miles in shark infested waters. He eventually landed in a Japanese controlled area and became a prisoner of war in several brutal, Japanese internment camps. For two and a half years he was enslaved, beaten, degraded, starved and tortured. Following the war, Zamperini initially struggled to overcome his ordeal, but eventually he managed to do so and went on to become an effective Christian evangelist. He died in 2014 aged ninety-seven. His story, which has attracted much media attention, illustrates what is the basic appeal of Hebrews: to show endurance in the face of extreme suffering.

Hebrews has been described as "a delight for the person who enjoys puzzles."[2] The comment, made by Lane, comes at the start of his discussion on introductory matters to the epistle, and alerts the reader to the challenge faced by scholars when trying to piece together an accurate picture of the historical background to this complex epistle.[3] With little solid evidence to work with, scholars must express their opinions tentatively when it comes to foundational issues. This applies to the identity of the original recipients of the epistle who it seems were largely, if not exclusively, long time Jews brought up in the Jewish faith but who had in addition confessed Jesus as the promised Messiah.[4] If

---

* PETER FIRTH (PhD Queen's University, Belfast, BD Hons Queen's University Belfast. Dr Firth currently lectures on the New Testament in the Irish Baptist College, N. Ireland). Email: peter@thebaptistcentre.org

** Unless otherwise stated quotations from the Bible are taken from the *English Standard Version* (2001). Quotations from the Greek Text are based on *NA28: Nestle-Aland Novum Testamentum Graece*. 28th ed. Stuttgart: Deutsche Bibelgesellschaft (2012).

[1] Laura Hillenbrand, *Unbroken: A World War II Story of Survival, Resilience and Redemption* (London: Fourth Estate, 2011).

[2] William L. Lane, *Hebrews 1–8*, WBC (Dallas: Word, 1991), xlvii.

[3] For a useful and informative discussion on the historical background of the epistle see D.A. Carson and Douglas J. Moo, *An Introduction to the New Testament*, 2nd ed. (Leicester: Apollos, 2005), 596–615. See also the introductory sections in the following commentaries: Harold W. Attridge, *The Epistle to the Hebrews* (Philadelphia: Fortress, 1989); Paul Ellingworth, *The Epistle to the Hebrews* (Grand Rapids: Eerdmans, 1993); Craig, R. Koester, *Hebrews* (New York: Doubleday, 2001); Peter T. O'Brien, *The Letter to the Hebrews (*PNTC, Grand Rapids: Eerdmans 2010) .

[4] Lane, *Hebrews 1–8*, liii–lv.

Guthrie is correct, they may have constituted a house church or group of house churches, in or near the city of Rome, perhaps in the mid-sixties CE.[5]

According to 10:32–34, the hearers had recently passed through an intense period of suffering.[6] Many had accepted this adversity "joyfully" but others had shrunk back from their earlier allegiance and had become apostates; some had not gone as far as this but were discouraged (vv. 35–39). Faced with ongoing opposition from fellow Jews (13:13), many of those who had remained faithful were in danger of succumbing to the temptation of compromising their faith, and lapsing back into their former religion as a way of escape. Aware of the situation, the author[7] identifies what it is that they needed (10:35–36):

> [35] Therefore do not throw away your confidence, which has a great reward. [36] For you have need of endurance (ὑπομονῆς), so that when you have done the will of God you may receive what is promised.

Later, he states it again (12:1):

> [12:1]Therefore, since we are surrounded by so great a cloud of witnesses, let us also lay aside every weight, and sin which clings so closely, and let us run with endurance (ὑπομονῆς) the race that is set before us.

In calling for endurance, the author uses the noun ὑπομονη. Hauck, in his detailed discussion of the etymology of the term, shows the difficulty translators face when trying to convey the fullness of the word's meaning in a single word.[8] The English term "endurance" is a good translation, but the actual essence and character of ὑπομονή is more clearly expressed by Barclay:

> It is not the patience which can sit down and bow its head and let things descend upon it and passively endure until the storm is past.... It is the spirit which can bear things, not simply with resignation, but with blazing hope ... the spirit which bears things because it knows that these things are leading to a goal of glory.... It is the quality which keeps a man on his feet with his face to the wind. It is the virtue which can transmute the hardest trial into glory because beyond the pain it sees the goal.[9]

The language of endurance in Hebrews is, of course, not confined to a single Greek noun or verb. A wide range of terms are used together with a rich array of literary devices including, admonitions, exhortations, metaphors, analogies, and examples. The author's concept intersects with many themes and ideas – temporal and eternal, visible and invisible, earthly and heavenly, human and divine. The result is a concept consistent with the rest of Scripture but one that is framed and expressed in a unique way.

The concept of endurance as reflected in Hebrews is made up of a number of interrelated elements. Of these, four are particularly noteworthy.

---

[5] George H. Guthrie, *Hebrews: The NIV Application Commentary* (Grand Rapids: Zondervan, 1998), 20.
[6] For a helpful analysis of the text and what the experience involved, see Bruce Winter, "Suffering with the Saviour: the reality, the reasons and the reward" in *The Perfect Saviour*, ed. Jonathan Griffith (Nottingham: Inter-Varsity Press, 2012), 147–67.
[7] It is assumed that the author is male. The use of the masculine participle διηγούμενον ("to tell") which refers to the author in 11:32 would, for example, rule out a female author.
[8] Friedrich Hauck, "μένώ ἐμ παρά περί προσμένώ μονή ὑπομένώ ὑπομονή" in *Theological Dictionary of the New Testament*, Vol. IV, eds. Gerhard Kittel and Gerhard Friedrich, trans. G. W. Bromiley, 10 vols. (Grand Rapids: Eerdmans, 1984), 574–88.
[9] William Barclay, *New Testament Words* (London: SCM 1964), 144–45.

Christology

Christology is said to be the theological epicentre of Hebrews.[10] The epistle offers a sublime exposition on the person, status, and ministry of Lord Jesus Christ. The preface (1:1–3) presents a magnificent vignette of the divine Son exercising his universal headship. "Amidst a variety of allusions to his deity" notes Walmark,[11] Jesus is presented as the one who fulfils the divinely ordained Old Testament offices of prophet, priest and king. Verses 1–2 introduce the prophetic office with Jesus being declared as God's Son and his supreme and final redemptive word. Next, comes his universal kingship, "he sat down at the right hand of the majesty in heaven" (v. 3). His position of exaltation on the throne is the result of his priestly work (v. 3b). It is this priestly ministry "that takes centre stage as the message of the Hebrews unfolds."[12]

The ensuing chapters develop the theme of the superiority of Jesus as eternal high priest. He is declared superior to the most important institutions of the ancient Hebrew faith. He is superior to the word of God spoken through the prophets since he is God's ultimate redemptive word. He is superior to the angels since no angel can lay claim to being fully divine (1:4–14) and also fully human (2:5–18). His deity and humanity uniquely qualify him to be the faithful and perpetual sin bearer of his people. Again because of his uniqueness, he is superior to Moses the great law-giver of Israel (3:1–6) as the creator is to the creature. The spiritual and eternal rest offered by Jesus is superior to that temporal rest offered through Moses and Joshua and experienced through the occupation of the Promised Land (4:1–11; esp. vv. 9–10).[13]

Beginning with chapter 5 the central theological concern of the epistle emerges: the eternal, spiritual, priesthood assumed by Jesus through the offering up of himself as the once-for-all sacrifice for sins. His ministry is infinitely superior to the temporal earthly ministry exercised by Aaron and his descendants (4:14–5:11; 7:1–10:18). It is at this point that the climax of the Christology is reached. Jesus the eternal, high priest enters the inner sanctuary of the universe and offers up his own body and blood in voluntary submission to God as a sacrifice for sins, once forever, on behalf of sinners. He is both priest and sacrifice; offerer and offering. His sacrifice cancels out all previous sacrifices for sins.

The detailed Christological exposition is fundamental to the author's appeal for endurance. Sachs comments on the relationship between the two:

> The author recognized that only an intensified, personal understanding of these truths would generate the resilience and determination needed to sustain them on their course.[14]

On two occasions during the course of the epistle, the author exhorts his hearers to focus sharply and think carefully on what he is teaching. The first is in chapter 3. The passage forms part of the first major block (3:1–4:16) in which the author maintains an extended and varied exhortation. Chapter 3:1–19 consists of two parts: verses 1–6 involve the use of *synkrisis*: a comparison between Moses's faithfulness as a servant and the filial faithfulness of Jesus. Verses 7–19 consist of a quotation from Psalm 95:7–11 and a commentary on it highlighting the unfaithfulness of the Israelites who were led out of Egypt by Moses. The author's aim is to present his listeners with a challenge to be faithful, but his method involves setting forth the exhortation first before providing the basis for it. In the present case the exhortation occurs in verse 1: "consider Jesus." The basis then follows (vv. 2–6). Jesus is the paradigmatic image of faithfulness. The imperative in verse 1 indicates that this is a command rather

---

[10] Leonard Walmark, "Hebrews, Theology of" in *Baker's Evangelical Dictionary of Biblical Theology,* ed. Walter A. Elwell (Grand Rapids: Baker, 1997), 335.

[11] Walmark, "Hebrews," 335.

[12] Walmark, "Hebrews," 335.

[13] Walmark, "Hebrews," 335.

[14] Stuart Sachs, *Hebrews Through a Hebrew's Eyes: Hope In The Midst Of A Hopeless World* (Baltimore: Lederer, 2014), 9.

than a suggestion, and the use of the verb κατανοέω implies deep concentration on what is being said. If the hearers are to persevere, they must rivet their attention on Jesus and think deeply about his faithfulness.

The second occasion occurs in chapter 12. Here the author employs the metaphor of an athletic contest when referring to the Christian life (v. 1). In verse 3 he writes:

> [3]Consider (ἀναλογίσασθε) him who endured (ὑπομεμενηκότα) from sinners such hostility against himself, so that you may not grow weary or fainthearted.

Again the imperative is used and the object of consideration is Jesus (v. 2), but this time the verb is changed to ἀναλογίζομαι which means "to consider thoughtfully."[15] The purpose of such thoughtful contemplation is that the hearers might be encouraged to keep on running with ὑπομονῆς "endurance."

The call to reflect carefully on such a sublime and extensive exposition of the person, status, and work of Christ seems to serve another purpose beyond that of reinforcing his listeners' theological understanding about Jesus. It would also help to remind them that the one in whom they had placed their faith is in fact worthy of their allegiance and worth suffering for. Apart from Jesus and his redemptive work they knew there is no eternal salvation. Furthermore, even though their discipleship involved experiencing opposition, they are could draw comfort from the fact that through Jesus there is access to God's throne of grace and therefore the divine resources necessary to help in their time of need (4:14–16; cf.13:20–21).

Eternal Realities

The verb μένω is important to the concept of endurance. In classical literature μένω often conveys the idea of remaining in one place. In the LXX, it frequently refers to something that remains fixed and is unchanging.[16] It is thus used with reference to God and the word of God. In contrast to nature which is transitory and changeable, God and his word are permanent and enduring. Theses notions of permanence and constancy are reflected in the Hebrews. Of particular relevance to the current theme is the way the author uses the term in texts to set up a contrast between something that is temporary and of little value and that which is permanent and of great worth.

Hebrews 10:34–36 is a case in point. The context of the passage involves a harsh word of warning (vv. 26–31) which the author then proceeds to mitigate by offering a positive example to his hearers; in this case their own past experience (vv. 32–34). He encourages them to remember former days when they endured great suffering and reminds them of how they responded to the harsh treatment meted out to them (v. 32). They remained faithful despite losing earthly possessions. What enabled them to persevere and accept this loss was their "knowledge:"

> [34] For you had compassion on those in prison, and you joyfully accepted the plundering of your property (ὑπαρχόντων), since you knew that you yourselves had a better possession (ὕπαρξιν) and an abiding one (μένουσαν). [35] Therefore do not throw away your confidence, which has a great reward. [36] For you have need of endurance (ὑπομονῆς), so that when you have done the will of God you may receive what is promised.

That aspect of knowledge which the author refers to was the realization that as well as temporary and material possessions they also had, through faith in Christ, a "better" and an "abiding" possession which could not be taken away. The play on words in verse 34 between ὑπαρχόντων, "possessions"

---

[15] Richard C. H. Lenski, *The Interpretation of The Epistle to the Hebrews and the Epistle to James* (Minneapolis: Augsburg, 1963), 430.

[16] Hauck, "μένώ," 574–79.

(v. 34b) and ὕπαρξιν, possession (v. 34c),[17] allows the author to make the contrast between what had been lost through seizure and that which cannot be taken away. The use of the present participle μένουσαν (from μένω) to describes this "better possession" explains what makes it better.[18] Bruce captures something of how the believers thought:

> [T]he eternal inheritance was so real in their eyes that they could light-heartedly bid farewell to material possessions which were short-lived in any case.[19]

Chapter10 shows that the concept of endurance in Hebrews extends beyond that of a human virtue. Other passages which indicate the same point will be considered shortly. However, before leaving Hebrews 10 we should also notice that having commended his hearers for their perseverance in the past the author immediately proceeds in verses 35–36 to exhort them to further displays of endurance (ὑπομονῆς). In this we see a connection being made between things that endure and the human virtue of endurance. Indeed the link is such that both affect each other. The relationship may be expressed thus: the knowledge of the enduring possession serves to engender the virtue of endurance whilst the virtue of endurance ultimately leads to the full enjoyment of the enduring possession.

The extending of the concept of endurance is further illustrated in Hebrews 12:27–28. This time the contrast is drawn between temporary kingdoms of men and the permanent kingdom of God. Verse 28 falls within a wider section (12:18–29) that marks the climax of the epistle in which the author draws together several strands of truth to arrive at an exhortation based on the uniqueness of the new covenant. In verses 25–29, a final warning is given exhorting the listeners to heed God. A noteworthy feature is the use of *a fortiori* argument. The lesser situation refers to those who refused to heed God's message in the desert and were therefore judged. The greater situation relates to the present hearers and their receptivity to the voice of God from heaven through the Son. If those under the old covenant did not escape the wrath of God when they turned from God's word, it follows that the judgment of those who reject his message of salvation under the new covenant will be even more certain. In describing the coming judgment (vv. 26–27) the author makes use of Haggai 2:6, "Yet once more, in a little while I will shake the heavens and earth." The first shaking of the earth (v. 26) refers to the event of terror at Mount Sinai when God manifested his presence to Moses (Exod 19:18). However, that shaking, notes the author, points to a more extensive shaking in the future that will include the heavens as well. This eschatological judgment will result in the removal of that which can be shaken in order that that which cannot be shaken μείνῃ "may remain" (v. 27).[20] After this cataclysmic event takes place only the kingdom of God will remain. This then leads the author to issue another challenge (vv. 28–29): to continue to worship God acceptably with reverence and awe. Yet implicit within the challenge is the theme of endurance. Indeed, as in 10:34–36, there is a connection (albeit oblique) being made between that which is eternal and enduring (the kingdom of God) and the virtue of endurance.

Other texts that illustrate the wider concept of endurance include 1:11 and 13:14. The first contrasts the temporal created order with the eternal Lord and involves the use of the verb διαμένω.[21] This verse falls within the first main movement of Christology (1:5–2:18). In this section the author quotes from several Old Testament passages. Verse 11 is part of a quotation from Psalm 102:25–17 which allows the author to affirm that the Son is the agent of creation but at the same time separate from it and sovereign over it. The creation will "perish" and "wear out like a garment;" the Son yet by contrast διαμένεις "remains" or "endures" (v 11), his "years will have no end" (v 12).

---

[17] Lane, *Hebrews 9–13*, 300.

[18] μένουσαν – participle, present, active, accusative feminine, singular of μένω.

[19] Frederick F. Bruce, *The Epistle To The Hebrews*, NICNT (Grand Rapids: Eerdmans, 1991), 271.

[20] Subjunctive aorist active, third person singular of the verb μένω.

[21] A compound verb composed of the preposition dia and μένω meaning "to remain, continue."

The second text sets up a contrast between an earthly city and an eternal city (13:14). This chapter serves as the conclusion of the letter and has several movements. Following a short list of practical guidelines for living (vv. 1–6) verses 7–17 provide an *inclusio* on the topic of leaders. Within this section there is a call to identify with the reproach of Jesus; this involves being an "outsider" in the world, and not living in accordance with the system of the world. Verse 14 gives the rationale for this: "For here we have no lasting (μένουσαν) city, but we seek the city that is to come."[22] The author is not saying that believers do not have an enduring city; to do so would contradict 11:10. Rather his point is that, as far as life here and now is concerned, believers do not have a permanent dwelling place. However, by implication, the city that they do seek (v. 14b) and which lies ahead is permanent and enduring.

Whilst not all of the aforementioned texts in this section make a direct link to the virtue of endurance, it is reasonable to assume that the repeated emphasis on eternal realities by itself would in some way help the hearers to think carefully about the actual virtue, especially given the fact that the verb ὑπομένω "I endure" is itself a compound verb combining the proposition ὑπο with the verb μένω.

Faith

The linking of faith with endurance is especially noteworthy in Hebrews.[23] Evidence for this is seen particularly in the way the author refers to key spiritual figures in Israel's past. Two figures in particular are noteworthy. In chapter 6, following a warning about the dangers of not persevering in the faith (vv. 4–8), the author goes on to express his confidence that his hearers would go on and serve God faithfully to the end (vv. 9–11). He calls them to be "imitators of those who through faith and patience inherit the promises" (v. 12), before presenting Abraham as a model of one who "having patiently waited, obtained the promise" (v. 15). In verses 12 "faith" is clearly linked to the noun μακ ροθυμία. The noun is used again in verse 15, "And thus Abraham, having patiently waited (μακ ροθυμήσας), obtained the promise." Although often translated "patience," μακροθυμία more accurately conveys "a steadfast spirit that never gives in,"[24] and is another term in the author's vocabulary of endurance.[25]

The second example is found in Hebrews 11. Whilst the whole of the eleventh chapter may be said to illustrate the connection between faith and endurance, it is particularly evident in the account about Moses. Beginning with Moses's parents, the author highlights their bold step of faith in saving their child from the king's edict (v. 23), before proceeding to talk about Moses and the boldness that he showed in Egypt (vv. 24–26) when choosing to identify with God's people rather than with the godless. As a result, Moses experienced "the reproach of Christ" (v. 26) or the same kind of reproach which Christ would later experience. He then took a further step of faith in deciding to leave Egypt. Despite incurring the king's wrath, the author affirms that Moses persisted in his course (v. 27):

> [27]By faith he left Egypt, not being afraid of the anger of the king, for (γὰρ) he endured (ἐ καρτέρησεν) as seeing him who is invisible.

The use of the conjunction γὰρ links faith and endurance together. The term "endured" translates the verb καρτερέω (v. 27) and, in the present context, indicates someone who remains steadfast in the face of opposition. This quality is further explained in the next phrase: "as seeing him who is invisible." For Lane[26] this is probably not to be taken as a reference to the event at the burning bush (Exod

[22] Μένουσαν – present active participle of μένω.
[23] Merland Ray Miller, "Seven Theological Themes in Hebrews," *Grace Theological Journal* 8.1 (1987): 131–40.
[24] Barclay, *New Testament Words*, 196.
[25] George V. Wigram and Ralph D. Winter, *The Word Study Concordance* (Cambridge: Tyndale House, 1979).
[26] Lane, *Hebrews 9–11*, 375. The key to the proper interpretation lies in the fact that v. 27b is a fixed Hellenistic idiom – ὁρῶν ἐκαρτέρησεν, "he kept seeing continually." The idiom, according to Lane, is frequently missed resulting in an inaccurate interpretation.

3:1–4:17), but rather refers to "a lifelong vision of God."[27] Such was the strength of Moses's consciousness of God, that he was not afraid to incur the wrath of the earthly king.

The examples of Abraham and Moses both indicate that the hallmark of genuine Christian faith is endurance. Both men exhibited great faith but both were flawed as were the other figures in Hebrews 11. The supreme example of faith, which the author sets before his hearers, is Jesus (v. 2). As τὸν τῆς πίστεως ἀρχηγὸν καὶ τελειωτὴν, "the founder and perfecter of faith" Jesus is both the initiator of faith and the one in whom faith reaches its perfection.[28] His whole life was characterized by unbroken and unquestioning faith in his heavenly Father. However, the supreme test of faith came as he faced the cross (Mark 14:36), a form of punishment reserved for those who were deemed of all men to be unfit to live. Yet "he ὑπέμεινεν (endured) the cross, despising the shame" (v. 2).[29] As a reward he now sits at the right hand of the throne of God (v. 2). Jesus is "the great Believer"[30] and the one whom believers are to continually fix their eyes upon.

Community

Whilst much of western Christianity is characterized by individualistic thinking, such a mentality is alien to the writers of the New Testament. For the author of Hebrews the outworking of the appeal for endurance is a community matter that involves corporate responsibility. Two texts, in particular, serve to illustrate the point.

The first is in chapter 3. Following the second warning passage employing Psalm 95:7b-11, and which records the fate of the Israelites when they failed to continue believing God at Kadesh Barnea (vv. 7–11), the author urges his hearers to apply the lesson from the past (vv. 12–14):

> [12] Take care, brothers, lest there be in any of you an evil, unbelieving heart, leading you to fall away from the living God. [13] But exhort one another (ἑαυτοὺς) every day, as long as it is called "today," that none of you may be hardened by the deceitfulness of sin.[14] For we share in Christ, if indeed we hold our original confidence firm to the end.

Two exhortations are given: one negative "take care ... lest there be" (v. 12); and the other positive "exhort one another" (v. 13). The first confronts the hearers with a general warning directed at the community. Believers should be careful because within any Christian community there may be those whose outward association does not reflect the inward condition of the heart. The danger lies in anyone who might possess an evil, unbelieving heart that they fall away from the living God. The second exhortation comes in the form of a positive command: "exhort one another every day."

Individual vigilance alone would not be sufficient. As Guthrie observes:

> For this community struggling with the problem of spiritual drifting, hardening of the heart was both a real and danger and avoidable. If it was to be avoided, however, the recipients of Hebrews had to relate to one another in an atmosphere of encouragement.[31]

The addition of the phrase "every day" may presuppose a daily gathering which would provide the occasion for this mutual encouragement.

The theme of mutual support is referred to again in chapter 10:

---

[27] Bruce, *Hebrews*, 314.

[28] Lane, *Hebrews 9–13*, 412.

[29] ὑπέμεινεν – aorist indicative 3rd person singular of ὑπομένω.

[30] James Moffatt, *A Critical and Exegetical Commentary on the Epistle to the Hebrews*, ICC (Edinburgh: T&T Clark, 1963), 192.

[31] Guthrie, *Hebrews*, 130.

[23]Let us hold fast the confession of our hope without wavering, for he who promised is faithful. [24] And let us consider how to stir up one another (ἀλλήλους) to love and good works, [25] not neglecting to meet together, as is the habit of some, but encouraging one another, and all the more as you see the Day drawing near.

The author at this point encourages his hearers to continue to hold on to the Christian hope without being moved by changing circumstances (v. 23). What follows is a call to exercise mutual encouragement. Κατανοέω "let us consider" is the main verb around which verses 24–25 revolve and means to "pay attention to or looking closely at."[32] The use of the present subjunctive indicates ongoing attention. His hearers should fasten their attention on the need for conscious activities of encouragement within their own community. They are to motivate one another to love expressed in good works which previously had characterized them (6:10). The context for this stimulation is explained by the use of contrasting expressions that indicate what the hearers must not and must do. What they must not do is stop meeting together on a regular basis. It would appear that some were abandoning their gathering together for worship which the author sees as fatal for perseverance in the faith. Since support cannot take place in isolation they must therefore continue to gather for mutual encouragement. Both consolation and encouragement to spiritual alertness are to be given in light of the great "day" of Christ's coming. The practical outworking of such becomes the focus of chapter 13.

Finally, the practice of such mutual care and support, in all probability, would have been especially important to those within the community who had experienced varying degrees of rejection and even ostracism particularly from family members because of their faith. The loss of such filial relationships would only be offset by the genuine love and support of their new spiritual family.

Practical Implications

Having briefly considered some of the interrelated elements critical to the author's understanding of endurance, a few brief comments of a practical nature on their relevance to Christians today is appropriate in closing.

When Paul and Barnabas revisited the newly founded churches of Galatia towards the end of what is commonly designated the "first missionary journey" their message to the new converts was that "through many tribulations we must enter the kingdom of God" (Acts 14:22). Today, some two thousand years on, the principle of suffering remains the same. The author's message about endurance is as relevant today as when it was first written. In seeking to apply his teaching five points may be made.

First, the basis of the concept of endurance as taught in Hebrews rests firmly upon God and what he has done in Christ. At the end of his epistle, the author focuses attention on the fact that God is both able and willing to equip his people with everything good for doing his will (13:21). Within the scope of the expression "everything good" lies the virtue of endurance. For the Christian this provides hope in the midst of trials and offers a reason for praise.

Second, the concept of endurance as taught in Hebrews informs the Christian that there is an onus on them to act responsibly in the light of God's word. Prayer is the starting point and the believer needs to ask God continually to work in them so that endurance may be produced and developed.

Third, the concept requires the Christian to recognize that the development of this virtue is also linked directly to the clarity with which they view the authentic Jesus. To overcome the temptation to lose heart and compromise one's faith, the believer must take seriously the need to develop an abiding preoccupation with the authentic Christ of Scripture. A superficial acquaintance with the truth of

---

[32] Guthrie, *Hebrews*, 345.

Scripture will not suffice. The prominent seventeenth century Puritan, emphasized the point when he said:

> If I have observed anything by experience it is this: a man may take the measure of his growth and decay in grace according to his thoughts and meditations upon the person of Christ, and the glory of Christ.[33]

The call in Hebrews to thoughtful and focused contemplation upon the person and work of Christ will undoubtedly present a real challenge for many Christian believers, especially in the western world where the pace of modern living continues to accelerate. Nevertheless, the need to slow down and engage with God's word in a meaningful way must be taken seriously if Christians are to be strong and resilient in times of adversity.

Fourth, as previously indicated the author's concept of endurance embraces eternal realities. The virtue of endurance is not an end in itself but a means to an end. Believers have a glorious hope. Hebrews draws our attention to a number of positive eternal realities which we shall one day fully enjoy. These too need to be studied and reflected on as a means of motivating endurance.

Fifth, the concept of endurance in Hebrews teaches that the development of endurance requires active participation a loving Christian community. Wesley wrote, "The Bible knows nothing of solitary religion."[34] Hebrews is a strongly relational book with a strong relational message. For theology to be done properly it requires community. Equally for authentic Christian community to function properly, it requires theology. It is in the interplay of both that Christians find themselves being empowered to go on and not give up. Christian fellowship according to Hebrews is not a luxury for believers; it is a necessity.

Bibliography

Attridge, Harold W. *The Epistle to the Hebrews*. Philadelphia: Fortress, 1989.

Barclay, William. *New Testament Words*. London: SCM Press, 1964.

Bruce, Frederick F., *The Epistle to the Hebrews*. New International Commentary on the New Testament. Grand Rapids: Eerdmans, 1991.

Carson, D. A., and Douglas J. Moo. *An Introduction to the New Testament*. 2nd ed. Leicester: Apollos, 2005.

Ellingworth, Paul. *The Epistle to the Hebrews*. Grand Rapids: Eerdmans, 1993.

Guthrie, George H. *Hebrews: The NIV Application Commentary*. Grand Rapids: Zondervan, 1998.

Hauck, Friedrich "μένω ἐμ παρά περί προσμένω μονή ὑπομένω ὑπομονη." Pages 574–588 in *Theological Dictionary of the New Testament*. Vol. IV. Edited by Gerhard Kittel and Gerhard Friedrich. Translated by Geoffrey W. Bromiley. Grand Rapids: Eerdmans, 1984.

Hillenbrand, Laura. *Unbroken: A World War II Story of Survival, Resilience and Redemption*. London: Fourth Estate, 2011.

Koester, Craig, R. *Hebrews*. New York: Doubleday, 2001.

Lane, William L. *Hebrews 1–8*. Word Biblical Commentary. Dallas: Word, 1991.

---

[33] John Owen, "The Excellency of Christ," in *The Works of John Owen* Vol. 9 (London: Banner of Truth, 1965), 475.

[34] John Wesley, *The Heart of John Wesley's Journal*, ed. Percy Livingstone Parker (Peabody: Hendrickson, 2008), 11.

Lane, William L. *Hebrews 9–13*. Word Biblical Commentary. Dallas: Word, 1991.

Lenski, Richard C. H. *The Interpretation of the Epistle to the Hebrews and the Epistle to James.* Minneapolis: Augsburg, 1963.

Miller, Merland Ray. "Seven Theological Themes in Hebrews." *Grace Theological Journal* 8.1 (1987): 131–40.

Moffatt, James. *A Critical and Exegetical Commentary on the Epistle to the Hebrews.* International Critical Commentary. Edinburgh: T&T Clark, 1963.

O'Brien, Peter, T. *The Letter to the Hebrews.* Pillar New Testament Commentary. Grand Rapids: Eerdmans, 2010.

Owen, John. "The Excellency of Christ." In *The Works of John Owen.* Vol. 9. London: Banner of Truth, 1965.

Sachs, Stuart. *Hebrews Through a Hebrew's Eyes*: *Hope in the Midst of a Hopeless World.* Baltimore: Lederer, 2014.

Walmark, Leonard. "Hebrews, Theology of." Pages 335–338 in *Baker's Evangelical Dictionary of Biblical Theology.* Edited by Walter A. Elwell. Grand Rapids: Baker, 1997.

Wesley, John. *The Heart of John Wesley's Journal.* Edited by Percy Livingstone Parker. Peabody: Hendrickson, 2008.

Wigram George V. and Ralph D. Winter. *The Word Study Concordance.* Cambridge: Tyndale House, 1979.

Winter, Bruce. "Suffering with the Saviour: the Reality, the Reasons and the Reward." Pages 147–167 in *The Perfect Saviour.* Edited by Jonathan Griffith. Nottingham: Inter-Varsity Press, 2012.

HEBREWS 13:15–16. THE NEW WORSHIP BY THE NEW PRIESTHOOD IN THE "TIME OF REFORMATION"

Hamilton Moore[*]

The Irish Baptist College, Constituent College of Queen's University

ABSTRACT: Hebrews 13:15–16 is the last of twelve exhortations in Hebrews in a chapter which has strong links with all that has gone before. The verses affirm that the sacrifices which were continually offered in the OT by the priests in the outer court have now ceased because of the effectiveness of the final sacrifice of Christ. By that sacrifice his people are "perfected forever" in this "time of reformation." The Aaronic priesthood has been superseded by the eternal priesthood of Christ and we now have direct access to God. The only sacrifices now required of us is to continually offer our praise for what God has done and live our lives showing compassion and generosity to others (as e.g., 13:1–3 reveal). In effect there is a new priesthood of his people which is implied but not clearly affirmed.

KEY WORDS: sacrifice of praise, time of reformation, priesthood, access to God, doing good.

It has been affirmed by some scholars that 12:14–29 is the point where Hebrews reaches its climax in the call to serve or worship God with reverence and godly fear and chapter 13 is really an appendix or supplement – almost an alien section. Yet on further examination scholars as William Lane[1] are convinced that one can affirm the integrity, authenticity and appropriateness of this final chapter. There are, for Lane, very evident links with the previous chapter both in content and thrust. There is a shared appeal to texts from the Pentateuch and the Psalms, the recurrence of key concepts plus considerations of structure and style which can be said to support the link to the previous chapters. It can be maintained that first, Hebrews 13:15–16 is strongly linked to the exhortation in 12:28 and also to the whole argumentation of the book. As we approach these verses we must be constantly thinking how the exhortation in 13:15–16 may look back to what the author has just been saying in the previous couple of chapters – and also the wider context of the whole book. It is possible that the exhortation here has not been given the prominence it should have as far as what many have understood as the one of the main themes of the book – access to God.

The Ground of This Statement

The statement begins with the phrase "through him" i.e., the Lord Jesus Christ. These words have an emphatic position in the Greek text. Here is the basis, the foundation of everything else. The author can exhort his readers to come to God in praise[2] because of all that the Christ of Hebrews is and has accomplished. The book of Hebrews is about the new way of access to God through Christ for the new community of his people, sons of God, those who he is not ashamed to call his "brothers," 2:10–12. Again, are the words "by or through him" here in this verse meant to serve as a contrast to v. 11 "by the high priest"?

The Exhortation of This Statement

"Let us." There are said to be twelve exhortations in Hebrews and this is one of them. But what are the readers being called upon to do? "Continually offer" – the author has used the present subjunc-

---

[*] HAMILTON MOORE, BD (QUB) MTh (QUB) PhD (QUB); Recognised Teacher Irish Baptist College, N. Ireland and Chester University, Chester; Adjunct Professor Emanuel University, Oradea.

[1] William L. Lane, *Hebrews 9–13*, Word Biblical Commentary 47b (Dallas: Word, 1991), 496–507.

[2] Lane explains that Early Christian documents from Rome and Asia Minor reveal that this formula was used in prayer and praise discourse e.g., 1 Clem. 61:3; 64; Mart. Pol. 14:3; cf. Hippolytus Apostolic Tradition 4; Lane, *Hebrews 9–13*, 549.

tive. In Hebrews 10:1–12 we are reminded that in the OT the priest was ministering and "offering repeatedly" the same sacrifices, which can never take away sins. But Christ's sacrifice did what they could never do – it was one sacrifice for sins *forever*. And so "there is no longer any offering for sin." This verse in Hebrews 13 is saying that the continually offered sacrifices (in the OT by the priests in the outer court – see 9:6) ceased and were to be replaced by the continually offered praise in the holiest – see 10:19–22.

The Focus of This Statement

"To God" – he is the focus of this praise. We have now access to God at any time. In the past 9:1–5 explains that under the first covenant there were ordinances – ordinances of divine service and an earthly sanctuary; also 9:6–10 reveals that the High Priest only could enter the sanctuary and then just once a year. That was "the present age" v. 9 – when the temple was still standing. There was no access. But now in the time of reformation there was access at any time by anyone (Heb 4:14–16; 10:19–25).

The Subject of This Statement: "A Sacrifice of Praise"

As we have affirmed earlier the other sacrifices had come to an end. But of course the community still had sacrifices to offer even if there remained no more sacrifice for sin. There must be praise to God. As Hanger[3] has stated, "There are forms of sacrifice – spiritual, and not literal – that are still pleasing to God. To these the author now calls his readers." It is clear that we have so much to praise him for as we see in all the epistle and particularly in the ultimate hope of the promised city of God (v. 14).

At this point we need to look more closely at this phrase, "a sacrifice of praise." Catholicism and Orthodoxy have attempted by forced reasoning to affirm that the verse actually was referring to the Eucharist. It is about the priest offering the mass – not the people offering their praise.

The phrase is used in the Septuagint in Lev 7:12, 13, 15; 2 Chron 29:31; 33:16; Ps 27:6; 29:14, 23; 106:22; 115:8. Also in Sir. 32:2; 1 Macc. 4:56. But the meaning is the expression of thanksgiving, no more than that. The Greek "sacrifice of praise" can be understood as an epexegetical genitive[4] i.e., praise is the sacrifice. Note also that in Ps 49[MT 50]: 14 LXX, the expression is used figuratively for the offering of cultic praise to God in contrast to animal sacrifice.[5]

John Gill[6] wrote: "The apostle having shown that legal sacrifices were all superseded and abolished by the sacrifice of Christ, which is the design of this epistle, points out what sacrifice believers should offer up to God, under the Gospel dispensation." He maintains that the Jews themselves explained that "in future time (i.e. in the days of the Messiah) all sacrifices shall cease, but, "the sacrifice of praise" shall not cease." Lane[7] also comments upon the use of ἀναφέρειν "to offer" here as a hortatory subjunctive, "let us offer." The author had used this verb in 7:27 of Jesus's offering of himself as the atoning sacrifice. "It may be conjectured that the choice of ἀναφέρειν in v. 15 is intended to underscore the homogeneity of the atoning sacrifice and the sacrifice of praise under the new covenant."

---

[3] Donald A. Hagner, *Hebrews,* NIBC (Peabody, MA: Hendrickson, 1993), 243.

[4] David L. Allen, *Hebrews: An Exegetical and Theological Exposition of Holy* Scripture, The New American Commentary, Vol. 35 (Nashville, TN: B&H Publishing Group, 2010), 622. See also Lane, *Hebrews 9–13*, 549, who writes of "a sacrifice consisting of praise."

[5] Lane, *Hebrews 9–13*, 549.

[6] John Gill, *Exposition of the Bible*, refers to Vajikra Rabba, sect. 9. fol. 153. 1. & sect 27. fol. 168. 4. See Also Philip E. Hughes, *A Commentary on the Epistle to the Hebrews* (Grand Rapids: Eerdmans, 1977), 583; A. Nairne, *The Epistle to the Hebrews*, The Cambridge Greek Testament for Schools and Colleges. Ed. R. John Parry (London: Cambridge University Press, 1922), 131.

[7] Lane, *Hebrews 9–13*, 549.

Notice also the phrase "The fruit of lips, that acknowledge his name." Clearly, for most readers, this cannot be the Eucharist; it is praise, "the fruit of lips," an allusion to Hosea 14:3 LXX.[8] It is praise for all that Christ has accomplished by his death. Those who advocate that here the reference is to priests offering the Eucharist link their assertion with v. 17, "obey your leaders and submit …." For them v. 17 is focusing upon the priests and so they affirm that only the priests are also the focus in vv. 15–16. But is it not simply that the exhortation we "offer" refers to all the believers – as the other exhortations throughout Hebrews? In the next verse the writer is simply reminding the whole community of vv. 15–16 of the need to respect their leaders. The addresses are the same in both verses – the Christians generally and NOT the supposed priests.

We should note that including "that is" provides the necessary explanation[9] since it makes clear that the previous phrase does not refer to animal sacrifices (or the Eucharist) but only praise. Lane[10] maintains that v. 15b "has been placed in apposition to v15a and confirms that the expression θυσία αἰνέσεως, "a sacrifice of praise" is to be interpreted figuratively as verbal praise." While it is true that ὁμολογειν is often translated "confess," Allen[11] also refers to Lane who explains that its interpretation must be determined by its usage in a clause that involves the "sacrifice of praise" and by its following object in the dative case in Greek – "giving thanks *to his name*." Connecting these phrases "fruit of lips" and "acknowledge his name" is found in a pre-Christian Jewish hymn in *Psalms of Solomon* 15:2–3.

> For who, O God, is strong except the one who praises you in truth;
> And what person is powerful except the one who acknowledges your name? A new psalm
> with song from a happy heart,
> The fruit of lips from the well-tuned instrument of the tongue,
> The first fruits of the lips from a devout and righteous heart.

The Fullness of This Statement

"Do not neglect to do good." The sacrifice of praise is not the only sacrifice we are called to make. There is the sacrifice of kindness or loving action, plus of generosity or sacrificial giving. They had been marked by these deeds of love (6:10); now they must not forget to continue in them (note the link between vv. 2a and 16a). These are also sacrifices which are pleasing to God. See Phil 4:14–18. Koester[12] points out that earlier in Hebrews the writer makes clear that God is not pleased with animal sacrifices (10:5, 8) but obedience and praise are the responses he now seeks from us. Pleasing God does not just happen through standing in church and singing hymns – it is something that must be manifest every day of the week in our relationships with others, exhibiting kindness, caring action or active support. Already in this chapter he has highlighted the service we can render, reaching out to the stranger, prisoners and those who are afflicted (13:1–3). Koester[13] also explains that the Greek word εὐποιΐα really signifying "acts of kindness" is rare, but the concept is not, (1 Pet 2:15, 20; 3:6, 17: 4:19; Acts 4:9). The word κοινωνία reminds us of Christ's sharing our human nature (2:11); his followers should also share with others. The motive here is that these acts of sharing and giving are further sacrifices which are acceptable or pleasing to God – he is mentioned emphatically at the end of the verse.

Ellingworth[14] points out that as the writer has earlier insisted on Christ's sacrifice as being unique and all-sufficient, he can employ the same term of how Christians are to respond in gratitude "with-

---

[8] Hughes, *A Commentary on the Epistle to the Hebrews*, 584: Bruce, *Hebrews*, 383, discuss the LXX and Hebrew text of this verse. The words of the Hebrew text can be translated either as "bullocks of our lips" or "fruit of our lips."

[9] Paul Ellingworth, *The Epistle to the* Hebrews, NIGTC (Grand Rapids: Eerdmans; Carlisle: Paternoster, 1993), 720.

[10] Lane, *Hebrews 9–13*, 550.

[11] Allen, *Hebrews: An Exegetical and Theological Exposition of Holy Scripture*, 623.

[12] Craig R. Koester, *Hebrews*, Vol. 36, The Anchor Bible (New York: Doubleday, 2001), 572.

[13] Koester, *Hebrews*, 572

[14] Ellingworth, *The Epistle to the Hebrews*, 722.

out any fear of confusion, or any suggestion that their good deeds automatically entail God's favour." For Hagner,[15] "This, and not through the sacrifice of animals (cf.9:8f.), is the way that faithfulness to God is to be manifested." This notion of being "pleasing to God" is expressed in other places in Hebrews (11:5; 12:28; 13:21). In fact, it seems clear that the exhortation to serve God acceptably in 12:28 is actually worked out here – in our praise and acts of kindness and generosity. These and these only are the sacrifices that are fitting or appropriate for the community of faith.

Calvin wrote:

> Christ ... once for all offered a sacrifice of eternal expiation and reconciliation; now having also entered the sanctuary of heaven, he intercedes for us. In him we are all priests (Rev 1:6; cf. 1 Pet 2:9), but to offer praises and thanksgiving, in short, to offer ourselves and ours to God. It was his office alone to appease God and atone for sins by his offering.[16]

Although believers as priests are not so named in Hebrews – as they are in Revelation and 1 Peter, in the above quotation from Calvin – this is basically what is being affirmed in Hebrews 12:28; 13:15–16. Believers are not like the Jerusalem priests who "serve the tent" (v. 10), but they are in effect priests who serve (or worship) God acceptably with "reverence and awe," (12:28). Cockerill[17] explains:

> The word translated "serve" is also used for "worship." The pastor has explained the work of Christ in priestly terms. Thus, the life of the faithful is a life of worship, a life of approaching God through Christ with the offerings of praise and good works, as chapter 13 will show.

Also in Westfall's work on *Discourse Analysis*[18] she affirms that the believers' priesthood is based on the fact that they share the heavenly calling of Christ (3:1). Again, Heb 4:14 makes clear that we can have access to the throne of grace and Heb 7–10 reveals how that Christ's sacrifice consecrates the believers to enter the holiest. Allen[19] seems convinced of this proposal when he writes:

> The author's conclusion in 12:28 and 13:15–16 is also expressed in unmistakable priestly language. Jesus is our high priest, and believers have been brought into such a relationship with Christ that they too are priests with the concomitant responsibilities and privileges that adhere to the priestly calling.

Thompson[20] also can make the same point when he writes, "Whereas it was once the task of priests to 'offer up a sacrifice,' now the whole community has taken over that role." Even while McKelvey[21] seems reluctant to go as far as other commentators and states that it is "unwarranted, however, to take access to God to mean that Christians are priests, as is the case in 1 Peter 2:5 ... the author's thought was moving in this direction (10:10, 14; cf. 9:19c)," but admits that here "we have a fascinating convergence of thought, inasmuch as both Hebrews and 1 Peter are thinking of the priesthood of the Christian community, not that of individual Christians." But really, is there any significant difference between the individual and the community here? One point is important. Exod 19:6 sets out God's original intention for the people redeemed from Egypt that they would be a "kingdom of priests." This has been realised through the sacrifice of Christ. Does not Hebrews see this as an ulti-

---

[15] Hagner, *Hebrews*, 244.
[16] *Institutes of the Christian Religion*, Vol.2 XXVIII Trans. From the Original Latin and Collated with the Author's Last Edition in French, by J. Allan (Eugene, OR: Wipf & Stock, 2010).
[17] Gareth Lee Cockerill, *The Epistle to the Hebrews*, NICNT (Grand Rapids: Eerdmans, 2012), 672. The word used for "serve" is λατρεύω used elsewhere for approaching God in worship as 8:5; 9:1, 6, 9; 10:2; 13:10.
[18] Cynthia Westfall, *A Discourse Analysis of the Letter to the Hebrews: The Relationship Between Form and Meaning* (London: T&T Clark, 2005), 287–291.
[19] Allen, *Hebrews: An Exegetical and Theological Exposition of Holy Scripture*, 623.
[20] James W. Thompson, *Hebrews* (Grand Rapids: Baker Academic, 2008), 284.
[21] Robert J. McKelvey, *Pioneer and Priest: Jesus Christ in the Epistle to the Hebrews* (Eugene, OR: Pickwick, 2013) 167.

mate goal, realised now in part in the Christian community – see Heb 2:12 – he declares God's name unto his brethren and announces 'I will sing your praise" in the midst of the church? So we come to offer the sacrifice of praise.

The Wider Context of the Statement

If we are to accept this interpretation of these verses, we need to find support in the earlier chapters of this letter, especially the meaning of the phrase which forms part of the title, "the time of reformation" (Heb 9:10). The thrust of the whole passage (9:1–10) is to demonstrate that temple service belonged to another time and to another people. Kurt Simmons[22] explains in his article on this phrase that those under the first covenant had ordinances imposed on them until the time of reformation but there is no indication that the writer identifies either himself or his readers with the Old Testament or the temple system.

For him, it is entirely a thing of the past. He does not say it is imposed upon us, but was imposed on them. This does not mean the temple service was not on-going, for indeed it was. Unbelieving Jews continued to cling to the dead body of Moses, supposing that in it they were justified with God. But for Christians, the ceremonial law had no claim or demand, but stood merely as a relic of the past with which they were not to become entangled in again. "For if I rebuild what I tore down, I prove myself to be a transgressor" (Gal 2:18).

Simmons then considers the substance of the reformation, the things Christ had come to reform. There were things that belonged to the former dispensation: the first covenant; the worldly sanctuary; the priestly service; the appointed days and ceremonies; the blood sacrifices; the washings; the dietary restrictions; miscellaneous carnal ordinances. He points out what the writer of Hebrews says in Heb 9:11–12: "But Christ being come an high priest of good things to come, by a greater and more perfect tabernacle, not made with hands, that is to say, not of this building; neither by the blood of goats and calves, but by his own blood he entered in once into the holy place, having obtained eternal redemption for us" (KJV).

Notice the verb tense in this passage: Christ being come (historical present, describing past events in the present voice); entered by his blood (past tense) having obtained eternal redemption (perfect tense, showing completed action in the past). In other words, the whole substance of the law looked to the work of Christ upon the cross, and was fulfilled in his death, burial, and resurrection. First the shadow; first covenant, worldly sanctuary, priestly service, appointed days and feasts, animal sacrifices, diverse washings, dietary restrictions, carnal ordinances. The shadow ended at the cross. Then the body and substance; new covenant, heavenly sanctuary, High Priesthood of Christ, his own blood, atonement, eternal redemption, perfected forever.

Hebrews reveals that there was a "time then present" – referring to the OT situation and also to the moment when the author was writing with the temple still standing in Jerusalem and the Jewish system of offerings and priests still operating. But the first coming of Christ brought a "time of reformation" of all this. We can say that in fact it signalled the end of the sacrifices and the ministry of the priests and High Priest. The sacrifices have no more any atoning significance, the Aaronic Priesthood has been superseded, and the temple is now obsolete. The reason is that it was only a shadow of the heavenly where our High Priest is now seated. We now have access to him directly – no need of a priest to go to God on our behalf (Heb 10:19–22). We can come to God with our sacrifices of praise. Koester[23] has stated that, "Christ has inaugurated the new covenant by his self-sacrifice, which provides complete cleansing. The way into the holiest part of the sanctuary was blocked under the first

[22] K. Simmons, "The Time of Reformation," in PreteristCentral.com.
[23] Koester, *Hebrews*, 398.

covenant, but Christ has now opened "the new and living way" into the sanctuary (10:19–20)." Ellingworth[24] also expresses the same point of view as he writes of 9:10–14:

> the effect of the OT sacrifices was (a) to do only with the sarx, and (b) temporary. In vv. 13f., the author reaffirms and develops point (a). The OT sacrifices are only πρὸς τὴν τῆς σαρκὸς καθαρότητα, but Christ's sacrifice is offered in the power of the eternal Spirit and is thus able to cleanse people inwardly, so that they can have true access to God in worship.

Tom Wells[25] in discussing worship in Hebrews, explains that:

> The whole Mosaic service "cannot perfect the conscience of the worshipper" (9:9). It could not give the sinner who was conscious of his sins the conviction that God wholeheartedly received him. It required a better priest, a better service and a better sacrifice to do that. That priest is Christ. His service is the service of the new covenant. His sacrifice is himself … Christ has entered the real "sanctuary," heaven (9:24).… What Jesus has done in dying has opened the door to God so fully that we may have utter confidence in approaching him. Our forgiveness is complete, since our sacrifice is perfect (10:15–18). There are no barriers between the believer and God - worship, praise, thanksgiving and prayer-all the things we address to God-are equally acceptable to him. Since that is the case, we can run to him at any time!

But we must go further back in Hebrews to chapters 5–7. Here we learn of the Aaronic priesthood which passed away and of the eternal priesthood of Christ. First we have in Heb 5:1–10 the qualifications for the priesthood. To take this role two things were necessary: (a) he must have sympathy vv. 2–3; (b) he must be divinely appointed (v. 4). He could not set himself up as High Priest. God alone chooses a person for this honour. It had to be by divine appointment (Exod 28:1ff; Lev 8:1ff; Num 16:5; 17:5; 18:1; Ps 105:26). He needed to have a direct and special call from God. The writer of Hebrews affirms that these were true also of Christ. First (a) divine appointment vv. 5–6. He did not assume this ministry by his own initiative but was called to it by God who acclaimed him as his Son, see 1:5 in the words of Ps 2:7. The second quotation from Ps 110:4 introduces two new features which affirm that Christ's priesthood is different/greater than that of Aaron's. It is "forever" and it is "after the order of Melchizedek." These will be expounded later, but they show that his priesthood is timeless. Two OT passages are cited to make the argument, vv. 5–6. In chapter 1:5 the unique sonship was affirmed by the citing of Ps 2:7. There also Ps 110:1 was applied to Christ in v. 13. Now we have a further quote from that Psalm. The person addressed in Ps 110:1 is also referred to as "a priest forever, after the order of Melchizedek" in v. 4. The quote from Ps 110:1 is not here, but the link has already been established in Hebrews 1. Jesus is the Son of God and raised to the right hand of God and at the same time appointed by God to be "a priest forever."

His second qualification was an ability to sympathise with those who need his help. This is because he is made like his brethren and has been exposed to all the trials/temptations/tests they have had to endure "in the days of his flesh" (see also Heb 4:15). Finally, v. 16 invites us to "with confidence draw near to the throne of grace." The later chapters of Hebrews will reveal how this access to the throne of God is now possible for us.

The author from 7:11f. sets out the imperfections of the Aaronic priesthood. The Levitical priesthood was something belonging to the age of preparation, which had now given way to the age of fulfilment. It seems clear that God had long ago decreed the supersession of the Levitical priesthood by another.

---

[24] Ellingworth, *The Epistle to the Hebrews*, 454.
[25] Tom Wells, "The Epistle to the Hebrews and Worship," *Reformation & Revival: A Quarterly Journal for Church Leadership*, Vol. 9 No. 2 Spring 2000, 126.

Verse 12 reminds us that the Aaronic priesthood was instituted under the Mosaic law. The writer of Hebrews is concerned with the ceremonial law – he will state later as we have noted that the sacrificial cultus is something which could never effectively remove sin. Here the teaching is that the ceremonial law was a temporary dispensation of God valid only until Christ came to inaugurate the age of perfection. Its supersession is seen here as implied in the emphasis that the Messiah is a priest after the order of Melchizedek.

That this is a radical change is clear since Jesus had nothing to do with the tribe of Levi but belonged to the tribe of Judah. Whatever hopes and promises were stated in the Pentateuch for this tribe there certainly was nothing about a member of this tribe officiating at the altar. Again in vv. 15–19 the quotation of the text of Ps 110 shows the imperfection or limitation of the old and the superiority of the new. "You are a priest forever." In the old order each one died in due course. The Christian's High Priest is immortal. He died once for all and is risen from the dead and lives in the power of an indestructible life. The law which established the Aaronic priesthood is called "a carnal commandment," (KJV) or "legal requirement" (ESV) being "a system of earth-bound rules" (NEB). It regulated the externalities of religion – the physical decent of priests, a material shrine, animal sacrifices. Everything in this system was marked by transience, but with Christ everything is characterised by permanence. Christ is said to have "become" a priest = at the time of the incarnation – eligible to be a priest because he has come to share their nature (2:17–18). Not as the other priests – the word used is "to arise" (7:11).

The author states in v. 19, "(The law made nothing perfect); but on the other hand, a better hope is introduced, through which we draw near to God." Its essential weakness was that it could not bring life. It could not bring the power but only show the standard to measure moral status. It could not make perfect but only focus/bring to light imperfection. A priesthood based upon this also had limitations. Christ accomplishes for us something better in that it brings about what was impossible under the old system – we can have access to or draw near to God (10:19–22; 13:15–16); seemingly, without a priest, but in reality, as a priest!

So Hebrews explains that under the Levitical system gifts and sacrifices were regarded as having a temporarily effect in enabling men to come to God, but not to attain perfection; the writer has in mind the superiority of the work of Christ (10:14). As F. F. Bruce[26] has stated, "in the earthly sanctuary sacrifices were indeed offered, but their efficacy was sadly restricted; they could not bring 'perfection' to the worshipper because they did not affect his conscience." It is only when the conscience is purified that a man is set free to approach God without reservation and offer him acceptable service and worship. For the superiority of the Christian way (see 9:14; 10:22. We noted earlier in 9:10 that the limitation under the old order is further seen in that many of the regulations imposed dealt only with the external issues. They existed "until the time of reformation" – only here in the NT and signifying something like "until the time of the new order," or better the "re-forming" of the worship of God.

Moving on to 9:11 we see that the author deals with the "good things that have come." Note the following:

(a) by virtue of his perfect sacrifice our High Priest has taken his seat at the right hand of the throne of God in the heavenly Zion, a sanctuary not made with hands. See Mark 14:58; Acts 7:48; 17:24.

(b) Whereas Aaron and his successors went into the earthly holy of holies "by means of the blood of calves and goats" Christ has entered literally "through" (διὰ), not as RSV "taking his own blood," as if he made atonement for us in the heavenly holy of holies by presenting his efficacious blood. On the cross he accomplished in reality what Aaron and his successors performed in type by the twofold act of slaying the victim and presenting its blood in the holy of holies. So the meaning is that by vir-

---

[26] Frederick F. Bruce, *The Epistle to the Hebrews,* NICNT (Grand Rapids: Eerdmans, 1990), 209.

tue of his shed blood he can appear as by right as his people's representative and High Priest. The Aaronic "redemption" had a token and temporary character and so the High Priests had to present themselves before God repeatedly. But Christ entered in once for all and is enthroned in perpetuity, because the redemption he procured is perfect in nature and eternal in effect.

(c) vv. 13–14 explains that the blood of slaughtered animals did possess a certain efficacy – the removal of ceremonial pollution. "The blood of goats and bulls" covers general sacrifices; "the ashes of a heifer," the ritual prescribed in Numbers 19. The unbroken heifer was slaughtered outside the camp and its blood was sprinkled 7 times in front of the tabernacle. The body was completely burned and water containing the ashes could be sprinkled upon someone who had been rendered unclean through touching a dead body (Num 31:21ff.). Christ's blood however, effected no mere ceremonial cleansing. Here we have one of the author's "how much more" in relation to Christ's sacrifice. These earlier rituals, as has been noted, may effect external purification, but the blood of Christ cleanses the conscience and so does the very thing they could not do. This is the perfection which the ancient ceremonial was unable to achieve. Once a defiled man was cleansed through the ashes of the red heifer he could approach the tabernacle where there was the symbol of the presence of God; so we can come right into his presence if we are cleansed.

(d) Christ is the mediator of the new covenant vv. 15–22. This is the New Covenant already foretold by Jeremiah (see also 8:6). The basis of the covenant and his mediatorship is now made plain – his sacrificial death.

By virtue of his death, redemption has been provided for those who had broken the law of God. As Bruce[27] can affirm, the first covenant provided a measure of atonement and remission for sins committed under it, but "it was incapable of providing 'eternal redemption;' this was a blessing which had to await the inauguration of the new covenant." He explains that this "redemptive death" had now taken place and "the promise of the eternal inheritance," the new covenant and all that the grace of God provides under it has been made good to all those who are called.

The author of Hebrews can then explain how Christ himself by fulfilling the will of God to the uttermost – this involved the offering of his body/himself - he has "sanctified" his people and provided the "perfection" which was unattainable on the basis of the ancient sacrifices. By the offering of his body and his blood (10:14–19) – his incarnate life – sanctification and access to God have been made available. In addition, his sacrifice was so perfect a sacrifice that no repetition of it is either necessary or possible; it was offered "once for all." The sanctification which his people receive is their inner cleansing from sin and being made fit for the presence of God.

We must take a little more time with 10:11–12. The unrepeatable sacrifice of Christ is contrasted with the sacrifices of the old order – but note with an appeal to the language of Ps 110 in v. 13. We have seen already the use of this Psalm in 1:3, 13; 8:1, but only now does he draw out its full significance. Aaronic priests never sat down throughout the performance of their duties. These duties were never done as sacrifices had always to be repeated. See v. 1 "every year," and 7:27 "daily." But whether annually or daily repetition was necessary, still not one of these sacrifices could remove sin or cleanse the conscience with permanent effect. The completion of one sacrifice meant that another one would also follow. But Christ sat down, in keeping with the perfection of his sacrifice. No further sacrificial service is required of a priest who appeared once to put away sin and perfect "for all time" his people. Our seated priest does indeed have a ministry to discharge at his father's right hand, but it is a ministry of intercession on the basis of the sacrifice presented and accepted. We can then have confidence of access to him and to his high-priestly aid. Probably most of the early converts had been accustomed to a form of worship involving animal sacrifices. The new form of worship had no place for such sacrifices, for they were not needed.

---

[27] Bruce, *The Epistle to the Hebrews*, 220.

Note also v. 14. In v. 10 "sanctified" is in the perfect tense; here as in 2:11 it is the present participle passive that is used. Bruce explains:

> In verse 10 the emphasis lay on the unrepeatable nature of the death of Christ as the sacrifice by which his people are set apart for the worship and service of God; here their character as the people thus set apart is simply indicated in "timeless" terms, because emphasis is now laid on the fact that by that same sacrifice Christ has eternally "perfected" his holy people.

Ellingworth[28] also writes of the significance of v. 14 which he sees as concerned with the consequences of Christ's death and exaltation for believers.

> Here, as elsewhere in Hebrews … τελειόω implies the fulfilment of the Christian goal, namely an access to God which was formally open only to the high priest. Hebrews emphasises the unique priesthood of Jesus … and thus does not speak explicitly of the priesthood of all believers; but he comes close to doing so here, in language which is not only cultic … but priestly…. Christ now has continuous and uninterrupted access to the Father … Christians though still on earth, share the same permanent access to the Father.

So by Christ's sacrifice his people have had their conscience cleansed from guilt; they have been fitted to approach God as worshippers; they have experienced the fulfilment of the promise of being brought into that perfect relation with God which is involved in the new covenant. Now we can see this stressed in vv. 19–25. Our link with Christ involves our access to God. There is a long sentence of sustained exhortation. What is stated is in view of all that has been accomplished for us by Christ. We are now encouraged to draw near to God. The "confidence" which believers in Christ have to enter into the heavenly sanctuary through him is set in contrast to the restrictions we noted earlier which hedged about the privilege of symbolic entry into the presence of God in Israel's earthly sanctuary. Not all the people could exercise this privilege, but the high priest only as their representative. He could not exercise this privilege any time he chose, but at fixed times and under fixed conditions. But those who have been cleansed within, made perfect by the sacrifice of Christ, have received a free right of access. We saw earlier that this invitation to draw near with boldness has already been issued in the epistle in 4:16 based on the assurance that our High Priest has passed through the heavens and that he is one whose own experiences of temptation enable him to sympathise with his people in their trials. Here the assurance is that the way by which the High Priest has entered into the presence of God remains open for his people to follow him there.

It is to the very throne of God that believers have entry. They do not need to ask "Who shall ascend the hill of the Lord?" We may enter the heavenly abode and hold communion with him "by the blood of Jesus." He thus entered (9:12) and we can follow. It is a new way and a "living" one, for in effect, the ever-living Christ himself as his people's sacrifice and priest is the way to God. So because Christ is our high priest and he is there, the author exhorts us in v. 22, "Let us draw near."

All this teaching is leading up to Hebrews 13:15–16. It is like a final summary or conclusion in light of all the earlier explanation. Guthrie[29] maintains that here in chapter 13:

> The epistle does not close without another use of priestly imagery. Having expounded in great detail the priestly office of Christ, the writer here employs the same imagery to describe the function of believers. There is a fundamental distinction in the type of sacrifices offered, for whereas Christ offered himself, the believer is to offer *a sacrifice of praise to God*…. Especially characteristic is the idea that such a sacrifice should be offered *continually* … in striking contrast to the once-for-all sacrifice of Christ.

---

[28] Ellingworth, *The Epistle to the Hebrews*, 511.
[29] Donald Guthrie, *The Letter to the Hebrews: An Introduction and Commentary* (Leicester: Inter-Varsity Press, 1988), 275.

Or, to sum up, as Cockerill[30] has expressed it:

> These verses are the pastor's final description of the life of faith so forcefully advocated throughout his sermon. Such sacrifices are not sacrifices for sin but sacrifices offered to God through the cleansing power of and in grateful response to the once-for-all, sin-removing sacrifice of Christ…. The sacrifices of the Old Covenant were offered perpetually because they were never effective in removing sin (10:1–4). The sacrifices of praise and right living described in these verses are to be offered perpetually because Christ's obedient self-offering has effectively done away with sin.

Therefore, let us draw near, let us offer the sacrifice of praise and let us live lives of compassion and loving care of others as the author of Hebrews exhorts us.

Bibliography

Allen, David L. *Hebrews: An Exegetical and Theological Exposition of Holy Scripture.* The New American Commentary. Vol. 35. Nashville, TN: B&H Publishing Group, 2010.

Bruce, Frederick, F. *The Epistle to the Hebrews.* NICNT. Grand Rapids: Eerdmans, 1990.

Cockerill, Gareth Lee. *The Epistle to the Hebrews.* NICNT. Grand Rapids: Eerdmans, 2012.

Ellingworth, Paul. *The Epistle to the Hebrews.* NIGTC. Grand Rapids: Eerdmans; Carlisle: Paternoster, 1993.

Guthrie, Donald. *The Letter to the Hebrews: An Introduction and Commentary.* Leicester: Inter-Varsity Press, 1988.

Hughes, Philip E. *A Commentary on the Epistle to the Hebrews.* Grand Rapids: Eerdmans, 1977.

Hagner, Donald A. *Hebrews.* NIBC. Peabody: Hendrickson, 1993.

Koester, Craig R. *Hebrews.* Vol. 36. The Anchor Bible New York: Doubleday, 2001.

Lane, William L. *Hebrews 1–8.* Word Biblical Commentary. 47a. Dallas: Word, 1991.

Lane, William L. *Hebrews 9–13.* Word Biblical Commentary. 47b. Dallas: Word, 1991.

McKelvey, Robert J. *Pioneer and Priest: Jesus Christ in the Epistle to the Hebrews* (Eugene, OR: Pickwick, 2013.

Nairne, A. *The Epistle to the Hebrews.* The Cambridge Greek Testament for Schools and Colleges. Edited by R. John Parry. London: Cambridge University Press, 1922.

Thompson, James W. *Hebrews.* Grand Rapids: Baker Academic, 2008.

Wells, Tom. "The Epistle to the Hebrews and Worship." *Reformation & Revival: A Quarterly Journal for Church Leadership* Vol. 9 No. 2 (Spring 2000): 126.

Westfall, Cynthia. *A Discourse Analysis of the Letter to the Hebrews: The Relationship Between Form and Meaning.* London: T&T Clark, 2005.

---

[30] Cockerill, *The Epistle to the Hebrews*, 705.

ECHOES AND INTERPRETATION IN HEBREWS[1]

GEORGE H. GUTHRIE[*]

Union University

ABSTRACT: Since the 1989 publication of *Echoes of Scripture in the Letters of Paul* by Richard Hays, fresh research has been done on a certain aspect of intertextuality between the Jewish Scriptures and the New Testament. The current article applies Hays's approach to the New Testament book of Hebrews, first identifying echoes previously recognized by various researchers (although at times those researchers did not use the term "echo") and then suggesting others that might be identified in the book. Particularly, the Nathan oracle of 2 Sam 7 (=1 Chron 17) and various contexts in Deuteronomy are investigated and a number of echoes in Hebrews are put forward for consideration.

KEY WORDS: echoes, Hebrews, allusions, intertextuality, Scripture.

A person would have to be deaf indeed not to have heard reverberating echoes of Richard Hays's 1989 work on a particular form of intertextuality in Paul. His *Echoes of Scripture in the Letters of Paul*,[2] which builds on the work of John Hollander,[3] addresses especially faint or less than obvious allusions, "recollections" according to Hays, drawn from Scripture and functioning as diachronic tropes.[4] The book has fostered energetic discussion, breathing fresh life into dialogue on the relationship between the New Testament and the Jewish Scriptures. Some, such as W. S. Green, J. Christian Beker, and Hans Hübner have found much to criticize in Hays's approach, pointing, for instance, to a lack of clarity in Hays's definition of echoes, his confusion of allegory and typology, or his methodology in isolating echoes.[5] Beker pointedly asks, "when are echoes whispers, when trumpets, when muffled, subliminal sounds?"[6] Others, including Craig Evans, S. C. Keesmaat, Karen Jobes, and

---

[1] This paper was presented at the New Testament Colloquium, University of Aberdeen, Scotland, Spring 2005. Reference is often made to the MT and Greek versions for "echoes" of the OT.

[*] GEORGE H. GUTHRIE serves as the Benjamin W. Perry Professor of Bible at Union University in Jackson, TN, USA. He holds the Ph.D. degree in New Testament from Southwestern Baptist Theological Seminary in Fort Worth, TX and the Th.M. degree in New Testament from Trinity Evangelical Divinity School in Deerfield, IL.

[2] Richard B. Hays, *Echoes of Scripture in the Letters of Paul* (New Haven: Yale University Press, 1989); see the collection of essays in Craig A. Evans and James A. Sanders, *Paul and the Scriptures of Israel*, Journal for the Study of the New Testament. Supplement Series, 83 (Sheffield: JSOT Press, 1993) and the survey of work on echoes by Kenneth D. Litwak, "Echoes of Scripture? A Critical Survey of Recent Works on Paul's Use of the Old Testament," in *Currents in Research: Biblical Studies* (Sheffield: Sheffield Academic Press, 1998). Also, see the reviews of Hays by Robert L. Brawley, "Echoes of Scripture in the Letters of Paul," *Cumberland Seminarian* 28 (1990), 94–5; Karl P. Donfried, "Echoes of Scripture in the Letters of Paul," *Theological Studies* 52 (1991), 732–34; Sharyn E. Dowd, "Echoes of Scripture in the Letters of Paul," *Lexington Theological Quarterly* 25 (1990), 125–28; James D G. Dunn, "Echoes of Scripture in the Letters of Paul," *Literature and Theology* 7 (1993), 88–90; Craig A. Evans, "Echoes of Scripture in the Letters of Paul," *Catholic Biblical Quarterly* 53 (1991), 496–98; David M. Hay, "Echoes of Scripture in the Letters of Paul," *Interpretation* 45 (1991), 88; Arthur Long, "Echoes of Scripture in the Letters of Paul," *Faith and Freedom: A Journal of Progressive Religion* 46 (1993), 125–26; Dale B. Martin, "Echoes of Scripture in the Letters of Paul," *Modern Theology* 7 (1991), 291–92; Ian Paul, "Echoes of Scripture in the Letters of Paul," *Anvil* 11, no. 3 (1994), 267–68; J Paul Pollard, "Echoes of Scripture in the Letters of Paul," *Restoration Quarterly* 36, no. 1 (1994), 53–4; Carol L. Stockhausen, "Echoes of Scripture in the Letters of Paul," *Journal of Biblical Literature* 111, no. 1 (1992), 155–57.

[3] John Hollander, *The Figure of Echo: A Mode of Allusion in Milton and After* (Berkeley: University of California Press, 1981).

[4] Hays, *Echoes of Scripture*, 20; Hayes states (p. 29), "*allusion* is used of obvious intertextual references, *echo* of subtler ones."

[5] J. Christiaan Beker, "Echoes and Intertextuality: On the Role of Scripture in Paul's Theology," in *Paul and the Scriptures of Israel*, 64–9; William S. Green, "Doing the Text's Work for It: Richard Hays on Paul's Use of Scripture," in *Paul and the Scriptures of Israel*, 58–63; Hans Hübner, "Intertextualität--Die Hermeneutische Strategie Des Paulus: Zu Einem Neuen Versuch Der Theologischen Rezeption Des Alten Testaments Im Neuen.," *Theologische Literaturzeitung* 116 (1991), 881–98.

[6] Beker, "Echoes and Intertextuality," 64.

Frank Thielman, have built on Hays's basic proposals and offered suggestive insights on specific points of NT interpretation.[7]

In this paper, I want to present preliminary findings stemming from an analysis of echoes in Hebrews. I define echoes as "faint allusions," holding that their presence in Hebrews witnesses, among other things, to the author's saturation with the language of his Greek text. Rather than exhaustive, I mean the paper to be suggestive of the fruit to be picked in such an endeavour, or at least a stimulus for discussion concerning one aspect of methodology when dealing with the OT in Hebrews. After a brief treatment of methodological issues, the presentation unfolds in two primary movements. The first concerns echoes in Hebrews that have been recognized previously, though not always labelled as such. The second movement focuses on the analysis of two passages in Hebrews, pointing out what might be considered echoes of OT material.

Methodology

At the heart of Hays's program, stand seven tests for hearing an echo in the text.[8] These are availability, volume, recurrence, thematic coherence, historical plausibility, history of interpretation, and satisfaction. "Availability" refers to whether the proposed source was indeed available to the author and/or the original readers. As Hays points out, when considering Paul's use of the Scriptures this is not a problem with which we have to be concerned for the most part, and the same, of course, is true for Hebrews. "Volume" concerns the degree of repetition, both of words and syntactical patterns, from the source text, but also the prominence of the source text and the rhetorical stress on the echo in Paul. Especially important for our study is the test of "recurrence," a criterion that considers how often the passage is used by Paul and includes the broader contexts of key passages. "How well does the alleged echo fit into the line of argument?" which Hays refers to as "Thematic Coherence," constitutes the fourth test, and "Historical Plausibility" the fifth. The latter analyses whether Paul and his readers, given their historical context, could have understood the alleged meaning of the echo. Sixth is the test of "History of Interpretation," or whether interpreters through the ages have heard the proposed echo. As Hays points out, however, this test is inherently unreliable as a primary guide, since traditions of interpretation may grow up that drown out nuanced hearings of the text. Finally, the test of "Satisfaction" considers whether the alleged echo makes sense in context, elucidating the argument.

As we identify echoes in Hebrews, we utilize Hays's tests. Yet, while cognizant of these criteria, as a methodological approach I have given special weight to aspects of the third, "Recurrence." In light of the extent and pervasiveness of the uses of the OT in Hebrews, I suggest the tracking of echoes might best begin with a consideration of the broader contexts of the book's citations and overt allusions. Of course, there may be places where an author uses echoes not originating in the contexts of his or her direct quotations and allusions. However, when stepping out on uncertain ground, it is better to step first on the firmer parts of a path rather than the softer spots of a wide-open field, and the contexts of the quotations are, at least, an appropriate place to begin our search, for we are assured of Hays's first and third criteria, availability and recurrence.

As Hays points out, "Allusive echo functions to suggest to the reader that text B should be understood in light of a broad interplay with text A, encompassing aspects of A beyond those explicitly echoed."[9] In his study on the influence of Isaiah 7–9 on Matthew's soteriology, Warren Carter, fol-

---

[7] Karen H. Jobes, "Jerusalem, Our Mother : Metalepsis and Intertextuality in Galatians 4:21–31," *Westminster Theological Journal* 55, no. 2 (1993) 299–320; Sylvia C. Keesmaat, "Exodus and the Intertextual Transformation of Tradition in Romans 8:14–30," *Journal for the Study of the New Testament*, no. 54 (1994) 29–56; Sylvia C. Keesmaat, "Paul and His Story : Exodus and Tradition in Galatians," in *Early Christian Interpretation of the Scriptures of Israel* (Sheffield, Eng: Sheffield Academic Pr, 1997); Frank Thielman, "Unexpected Mercy : Echoes of a Biblical Motif in Romans 9–11," *Scottish Journal of Theology* 47, no. 2 (1994) 169–181.

[8] Hays, *Echoes of Scripture*, 29–32.

[9] Ibid., 20.

lowing Lars Hartman, suggests intertextual elements invoke the authority of the source text, using the words of that text but at times pointing beyond the intertextual element to a larger complex of ideas.[10] This is similar to the suggestions of C. H. Dodd, who proposed that a quotation from the Old Testament serves to bring to mind a broader OT context, invoking the authority of the whole.[11] It also makes sense in communication contexts, such as the preaching of sermons today. Imagine, for instance, a preacher, expounding on the theme of the need for love in the church, who exhorts, "let's not be clanging cymbals!" Such a reference calls to mind, of course, the whole of 1 Corinthians 13. That chapter is so fore-grounded in the conscience of most Christian congregations today, both by its distinctiveness and its popularity, the allusion would be readily identifiable and the collateral material brought to mind as well.

In line with this dynamic, it may be suggested that the author of Hebrews, rather than an atomistic approach to citations from Israel's Scriptures, had in mind, and at times used, OT references in light of their broader contexts. For instance, the author's reasons for using the brief quotation from Isaiah at Heb 2:13 are barely discernible until one considers the broader, messianic context from which the quotation hails. The broader contexts of many Hebrews quotations, moreover, would have been familiar to the hearers, stemming from their Scriptures, though some contexts certainly would have been more familiar than others, depending on the level of popularity and use. Such a circumstance, therefore, challenges us not to be atomistic in our analysis of the OT citations and allusions. In my study of the uses of the OT in Hebrews in recent years, therefore, I have systematically examined the broader contexts of every quotation, looking for elements that might be echoed elsewhere in Hebrews.

Previously Heard Echoes in Hebrews

First, there are those places where interpreters have already noted what might be considered echoes of the OT text. For instance, William L. Lane, in the first volume of his commentary on Hebrews, points to Ps 92:1/93:1 MT and Ps 95:10/96:10 MT as the source for the phrase τὴν οἰκουμένην mentioned at Heb 2:5, which he equates with the age to come (6:5) and the city to come (13:14). Both psalm passages proclaim that this "world" established with the reign of God, "shall not be shaken," a part of these psalms echoed at Heb 12:28. Lane comments, "The explicit allusion to 'a kingdom that cannot be shaken' in Heb 12:28 indicates that these passages were not far from the writer's mind when he penned [2:]5.[12] Thus, the use of τὴν οἰκουμένην at 2:5 echoes Ps(s) 92/95 (LXX)."

Similarly, several commentators have found in the reference to τόν πρωτότοκον in the IF of Heb 1:6, an allusion to Ps 88:28 LXX.[13] This, IF, of course, follows fast on the heels of the paired quotation of Ps 2:7 and 2 Sam 7:14, which emphasize the Son's superiority over the angels by virtue of his unique filial relationship with the Father. Beginning at 88.27, the psalm reads, "He will call to me, "You are my Father, my God, and the helper of my salvation." And I will appoint him as my firstborn (πρωτότοκον), exalted beyond the kings of the earth." This proclamation concerning David reverberates themes from the Nathan oracle in 2 Sam 7, and, with Ps 88's theme of world domination, scholars such as Kraus also have suggested its association with Ps 2.[14] N. M. Sarna, who is supported by

---

[10] Warren Carter, "Evoking Isaiah: Matthean Soteriology and an Intertextual Reading of Isaiah 7–9 and Matthew 1:23 and 4:15–16.," in *Journal of Biblical Literature* (Society of Biblical Literature, 2000), 505.

[11] C. H. Dodd, *According to the Scriptures: The Sub-Structure of New Testament Theology* (London: Nisbet, 1961), 126. Dodd notes:

> The method included, first, the selection of certain large sections of the Old Testament Scriptures, especially from Isaiah, Jeremiah and certain minor prophets, and from the Psalms. These sections were understood as wholes, and particular verses or sentences were quoted from them rather as pointers to the whole context than as constituting testimonies in and for themselves.... But in the fundamental passages it is the total context that is in view, and is the basis of argument.

[12] William L. Lane, *Hebrews 1–8*, Word Biblical Commentary; V. 47a (Dallas: Word, 1991), 45–6.

[13] E.g. Weiss, *Der Brief an die Hebräer*, 163.

[14] Hans-Joachim Kraus, *Psalms 60–150: A Commentary*, trans. Hilton C. Oswald (Minneapolis: Augsburg, 1989), 209.

Michael Fishbane, suggests that Ps 89 MT is an adaptation of the Nathan oracle in 2 Sam 7.[15] The psalm may have been called to mind by the author of Hebrews as he quoted 2 Sam 7:14 in the previous verse. Just a few verses prior to the psalm's mention of the πρωτότοκον, in v. 12 of the Greek version, the psalmist writes, "Yours are the heavens and yours the earth, the world (οἰκουμένην) and its fullness."

The author's use at 3:16–19 of *subiectio*, a rhetorical pattern of asking and answering a series of questions in rapid-fire manner, takes its questions from Ps 95:7b–11 and its answers from a network of passages bemoaning the wilderness rebellion. That those who came out of Egypt with Moses were the ones who rebelled against the Lord (Heb 3:16) may be concluded from Ps 106, Num 14:1–38, or Deut 9. That it was "those who sinned, whose bodies fell in the desert" with whom God was upset (Heb 3:17) echoes either Ps 106 or Num 14:1–38. The concept of the disobedient ones as those to whom God swore that they would not enter his rest (Heb 3:18) finds expression in Deut 9:7, 24. Finally, the unit concludes with a summary statement in 3:19, explaining that at its core the wanderers' inability to enter God's rest stemmed from their unbelief, thus linking the concepts of unbelief and disobedience. This important "unbelief" motif occurs in Deut 9:23, Num 14:11, and Ps 78:22, 32. These allusions, rather than overt—some of them cannot be pinpointed as to exact location— constitute recollections, to use Hays's word, of prominent concepts. Thus, these interrelated passages form somewhat a hall of echoes from which the author draws, and this observation will be important as we go further.

Other examples can be given. My interest in Hebrews research originates from a 1954 article by August Strobel, in which he suggests the "cries and tears" of Heb 5:7, although not part of the Gethsemane accounts, probably stem from Ps 116, a "prayer of righteous suffering."[16] The faintness of the allusion, however, would suggest that these be considered echoes expressing, however faintly, reflection on Jesus's experience in Gethsemane in light of early Christian appropriation of "righteous-sufferer" psalm material.

More recently, Dave Matthewson has offered a highly suggestive article entitled, "Heb 6:4–6 in Light of the Old Testament."[17] In this article, Matthewson argues that "the author's language in 6.4–6 is coloured by OT references by means of allusion and echo apart from direct citation."[18] Thus, the descriptions of those who have fallen away, descriptions so elusive and divisive in the history of interpretation, stem from the wilderness wandering passages, continuing a prominent contextual framework for exhortation begun in 3:7–19. For instance, Mathewson suggests those who were "enlightened" echoes the pillar of fire by which the Israelites were "enlightened" on their way (Neh 9:12, 19; Ps 105:39).[19] The "heavenly gift" that those under consideration had tasted echoes those passages that refer to the heavenly gift of manna, which the Lord gave to people of the wilderness generation. In passages such as Exod 16:15; Ps 78 (77):24; and Neh 9:15, the heavenly bread is said to have been given (ἔδωκεν) to them. For Mathewson, that those who have fallen away had become companions of the Holy Spirit (Heb 6:4c), echoes the experience of the wilderness wanderers, who

[15] N. M. Sarna, "Psalm 89: A Study in Inner Biblical Exegesis," in *Biblical and Other Studies*, ed. A. Altmann (Cambridge, MA: Harvard University Press, 1963) 29–46; Michael Fishbane, *Biblical Interpretation in Ancient Israel* (Oxford: Clarendon Press, 1985) 466–7.

[16] E.g., August Strobel, "Die Psalmengrundlage der Gethsemane-Parallele Hbr. 5,7ff.," *Zeitschrift für die neutestamentliche Wissenshaft* 45 (1954), 252–66. Strobel suggests Psalm 116 forms the basis for Hebrews 5:7–8. That Psalm states in part, "I love the Lord, for he heard my voice; he heard my cry for mercy…. The cords of death entangled me, the anguish of the grave came upon me; I was overcome by trouble and sorrow … you, O Lord, have delivered my soul from death, my eyes from tears, my feet from stumbling." Psalm 22, a psalm the early church understood as referring to the Gethsemane experience, offers another viable backdrop, placing great emphasis on the "cry" of the righteous sufferer.

[17] Dave Mathewson, "Reading Heb 6:4–6 in Light of the Old Testament," *WTJ* 61 (1999), 209–25. One caveat is in order. Matthewson identifies the whole of 12:14–29 as a warning. Rather, the warning comes at 12:25–29 and follows the pattern of *a fortiori* argument common elsewhere in the warning passages. See Guthrie, *The Structure of Hebrews*, 135.

[18] Mathewson, "Heb 6:4–6 in Light of the Old Testament," 214.

[19] Ibid., 216–17.

had extensive interaction with the Spirit of God, as witnessed in numerous passages, such as Num 9:20, 11:17, 25, and Isa 63:11. Having considered the elements describing the fallen in Heb 6:4–6, Matthewson concludes: "the author is not just alluding to snippets of texts and isolated vocabulary for rhetorical colour, but by alluding to texts which belong to a larger matrix of ideas he is evoking the entire context and story of Israel's experience in the wilderness."[20] Thus, the author of Hebrews utilizes the language of the OT, specifically failures of the wilderness generation, to speak of a particularly grievous abandonment of the Christian community in his day. Mathewson's identification of echoes here has enormous implications for discussions of this passage's interpretation, giving ambiguous language a grounding and context not previously recognized.

Hebrews 3:1–6, a notoriously difficult passage at points, offers another example of the importance of identifying echoes in the text. In the second through sixth verses of Heb 3, the author argues that

a.   Jesus is faithful to the one who appointed him (v. 2).

b.   Jesus is worthy of more glory than Moses (v. 3a).

c.   This is analogous to the builder of a house receiving more honour than the house itself (v. 3b) .

d.   Every house is built by someone (v. 4a).

e.   Yet, God is the builder of everything (v. 4b).

f.   And, finally, Christ was faithful as a son over his house (v. 6).

It could be that the author is pulling the analogy of v. 3 out of thin air, or that the whole grows out of a parallel to Philo's truism, "But the Mind of all things has brought the universe into existence; and that which has made is superior to the thing made." (*Migr. Abr.* 193). Yet, Mary Rose D"Angelo, playing off a 1961 *NTS* article by Sverre Aalen, considers the argument in light of 2 Sam 7 and its parallel in 1 Chron 17.[21] In 2 Sam 7 we are told that David's son would build a house for God's name (7:13), and that the son's house would be made faithful forever. The term οἶκος is prominent in this chapter, used fourteen times by the author to speak variously of the Lord's house, David's house, and the house of David's heir. Further, the chapter proclaims that the Lord would build the son's house and that the son would build a house for the Lord (v. 13).

Yet, this is not all. In 2 Sam 7:16, and the parallels in 1 Chron 17:14, God promises to "confirm" or "show faithful" the house of David's son, the author using the verb πιστόω.[22] In the Greek version of 2 Sam 7.16 we read, "And his house shall be shown faithful, and his kingdom forever before me." Further, it is interesting that the Targum on the parallel passage in 1 Chron 17 emphasizes the faithfulness of David's son and God's promise to establish that son as faithful in God's house and kingdom. Verse 14 reads, "And I shall establish him as a faithful one among my people in my sanctuary house and in my kingdom forever, and the throne of his kingdom will be established for ever." Though the targum probably is late, the parallel with the statement in Hebrews 3:2, which reads, "being faithful to the one having appointed him," is striking.

Also, in the Greek version of 1 Chron 17:23, we find the phrase ἐπις τὸν οἶκον αὐτοῦ, a phrase mirrored exactly in Heb 3:6.[23] Only four places in the LXX match this phrase exactly (2 Sam 21:1; 1 Kings 2:46, 16:7; 1 Chron 17:23), and the passage in 1 Chron 17 constitutes the only use having to do with David's house.

---

[20] Ibid., 223.

[21] Mary Rose D"Angelo, *Moses in the Letter to the Hebrews*, SBLDS 42 (Missoula, MT: Scholars Press, 1979), 70–93 develops the argument for the Nathan oracle as the backdrop for Heb 3:1–6, building on the earlier work of Sverre Aalen, "'Reign' and 'House' in the Kingdom of God in the Gospels," *NTS* 8 (1961–62), 234–37.

[22] 2 Sam 7:25 and 1 Chron 17:23 also use the verb, but in these verses David asks the Lord to confirm his word over his house.

[23] Only four places in the LXX match this phrase exactly (2 Sam 21:1; 1 Kings 2:46, 16:7; 1 Chron 17:23), and the passage in 1 Chron 17 constitutes the only use having to do with a Davidic house.

Finally, in light of the broader context of Heb 3–4, it also is interesting that 2 Sam 7 speaks of the promised rest for the people of Israel in v. 11, a topic to which the author of Hebrews shortly turns. So the fact that Jesus has been appointed as faithful, that he is a builder of a house, that God also is a builder of houses, and that Jesus is "over his house," all find expression in the Nathan oracle of 2 Sam 7/1 Chron 17. In light of Hays's tests for echoes, this suggestion meets the criteria of availability, volume, recurrence, thematic coherence, historical plausibility, and satisfaction.

What this does for our process of interpreting this passage is clear. The statements about Jesus's faithfulness over his house anchor the *synkrisis* of 3:1–6 in the context of the oracle by Nathan, delivered to David concerning David's house and his son. In Second Temple Judaism the oracle was used especially to emphasize the dynastic permanence of David's line (4QpGen[a] 5.1–6; *Sir.* 47.11, 22; *Pss. Sol.* 17.4), and 4Q*Flor.* 1.10–11 specifically interprets 2 Sam 7:14 as speaking of the "branch of David, who will arise with the Interpreter of the law … in the last days." Thus, it may be no accident that the title Χριστός appears in Hebrews for the first time at 3:6.

Yet, several recent commentators have missed or rejected the point. For example, Harold Attridge rejects D'Angelo's conclusions as unconvincing, and even writes that Jesus is not here considered the builder of the house, concluding that the house metaphor simply refers to the people of God.[24] Yet, he offers no clear explanation for the interplay of "house" language in the passage.

Each of the cases mentioned above suggest further study of echoes in Hebrews might prove fruitful. What we need at this point in this field of inquiry would be, at least, the following: 1) continued reflection on methodology; and 2) continued investigation into specific uses of echo. I have already offered a modest suggestion on the first of these issues by suggesting the broader contexts of overt quotations and allusions offer a beginning place for investigation into an author's use of echoes. In the balance of this article, I would like to proceed by considering the second issue, pointing out yet other material in Hebrews that might constitute echoes.

Further Echoes

More from the Nathan Oracle

First, consider further 2 Sam 7 and its parallel in 1 Chron 17, as a repository from which the author of Hebrews draws.[25] We have already noted the influence of this passage and its parallel in 1 Chron 17 on Hebrews 3:1–6, and the author quotes 2 Sam 7:14 at Heb 1:5. What then of other possible echoes from this important OT context?

At Hebrews 1:4 the author speaks of the superior "name" (ὄνομα) inherited by the Son. Recent commentators have given various interpretations of this ὄνομα, but most understand it as a stylistic replacement for the title "Son."[26] Others have suggested the title "Lord"[27] or even "High Priest"[28] is in

---

[24] Attridge, *Epistle to the Hebrews*, 109–111.

[25] In terms of its relationship to other OT quotations in Heb 1, 2 Sam 7:14, quoted at Heb 1:5, has a number of parallels with Ps 110 and Ps 2, parallels related to the theme of a royal heir being invested to rule. The context of 2 Sam 7 begins by stating that the Lord had "given" King David "an inheritance" (κατακληρονομέω) (7.1/Ps 2:8) and provided freedom from his "enemies" (ἐχθρός) (7:1, 9, 11/Ps 2:2 in concept 110:1). Further, David's seed would be given a throne (7:13, 16/implied in Pss 2 and 110) forever (7:13, 16/110:4). Each of the passages also mentions a "rod" (7:14/Ps 2:9/110:2). Thus, the connections between these psalms extend beyond the verbal analogy between 2 Sam 7:13 and Ps 2:7, and it may be that they had been pulled together already in Christian tradition, prior to their use in Hebrews.

[26] So e.g., Lane, *Hebrews 1–8*, 17; Jean Héring, *L'Épître aux Hébreux*, Commentaire du Nouveau Testament (Paris: Delachaux & Niestlé, 1954), 24; Graham Hughes, *Hebrews and Hermeneutics: The Epistle to the Hebrews as a New Testament Example of Biblical Interpretation*, Monograph Series (Cambridge: Cambridge University Press, 1979) 7; F. F. Bruce, *The Epistle to the Hebrews*, New International Commentary on the New Testament, rev. ed. (Grand Rapids: Eerdmans, 1990) 50; Craig R Koester, *Hebrews: A New Translation with Introduction and Commentary*, The Anchor Bible, 36 (New York: Doubleday, 2001), 182. Paul Ellingworth also opts for the title "Son," but with enough flexibility built into the use here that other titles, such as "high priest," may be anticipated as well. See Paul Ellingworth, *The Epis-*

mind. Of these suggestions, the first has the strongest basis in the text. The ὃν ἔθηκεν κληρονόμον πάντων of 1:2 might be understood as the opening of an *inclusio* closed with the κεκληρονόμηκεν ὄνομα of 1:4. The statement of the Son having been made heir of all things in v. 2, moreover, clearly alludes to the context of Ps 2:7, quoted at 1:5, where God says, "You are my son." Further, the theme of the Son's superiority pervades this section in Hebrews. Consequently, many have suggested the inherited name of 1:4 refers to the title υἱός.

Yet, this position is not as strong as it may seem at first sight. First, it is clear from certain passages in Hebrews that the author considered Jesus as Son of God prior to the exaltation, indeed prior to the incarnation. It is the Son through whom the created order was made (1:2, 10), who laid the foundations of the earth and crafted the heavens with his hands. Moreover, Heb 5:8 tells us, "Although he was a son, he learned obedience through the things he suffered," speaking of his passion.

Second, the use of "son" in v. 2 is not titular; and in the collection of quotations which follow in 1:5–14 the title "son" is joined by the titles "God" (v. 8) and "lord" (v. 10). Furthermore, Jesus as Son not only pervades the string of pearls in 1:5–14, which flows from the exaltation statement in the book's introduction, but it continues through the section that follows on his humiliation (2:10–18). What seems to be in focus in Hebrews 1:4, as well as the string of texts in the balance of chapter 1 is the Son's prominence of place, his position, vis-à-vis the angels. He is the one who deserves worship (v. 6), has a throne and a sceptre (v. 8), has been anointed (as a king?) (v. 9), has made the earth and heavens and will wrap them up like a garment in the end (v. 10), and has been exalted to the right hand of God (v. 13). The angels, by contrast, are ministering spirits sent out to do his bidding (1:6–7). The word translated here as "name" has a broad range of meanings, including "name," "status," "title," "rank," "reputation," or even "person." Richard Longenecker has pointed out "the name," initially used as a pious reference to God, came to be employed among early Jewish Christians as a designation for Jesus.[29] Both Eph 1:21 and Phil 2:9, for example, speak of the exaltation of Christ over powers of the universe, as does the author of Hebrews. In each of those texts Jesus's "name" is said to be above every other. The term is used absolutely at Acts 5:41, where the disciples rejoiced that they were counted worthy to suffer shame for "the name."[30] The designation connoted the Messiah's power, divinity, and rank. In Heb 1.4 what the Son inherited was the title "the name," a designation, or rank, formerly reserved for God.

Further, what interpretations of the use of ὄνομα at Heb 1:4 overlook is the broader context of several of the OT passages in the "string of pearls" found in Heb 1:5–14, among them 2 Sam 7:14 (2 Kgs 7 LXX), quoted by the author in the book's next breath at Heb 1:5. The Nathan oracle of 2 Sam 7 and 1 Chron 17 plays a vital role in OT thought concerning the house of David. In the Samuel version, the passage is introduced saying, among other things, that the Lord had given David an inheritance on every side (2 Sam 7:1). The passage continues with God telling David, "I made a name for you according to the names of the great ones of the earth" (v. 9 = 1 Chron 17:8). In 2 Sam 7:13, the verse immediately prior to the quotation used by the author of Hebrews in 1:5, we find this promise concerning David's son, "He shall build a house for me for my name (τῷ ὀνόματί μου), and I will establish his throne forever." Here the author associates the name of the Lord and the throne of David's son, as is the case in Heb 1:3–4. At 7:23, David says to the Lord, "What other nation on earth is like your people Israel, in that God guided him, to redeem for himself a people, to make himself a name,

---

tle to the Hebrews: A *Commentary on the Greek Text*, The New International Greek Testament Commentary (Carlisle: Paternoster; Eerdmans, 1993), 105–06.

[27] On the interpretation of ὄνομα as κύριος see J. H. Ulrichsen, "Διαφορώτερον ὄνομα in Hebr. 1,4: Christus als Träger des Gottesnamens," *Studia Theologica* 38 (1984), 65–75.

[28] Albert Vanhoye, *Prêtres anciens, prêtre nouveau selon le Nouveau Testament*, Parole de Dieu (Paris: Éditions du Seuil, 1980), 105–06.

[29] Richard Longenecker, *The Christology of Early Jewish Christianity* (Grand Rapids: Baker, 1981), 41–6. E.g., Acts 3:16; 4:7, 10; 16:18; 19:13–17; Eph 1:21; Phil 2:9.

[30] *Theological Dictionary of the New Testament*, ed. Gerhard Friedrich, trans. and ed. Geoffrey W. Bromiley, vol. 5 (Grand Rapids: Eerdmans, 1967; reprint 1987), s.v. "ὄνομο," by Hans Bietenhard.

to accomplish greatness and visibility," and in v. 26, "Let your name be magnified forever." In each of these last two uses of ὄνομα, the name of the Lord is emphasized. Thus, the author of 2 Sam 7 uses ὄνομα four times (vv. 9, 13, 23, and 26), the name of David and the name of the Lord both coming into play. Earlier we noted the association of Ps 88 with the Nathan oracle of 2 Sam 7/1 Chron 17, suggesting the psalm as the possible origin for the use of πρωτότοκον in the IF of Heb 1:6. That psalm also places emphasis on the name of the Lord in vv. 17 and 25. In v. 25 (89:24 MT) God says of David, "and my truth and my mercy will be with him, and in my name, his horn will be exalted" (ἐν τῷ ὀνόματί μου ὑψωθήσεται τὸ κέρας αὐτοῦ).[31]

The proposition that the ὄνομα of Heb 1:4 echoes 2 Sam 7, finds further support by the occurrence of μεγαλοσύνη in both Heb 1:3–4 and 2 Sam 7. In Heb 1:3, the author makes an allusion to Ps 110:1 with the words, ἐκάθισεν ἐν δεξιᾷ τῆς μεγαλωσύνης ἐν ὑψηλοῖς. Many commentaries, following Spicq, take μεγαλωσύνης here as a periphrasis for God himself, but this is not how the LXX normally uses the term. Almost universally in the Greek OT, the word refers to the greatness of God or an attribute of something related to God. I would suggest that it be translated at 1:3 as a genitive of quality, or an attributive genitive, the "right hand of majesty," or "the majestic right hand." At this position of the right hand of majesty, Jesus has been exalted, having become as much better than the angels, as his inherited name is superior to theirs.

The term μεγαλωσύνης, found in the NT twice in Hebrews (here and at 8:1) and at Jude 25, occurs fairly infrequently in the Greek version of the Jewish Scriptures as well. It occurs only in about nine contexts in some form of association with the name of God (Deut 32:3; 1 Chron 17:19–21; 22:5; 29:11–13; Dan 2:20; Prov 18:10; Odes 2.3, Sir 39.15, and, in our text under consideration, 2 Sam 7:21–23). At 2 Sam 7:21–23, in the prayer in which David answers the oracle of God given through Nathan, David praises God that God has brought about all this greatness (μεγαλωσύνην) (v. 21), speaking of the establishment of David's royal house, his kingdom, and his throne. Indeed, according to the passage, God has made a name for himself by accomplishing the greatness (μεγαλωσύνην) of David's reign (v. 23). Further, the cognate verb is used in 2 Sam 7:22, 26. In v. 22 David proclaims that God has worked great things on David's behalf that he might magnify (μεγαλύναι the Lord, and in v. 26, David, speaking to the Lord, says, "Let your name be magnified (μεγαλυνθείη) forever." The greatness of a name also is expressed at 7:9, where God says to David, "I will make your name like the names of the great ones (τῶν μεγάλων) of the earth." Although the evidence should not be pressed too far, it may be that the descriptor of God's right hand as τῇ μεγαλωσύνη is picked up from this context and used by the author of Hebrews to describe God's work in the exaltation.

Thus, the use of ὄνομα in Heb 1:4, in association with God's right hand as τῆς μεγαλωσύνης, could be understood as an anticipatory echo of that broader messianic context of 2 Sam 7 to which the author immediately will point in Heb 1:5. The inherited "name," then, mentioned in 1:4, is, on this reading, not to be understood as an allusion to the title "Son," but rather an honour conferred by God on Messiah as the Davidic heir, at the establishment of his throne, and in association with God himself. This fulfils Hay's criteria of availability, volume (especially in terms of source text), recurrence, thematic coherence, historical plausibility, and satisfaction.

Deuteronomy and Echoes in Hebrews

Another section of Scripture that should be read carefully for its influence on Hebrews is Deuteronomy. Scholars have pointed out at least eighteen passages in Hebrews that contain quotes or allusions

---

[31] See Luke 1:69 where Jesus is call the "horn of salvation." Further, the ὄνομα of the Lord comes into the broader context of other passages in the catena of Hebrews 1, including the Greek versions of Deut 32:3, Ps 101:16, 22; and, if we add Ps 8, quoted at 2:5–7, vv. 2 and 10 of that passage. Deut 32:3 "For I called upon the name of the Lord; give greatness to our God;" Ps 101:16, "and the nations will fear the name of the Lord, and all the kings of the earth Your glory;" Ps 101:19–22, "The Lord looked upon the earth out of heaven ... to proclaim the name of the Lord;" Ps 8:2, 10 "O Lord, our Lord, how majestic is your name in all the earth ... O Lord, our Lord, how majestic is your name in all the earth."

to Deuteronomy. These are displayed in the figure below, and note the influence especially of the final movement of Deuteronomy.

Q= Quotation

Deut	*32:43?*	*32:46*	*32:8*	*29:18*	*9: 32*	*31:7*	*32:15*	*10:3–5*	*32:4*	*17:6; 19:15*
Heb	*1:6 (Q)*	*2:1*	*2:5*	*3:11–12*	*3:16–19*	*4:8*	*6:9*	*9:4*	*10:23*	*10:28*

32:35–36	*1:10; 10:22*	*8:5*	*29:17; 32:32*	*4:11–12; 5:22–27*	*9:19?*	*4:24; 9:3*	*31:6, 8*
10:30 (Q)	*11:12*	*12:7*	*12:15*	*12:18–19*	*12:21 (Q)*	*12:29*	*13:5(Q)*

Paul Ellingworth, for instance, suggests that Heb 2:1, with its use of προσέχω may allude to Deut 32:46, where Moses exhorts the people, "Pay attention with your heart to all these words."[32] Given the faintness of the allusion, we could label it an echo. At Heb 2:5, the author of Hebrews echoes Deut 32:8, which says that the Lord set the boundaries of the nations according to the number of the angels. The author implies a contrast of the angels with the Son of God to whom the coming world has been submitted. Also, Deut 32 was originally given as a powerful word just prior to Israel's entrance to the promised land, and, of course, "entrance into the rest" or "the inheritance" is an important theme for Hebrews (3:7–4:11). In Deut 32 Moses, leader of the people of God, confronts the people concerning the consequences of a lack of faithfulness to covenant with God. Hebrews too is concerned with a lack of faithfulness to covenant and quotes Deut 32:35–36, later in the book, at 10:30, to speak of judgment against those who have "regarded the blood of the covenant as common" (10:29). On the other hand, God is called "faithful" at Deut 32:4, a sentiment perhaps echoed in Hebrews at Heb 10:23, where it says, "The one who promised is faithful." Furthermore, the "root of bitterness" of Heb 12:15 alludes to Deut 29:17 (LXX), and that bitterness is reiterated in Deut 32:32. Further, the author presents an overt allusion to Deut 31:6, 8 at Heb 13:5. Deut 31:8 reads, "And the Lord who goes with you shall not forsake you nor abandon you." It is clear, therefore, that this portion of OT Scripture was very much in mind as the author of Hebrews wrote the book.

It may be suggested that there exists another image in the broader context of Deuteronomy, and chapter 32 specifically, that might be echoed in Hebrews. The agricultural imagery of Heb 6:7–8 stands as a striking picture of God's blessing for those who respond to his word and God's curse on those who do not. Several passages have been proposed as possible OT origins for the imagery, including Gen 3:17–18 for the curse of the ground, Isa 5:1–5 for the image of the failed crop and thorns growing up, Hos 10:8, 12, also for the thistles coming up, and Ezek 19:10–14, which depicts a vine being torn down and burned.[33] Yet, to this list should be added several passages in Deuteronomy, as shown in Fig. 3, and these occur in a context of blessing for those who receive and live out the covenant, or a curse for those who reject it.

---

[32] Ellingworth, *Epistle to the Hebrews*, 136.
[33] Attridge, *Epistle to the Hebrews*, 172.

It may be suggested there are four elements from the agricultural imagery of Heb 6:7–8 that stem from Deuteronomy and a fifth that serves as a wellspring from which the curse framework of the Deuteronomy material comes.

First, earlier in the book, at Deut 11:11, the blessing of the promised land is described as follows: "but the land into which you go to inherit it, is a land of mountains and plains; it shall drink water of the rain of heaven." The Greek terms used here are γεωπγειται, and πίνω, the same terms used at Heb 6:7. To my knowledge, this is the only place in the LXX that speaks of the land drinking rain. However, similar imagery exists in Deut 32. Deut 32:1–2, the introduction to Moses's speech, the word he is about to speak to the people, is compared to rain as follows,

> Listen, O heaven, and I will speak; and let the earth hear the words out of my mouth. Let my speech be looked for as the rain, and my words come down as dew, as the shower upon the plants, and as snow upon the grass.

Thus, Heb 6:7 uses the image of rain often coming on the land as an image of blessing.

Second, the dichotomy of land that either is blessed or cursed is prominent in Deuteronomy. For example, at Deut 28:12 the rain from God is a gift and works with the blessing of the works of one's hands. On the other hand, there are those passages that emphasize curse. I have already mentioned the allusion to Deut 29:17 (LXX) at Heb 12:15. That passage continues a few verses later:

> All its land is brimstone and salt, a burning waste, unsown and unproductive, and no grass grows in it, like the overthrow of Sodom and Gomorrah, Admah and Zeboiim, which the LORD overthrew in his anger and in his wrath.[24] All the nations will say, "Why has the LORD done thus to this land? Why this great outburst of anger?"[25] Then *men* will say, "Because they forsook the covenant of the LORD, the God of their fathers, which he made with them when he brought them out of the land of Egypt.[26] They went and served other gods and worshiped them, gods whom they have not known and whom he had not allotted to them.[27] Therefore, the anger of the LORD burned against that land, to bring upon it every curse which is written in this book." (NAS)

Thus, the curse on the land is brought on by a rejection of the covenant, and that curse consists of burning.

Third, the image of fire as a form of judgment occurs in Hebrews at three places. At Heb 10:27 the author proclaims that for those who keep on sinning after receiving a knowledge of the truth, their remains only imminent judgment and a jealousy of fire, perhaps alluding to Isa 26:11 or Zeph 1:18, but also consonant with Deut 29:19, where God's inflamed jealousy burns against those cursed ones who turn away from the covenant. At Heb 12:29 we find a second place where fire is form of judgment in Hebrews, here in an overt allusion either to Deut 4:24 or 9:3, where God is called a "consuming fire." Again we are moved decisively back into the orbit of Deuteronomy. The third place where fire occurs as a form of judgment is in Heb 6:8. The unproductive land ends up being burned. The burning of land also occurs in Deut 32. At v. 22, Moses says, "For a fire has been kindled out of my wrath, it shall burn to hell below; it shall devour the land, and the fruits of it."

Finally, Heb 6:8 says that such land is κατάρας ἐγγύς, "about to be cursed." There are a number of places in the LXX where the term ἐγγύς is used to speak of the immanence of judgment—all of these but two in the prophets, who speak of the nearness of the Day of the Lord (e.g., Joel 1:15; 2:1; 4:14; Obad 1:15; Zeph 1:7,14; Isa 13:6; Ezek 30:3). The only other places that the imminence of judgment is mentioned, using ἐγγύς is at Deut 32:35, where God says of his enemies, "the day of their calamity is near," and the restatement of this verse in Ode 2:35. This small portion of Scripture from Deut 32:25 happens to be wedged between the two parts of Deut 32:35–36 quoted at Heb 10:30: "Vengeance is mine, I will repay," and again, "The Lord will vindicate his people." Therefore, a case can be made that Hebrews has in mind this Deuteronomy passage specifically at Heb 6:8, and the nearness of a curse fits the context of Deuteronomy, with its "blessing or curse" framework.

Thus, several elements from Deuteronomy seem to be echoed in the proverbial imagery of Heb 6:7–8, including the earth that drinks the rain, the blessed over against the cursed land, firing of the land as an image of judgment, and the nearness of God's judgment.

What then of the "thorns and thistles" of Heb 6:8? The exact form of the words as they occur in Heb 6:8 (ἀκάνθας καὶ τριβόλους) occurs also in Gen 3:18, the statement of judgment on Adam, which involved the curse on the ground. It would grow thorns and thistles for him. It seems that Hebrews may be utilizing the curse on the land material in Deuteronomy, and incorporating into it the curse on the ground from Gen 3:18. Indeed, a number of Pentateuch scholars suggest that the Genesis passage is one wellspring from which the curse on the land in Deuteronomy flows, and a rabbi of the first century certainly would see the verbal analogy between the curse on the earth in Gen 3:18 and the terminology of curse and land in Deuteronomy. Therefore, it may be that Hebrews borrows from both to craft the proverbial statement we have in 6:7–8. This identification of Deuteronomy echoes behind Heb 6:7–8 fulfills Hays's criteria of availability, volume, recurrence, thematic coherence, historical plausibility, and satisfaction.

What difference does this make to interpretation? It places the harsh warning of Heb 6:7–8 squarely in the context of Deuteronomy's blessing and curse framework. Moreover, if Dave Mathewson is correct about the wilderness echoes in Heb 6:4–6, the agricultural imagery of Heb 6:7–8 provides a culmination of that imagery in the immediate context, much as Deuteronomy generally and its Song of Moses in chapter 32, provide for the Pentateuch. Moreover, the ambiguous language of Heb 6:4–8 now has a grounding in the scriptural text and the imagery from Israel's history, much like and in line with, the other warnings in Heb 2:1–4, 3:7–19, 10:26–31, and 12:25–29.

Conclusion

The examples delineated in this presentation are offered as suggestive of the stimulating data afforded by a consideration of echoes, found in the broader contexts of common OT texts. Obviously, much work remains to be done on echoes in Hebrews. The fruit from the consideration of echoes is neither obtained nor verified easily—it tends to be hidden in the branches of the tree, and, having made the climb, you often find yourself empty-handed on your way back down. Nevertheless, it is the rare fruit of extensive toil, which tastes the sweetest. The ultimate goal, however, has little to do with mere finding, and everything to do with elucidation of the text. For, the test of echoes, at the end of the day, rests in the help they bring to our understanding of the author's statements, exhortations, promises, and logic. May we grow ever more attuned to hear the echoes reverberating from the Scriptures of Israel.

Bibliography

Aalen, Sverre. "'Reign' and 'House' in the Kingdom of God in the Gospels." *NTS* 8 (1961–62): 234–37.

Attridge, Harold W. *Epistle to the Hebrews.* Fortress Press, 1989.

Beker, J. Christiaan. "Echoes and Intertextuality: On the Role of Scripture in Paul's Theology." Pages 64–69 in Evans, Craig A. and James A. Sanders. *Paul and the Scriptures of Israel.* Journal for the Study of the New Testament. Supplement Series, 83. Sheffield: JSOT Press, 1993.

Bietenhard, Hans. "ὄνομὸ" Pages 242–282 in *Theological Dictionary of the New Testament.* Edited by Gerhard Friedrich. Translated and edited by Geoffrey W. Bromiley. vol. 5 Grand Rapids: Eerdmans, 1967; reprint 1987.

Brawley, Robert L. "Echoes of Scripture in the Letters of Paul." *Cumberland Seminarian* 28 (1990): 94–5.

Bruce, F. F. *The Epistle to the Hebrews*. New International Commentary on the New Testament. rev. ed. Grand Rapids: Eerdmans, 1990.

Carter, Warren. "Evoking Isaiah: Matthean Soteriology and an Intertextual Reading of Isaiah 7–9 and Matthew 1:23 and 4:15–16." *Journal of Biblical Literature* 119/3 (2000): 503–520.

D'Angelo, Mary Rose. *Moses in the Letter to the Hebrews*. SBLDS 42. Missoula, MT: Scholars Press, 1979.

Dodd, C. H. *According to the Scriptures: The Sub-Structure of New Testament Theology*. London: Nisbet, 1961.

Donfried, Karl P. "Echoes of Scripture in the Letters of Paul." *Theological Studies* 52 (1991): 732–34.

Dowd, Sharyn E. "Echoes of Scripture in the Letters of Paul." *Lexington Theological Quarterly* 25 (1990): 125–28.

Dunn, James D. G. "Echoes of Scripture in the Letters of Paul." *Literature and Theology* 7 (1993): 88–9.

Ellingworth, Paul. *The Epistle to the Hebrews*: *A Commentary on the Greek Text*. The New International Greek Testament Commentary. Carlisle: Paternoster; Eerdmans, 1993.

Evans, Craig A. "Echoes of Scripture in the Letters of Paul." *Catholic Biblical Quarterly* 53 (1991): 496–98.

Evans, Craig A. and James A. Sanders. *Paul and the Scriptures of Israel*. Journal for the Study of the New Testament. Supplement Series, 83. Sheffield: JSOT Press, 1993.

Fishbane, Michael. *Biblical Interpretation in Ancient Israel*. Oxford: Clarendon, 1985.

Green, William S. "Doing the Text's Work for It: Richard Hays on Paul's Use of Scripture." Pages 58–63 in Evans, Craig A. and James A. Sanders. *Paul and the Scriptures of Israel*. Journal for the Study of the New Testament. Supplement Series, 83. Sheffield: JSOT Press, 1993.

Guthrie, George H. *The Structure of Hebrews*. Grand Rapids: Baker, 1998.

Hay, David M. "Echoes of Scripture in the Letters of Paul." *Interpretation* 45 (1991): 88.

Hays, Richard B. *Echoes of Scripture in the Letters of Paul*. New Haven, CT: Yale University Press, 1989.

Héring, Jean. *L'Épître aux Hébreux*. Commentaire du Nouveau Testament. Paris: Delachaux & Niestlé, 1954.

Hughes, Graham. *Hebrews and Hermeneutics*: *The Epistle to the Hebrews as a New Testament Example of Biblical Interpretation*. Monograph Series. Cambridge: Cambridge University Press, 1979.

Hollander, John. *The Figure of Echo: A Mode of Allusion in Milton and After*. Berkeley: University of California Press, 1981.

Hübner, Hans. "Intertextualität--Die Hermeneutische Strategie Des Paulus: Zu Einem Neuen Versuch Der Theologischen Rezeption Des Alten Testaments Im Neuen." *Theologische Literaturzeitung* 116 (1991): 881–98.

Jobes, Karen H. "Jerusalem, Our Mother: Metalepsis and Intertextuality in Galatians 4:21–31." *Westminster Theological Journal* 55.2 (1993): 299–320.

Keesmaat, Sylvia C. "Exodus and the Intertextual Transformation of Tradition in Romans 8:14–30." *Journal for the Study of the New Testament* 54 (1994): 29–56.

Keesmaat, Sylvia C. "Paul and His Story: Exodus and Tradition in Galatians." in *Early Christian Interpretation of the Scriptures of Israel*. Sheffield: Sheffield Academic Press, 1997.

Koester, Craig R. *Hebrews: A New Translation with Introduction and Commentary.* The Anchor Bible 36. New York: Doubleday, 2001.

Kraus, Hans-Joachim. *Psalms 60–150: A Commentary.* Translated by Hilton C. Oswald. Minneapolis: Augsburg, 1989.

Lane, William L. *Hebrews 1–8.* Word Biblical Commentary. Vol. 47a. Dallas: Word, 1991.

Litwak, Kenneth D. "Echoes of Scripture? A Critical Survey of Recent Works on Paul's Use of the Old Testament." in *Currents in Research: Biblical Studies*. Sheffield Academic Press, 1998.

Long, Arthur. "Echoes of Scripture in the Letters of Paul." *Faith and Freedom: A Journal of Progressive Religion* 46 (1993): 125–26.

Longenecker, Richard. *The Christology of Early Jewish Christianity.* Grand Rapids: Baker, 1981.

Martin, Dale B. "Echoes of Scripture in the Letters of Paul." *Modern Theology* 7 (1991): 291–92.

Mathewson, Dave. "Reading Heb 6:4–6 in Light of the Old Testament." *WTJ* 61 (1999): 209–25.

Paul, Ian. "Echoes of Scripture in the Letters of Paul." *Anvil* 11.3 (1994): 267–68.

Pollard, J. Paul. "Echoes of Scripture in the Letters of Paul." *Restoration Quarterly* 36.1 (1994): 53–4.

Sarna, N. M. "Psalm 89: A Study in Inner Biblical Exegesis." Pages 29–46 in *Biblical and Other Studies.*, Edited by A. Altmann. Cambridge, MA: Harvard University Press, 1963.

Strobel, August. "Die Psalmengrundlage der Gethsemane-Parallele Hbr. 5,7ff." *Zeitschrift für die neutestamentliche Wissenshaft* 45 (1954): 252–66.

Stockhausen, Carol L. "Echoes of Scripture in the Letters of Paul." *Journal of Biblical Literature* 111.1 (1992): 155–57.

Thielman, Frank. "Unexpected Mercy: Echoes of a Biblical Motif in Romans 9–11." *Scottish Journal of Theology* 47.2 (1994): 169–181.

Ulrichsen, J. H. "Διαφορώτερον ὄνομα in Hebr. 1,4: Christus als Träger des Gottesnamens." *Studia Theologica* 38 (1984): 65–75.

Vanhoye, Albert. *Prêtres anciens, prêtre nouveau selon le Nouveau Testament.* Parole de Dieu. Paris: Éditions du Seuil, 1980.

Weiss, Hans-Friedrich. *Der Brief an die Hebräer.* Göttingen: Vandenhoeck & Ruprecht, 1991.

PILGRIMAGE IN THE BOOK OF HEBREWS

ISTVÁN BORZÁSI[*]

Emanuel University

ABSTRACT: The article is an examination of the concept of pilgrimage in the Book of Hebrews. The theme is shown to be an important feature throughout the Old Testament and has a pervasive presence in Hebrews. Hebrews 3:1–4:16; 5:11–6:12; 10:19–39; 11:8–16; 12:1–3; and 12:4–13:21 in particular are examined, not to offer a full commentary on these texts, but only to point out their major contribution to the motif of pilgrimage. The conclusion is that while this motif can be regarded as one of the leading themes of the letter, it is not regarded as *the* theme of Hebrews.

KEY WORDS: pilgrimage, theology of rest, perfect, perseverance, eschatology.

John Bunyan imagined the Christian life as a pilgrimage, in his well-known *Pilgrim's Progress*. It is true that all of us are on a journey, no matter if we are righteous or wicked: only the goal of our wanderings differ.

According to Don A. Carson and Douglas J. Moo it was Käsemann who "introduced us to the pilgrim theme in Hebrews, in *The Wandering People of God*."[1] After Käsemann's book many other commentators started to consider this point of view.[2] In the same time more and more critical evaluations were presented about the legitimacy of Käsemann's arguments.[3] I am much indebted to Pál Borzási's thoughts and writing,[4] in presenting this article.

The Origins of the Pilgrimage Motif in the Old Testament

We began with the assumption that pilgrimage is a motif that can be demonstrated from Hebrews. It should now be noted that this theme is an important feature of both the Old and New Testament history and theology.

Pilgrimage in the Pentateuch

The Pentateuch begins with the creation of human beings, but the disobedience of Adam and Eve resulted in divine curses and expulsion from Eden. Right after this we read about Cain's murderous act, as a repetition of the fall,[5] and God's sentence that Cain is "driven from the ground" (Gen 4:11), or "from the land" (Gen 4:14). He became "a restless wanderer on the earth" (Gen 4:12; cf. v. 14).

---

[*] ISTVÁN BORZÁSI (PhD Babeş-Bolyai University, Cluj-Napoca, BD Baptist Theolgical Institute Bucharest. Dr Borzási currently lectures on the Old Testament in Emanuel University from Oradea, and is pastor of Hungarian Baptist Church from Crasna, Romania). He finished further studies at MABS Central Baptist Seminary, Minnepolis, Minnesota, MTh International Baptist Theological Seminary, Prague, and MA Emanuel University from Oradea.

[1] D. A. Carson and Douglas J. Moo, *An Introduction to the New Testament*, 2nd ed. (Leicester: Inter-Varsity Press, 2005), 614.

[2] Ernest Käsemann, *The Wandering People of God: An Investigation of the Letter to the Hebrews*, translated from the second edition by Roy A. Harrisville and Irving L. Sandberg (Minneapolis: Augsburg, 1984).

[3] Carson and Moo suggest that "the most comprehensive and nuanced treatment is still that of Hurst," op. cit. See Lincoln D. Hurst, *The Epistle to the Hebrews: Its Background of Thought*, SNTSMS 65 (Cambridge: Cambridge University Press, 1990).

[4] Pál-Zoltán Borzási, *An Examination of the Motif of Pilgrimage in the Epistle to the Hebrews with Reference to its Origins and Significance*, 2006. Unpub. Manuscript.

[5] According to G. J. Wenham, this echoes Genesis 3, "showing that his [i.e. Cain's] offence was a repeat of the Fall." See also his article "Cain and Seth," in *NIDOTTE* 4, 455; and John H. Walton, *Genesis*, in NIVAC (Grand Rapids: Zondervan, 2001), 265.

As a consequence, *"Cain went out from the LORD's presence and lived in the land of Nod, east of Eden"* (Gen 4:16).[6]

Interestingly, the name *"Nod"* means *"wandering."*[7] This has a symbolic sense here, evoking "a "homeless" or "aimless" place," and "Nod" (נוד) is the Hebrew root of the verb "to wander" (לנדוד) implying a movement "to and fro."[8] Cain being cursed, because of his own sin, is departing further away from God's presence toward the East, and is wandering in the whole world without any divine purpose or direction. This is the opposite of what pilgrimage means.

But *Abraham* left the city of Ur, his homeland, to become a pilgrim, and settled in the land that finally became the place of God's presence. In utter contrast with Cain's wandering in Genesis 4, Abraham's pilgrimage: (1) had its origin in God's *gracious call*; (2) it was a journey starting *from* the East (going to the west); (3) it was undertaken under God's *guidance and direction*; (3) it had a specific *goal* and God-given *destination*; and (4) anticipated God's many-sided *promises and blessings* (Gen 12:1–3).

The hallmark of Abraham's relationship with God was his *faith expressed in obedience* (especially in starting a "pilgrimage"). Arriving to Canaan, he never fully settled in the land but obeyed God's further command for a *renewed* pilgrimage, walking "through the length and breadth of the land" (Gen 13:17) as a constant traveller, without actually inheriting it. According to ancient customs and traditions this "symbolized his legal acquisition" of the land.[9] Abraham may be considered as the archetype of all pilgrims in both Testaments.

In the *Isaac* narratives the main themes are similar to what we observed in the case of Abraham.[10]

Jacob also viewed himself as a pilgrim: in Gen 47:9, after being asked by the Pharaoh how old he was.

Exodus and the rest of the *Pentateuch* focus mainly: (1) on Israel's exodus from Egypt; (2) on her pilgrimage toward the Promised Land; and (3) on various developments that occurred prior to her taking possession of it. The Passover ritual and the Exodus event constitute the definite *starting point* of Israel's pilgrimage. The pilgrimage the Israelites had as its *initial goal* was not the Promised Land, but Mount Sinai in the wilderness.

Until Kadesh (Num 13–14) the Israelites firmly believed, that all of them would *pass through* the wilderness, in spite of any occasional obstacles or opposition.[11] This confidence is expressed in the song of Moses (Exod 15:13–14, 16).[12]

Obviously, the divine guidance and triumphant pilgrimage was going to be actualized and guaranteed: (1) by "the angel of God, who had been travelling in front of Israel's army" (Exod 14:19a); (2) by the pillar of the cloud and of fire (Exod 13:21–22; 14:19b–20; 16:10; etc.);[13] and (3) by the divinely authorised leadership of Moses, the servant of the LORD (Exod 3:10; 14:31; cf. Num 10:13).[14]

---

[6] Quotations in this article are taken from the New International Version.

[7] See Bruce K. Waltke, *Genesis: A Commentary* (Grand Rapids: Zondervan, 2001), 99.

[8] T. C. Mitchell, "Nod," in D. R. W. Wood, ed., *NBD*, 3rd ed. (Downers Grove: InterVarsity Press, 1996), 827.

[9] Waltke, *Genesis*, 222.

[10] See John H. Sailhamer, "Genesis", in *Expositor's Bible Commentary*, Tremper Longman III and David E. Garland, eds. (Grand Rapids MI: Zondervan), 2008. 36.

[11] See also the comments below under "Numbers."

[12] Cf. Alec Motyer, *The Message of Exodus: The Days of Our Pilgrimage* (Leicester: Inter-Varsity Press, 2005), 168.

[13] For the many-sided function of the pillar of cloud, cf. Ian Wilson, "Pillar of the Cloud and of Fire," in *NIDOTTE* 4, 1052–5.

[14] In connection with God guiding the Israelites see the comments of Motyer, *Exodus*, 177–8.

Moreover, there was the indispensable aspect of the LORD's special presence during Israel's journey, which is highlighted by the request of Moses in Exod 33:15–16.[15]

The *final destination* of Israel's pilgrimage was entering and possessing the Promised Land. This too is implied in the song of Moses (Exod 15:13). The "dwelling" place of the LORD becomes even more precise: the Israelites had in mind not only Canaan in general[16] but a mountain in particular:[17] *"You will bring them in and plant them on the mountain of your inheritance – the place, O LORD, you made for your dwelling, the sanctuary, O LORD, your hands established"* (Exod. 15:17).[18] According to later developments in Israel's history, this mountain was no other than Mount Zion. The pilgrimage of the Israelites is marked by two distinct mountains: by Mount Sinai and Mount Zion. Moses expressed his optimism in their pilgrimage, asking Hobab to join Israel in her journey (Num 10:29; cf. v. 31), an optimism which is expressed in his battle cry also (Num 10:35). With her LORD in the foreguard, Israel was now "prepared for the march, the battle, and the victory."[19]

In Deut. 16:16–17, we find that: (1) every male Israelite was obliged to present himself three times a year before the LORD (Exod 34:24); (2) Israel should assemble only at the God-appointed place, where the LORD chooses to put his name (vv. 2, 5–7, 11, 15–16),[20] a strict limitation of sacrifice to Jerusalem which created the imperative of the pilgrimage; (3) nobody was allowed to present himself before the LORD empty handed, meaning that the pilgrimage feasts were opportune times for bringing a gift "in accordance with the blessing of Yahweh" to the place which he chose (Deut 16:16–17)."[21]

In Deut 26:5 God commanded the Israelites to acknowledge before their LORD: "My father was a wandering Aramean." According to Gordon McConville: "The phrase refers to his relatively unsettled life and migration to Egypt, and also to his years spent in the area of Aram, or Syria, where he married Rachel and Leah, daughters of Laban the Aramean (Gen 28:5; 29). The confession continues by recalling the migration to Egypt… The whole life of Jacob and the life of the other patriarchs as well can be described as a lifelong pilgrimage which is now remembered by their descendants."

Pilgrimage in the Historical Books

In Josh 11:23 we read: "So Joshua took the entire land, just as the LORD had directed Moses, and he gave it as an inheritance to Israel according to their tribal divisions. Then the land had rest from war." This implies that "Israel's wanderings were over."[22] The people reached the goal of their pilgrimage by arriving at the Promised Land and thus resting from their tiresome wandering.

In 1 Samuel in connection with Elkanah, we read: *"Year after year this man went up from his town to worship and sacrifice to the LORD Almighty at Shiloh"* (1 Sam 1:3). Accordingly, *"Elkanah made an annual pilgrimage to sacrifice at Shiloh"* (cf. Judg 21:19). This seems to be a private, personal

---

[15] See Mark Dever, *The Message of the Old Testament: Promises Made* (Wheaton: Crossway, 2006), 97–8.
[16] As Alan Cole suggests in *Exodus: An Introduction and Commentary* (London: Inter-Varsity Press, 1973), 126.
[17] See Walter C. Kaiser, Jr., "Exodus," Pages 64–125 in *Expositor's Bible Commentary,* Tremper Longman III & David E. Garland, eds. (Grand Rapids, MI: Zondervan, 2008). See especially his comments on verse 13.
[18] Emphasis added.
[19] Allen, Leslie C., *Psalms 101–150,* in WBC Vol. 21 (Dallas: Word, 1998), Electronic edition. From this time on, it was commonplace for Israel to use the ark of the LORD's covenant in war. For later examples see 1 Sam 4:1–22; 2 Sam 11:11.
[20] W. A. VanGemeren, "Feasts and Festivals, Old Testament," in W. A. Elwell (ed.), *Evangelical Dictionary of Theology,* 2nd ed. (Grand Rapids: Baker Academic, 2012), 410.
[21] Ibid.
[22] Bruce K. Waltke, "Joshua," in *NBC* (electronic ed.), ad loc.

pilgrimage, distinct from the requirement for males to appear three times a year before Yahweh as part of a national festival (Exod 23:15–17; 34:18–24; Deut 16:16).[23]

In 2 Samuel 7 we find "the theological highlight of the Books of Samuel"[24] where we find David's desire to build a house for the LORD and the LORD's reaction to it. We read that to David was granted rest from all his enemies (2 Sam 7:1, 11) and to the people of Israel were given their own land (2 Sam 7:10). These all point to the fulfillment of the divine promises given to the patriarchs.

In 1 Kings, Solomon used to make pilgrimages: he "went to Gibeon to offer sacrifices, for that was the most important high place" (1 Kgs 3:4). The reason why the king was worshipping in this place and not in Jerusalem is, "because the temple had not yet been built for the Name of the LORD" (1 Kgs 3:2). This not only acquits Solomon for making pilgrimage to Gibeon, but also shows that by this time it was a custom to undertake individual and corporate pilgrimages by people and king to worship God in a particular place. Later in 1 Kgs 12:26–30 we read about the unfortunate decision of Jeroboam in declaring *Bethel and Dan as new centres of pilgrimages* in order to stop the ten northern tribes going up to Jerusalem to worship the LORD. He instituted other festivals, like the festivals held in Jerusalem, and encouraged the people to offer sacrifices on the newly-set-up altars of these places. Clearly, this was the most notorious countermovement against God in the book of Kings and against the law of pilgrimage given in Deuteronomy 16.

The motif of pilgrimage is present in a unique way in the narratives concerning Hezekiah (2 Chron 30:1–13) and Josiah (2 Chron 35:1–19). The Chronicler highlights how these two kings have celebrated the Passover and assembled the whole people to Jerusalem to repent of their idols and to worship the LORD.[25]

Pilgrimage in the Wisdom Books

Pilgrimage receives considerable emphasis only in the Psalms.[26] In *Psalm 15* the expression "to dwell" is actually "to dwell as a sojourner, one who is distinguished from the native citizen."[27] Accordingly, the psalmist is interested "not about taking up permanent residence as a priest or Levite but about making a pilgrimage."[28] In answer to the question, the inquirer is given ten[29] moral conditions and a final promise (cf. Ps 24; Isa 33:14b–16).[30]

Psalm 23 is perhaps the most well known psalm in the Bible. Its relevance to the motif of pilgrimage is evident from the comments of Broyles:

> Psalm 23 is a psalm of journey and of nourishment, both along the way and at the final destination. When we think of believers on a journey, we think of pilgrimage, and that is probably the situation portrayed here.[31]

---

[23] Ralph W. Klein, *1 Samuel*, WBC, vol. 10. Electronic ed., ad loc. Joyce Baldwin is agnostic about the occasion of Elkanah's pilgrimage. See *1 and 2 Samuel: An Introduction and Commentary* (Leicester: Inter-Varsity Press, 1988), 51.

[24] A. A. Anderson, "2 Samuel," in WBC, vol. 11, electronic ed., ad loc., and others quoted by him. See also Baldwin, *1 and 2 Samuel*, 213.

[25] See Hill, *1 & 2 Chronicles*, 586–9, 624–8.

[26] For the possible contribution of Proverbs to pilgrimage see Eugene Merrill, "גור," in *NIDOTTE* 1:991.

[27] Konkel, "גור," 837. Cf. also Gen. 47:4.

[28] Craig C. Broyles, *Psalms*, New International Biblical Commentary (Peabody: Hendrickson, 1999), 91. In what follows, I am much indebted to his comments on pilgrimage. See also Gerald H. Wilson, *Psalms*, vol. 1, NIVAC (Grand Rapids: Zondervan, 2002), 297.

[29] Contra Wilson, *Psalms*, 298.

[30] See the comments of Peter C. Craigie, *Psalms 1–50*, WBC, electronic ed., vol. 19, ad loc.

[31] Broyles, *Psalms*, 123. See also the theological and pastoral reflections of Wilson, *Psalms*, 441–3.

Psalm 24 also contains allusions to pilgrimage. A question is raised as to who may join the procession of the Temple entry, and a promise is given to those who accordingly are willing to become pilgrims and ascend the LORD's hill (cf. Ps 15; Isa 33:14b–16).[32]

In *Psalms 42 and 43* the psalmist is speaking about pilgrimage, using the verb "go" in Ps 42:2, which "is the usual term for "entering" the temple,"[33] and in Ps 42:4 "a term used to denote making a pilgrimage."[34]

Psalm 68 opens with echoes of the Battle Cry of Moses as the ark of the LORD set out on its journeys (Num 10:33–36)[35] and expresses rich memories of Israel's pilgrimage through the wilderness.[36]

Psalm 78 reviews Israel's history with educational purposes, where the psalmist mentions the same basic elements of pilgrimage we encountered within the Pentateuch. He points out: (1) the start or commencement of the journey – "he brought his people out" of Egypt; (2) the course or continuation of the journey – "he led them like sheep through the desert;" and (3) the finish or completion of the journey – "he brought them to the border of his holy land."

Psalm 84 lets us know who the really blessed people are: those "who have set their hearts on pilgrimage" (Ps 84:5), *longing* for the experience of God's presence (vv. 1–4), *journeying* through a transformed oasis into his presence (vv. 5–8) and *resting* in his blessed presence in Zion (vv. 9–12).[37]

Psalm 95 was "perhaps composed for the Feast of Tabernacles, when God's people re-lived, in token, their time of encampment in the wilderness."[38] After a call to praise and worship God (vv. 1–7c), the psalmist challenges Israel to learn from the lessons of her wilderness experience (vv. 7d–11). A new call is issued, so that Israel should not harden her heart "today" as the exodus generation did in the wilderness. The far-reaching implications of this fact will be worked out later by the author of Hebrews.

There is no need to prove that *Psalms 120–134*, the "Songs of Ascents" point to a Zionward movement, having a clear relevance to pilgrimage.[39]

Pilgrimage in the Prophetic Books

Among the prophetic material we find the roots of pilgrimage in the books of Isaiah, Hosea and Zechariah.

In *Isa 2:1–5* (and Mic 4:1–5)[40] we read about God's glorious promise that in the last days the mountain of the LORD's temple (Zion) will be the highest among the mountains of the world.[41] Isaiah prophesies about a worldwide movement with a *centripetal* orientation: "all nations will stream to it" (Isa 2:2; cf. Mic 4:1–2). This "anti-gravitational anomaly of this human river flowing uphill to wor-

---

[32] See Wilson, *Psalms*, 450.

[33] Ibid., 197n.

[34] Ibid., 196.

[35] Derek Kidner, *Psalms 1–72: An Introduction and Commentary on Books I and II of the Psalms*, TOTC (London: Inter-Varsity Press, 1973), 238.

[36] Of course, David does not speak only about the past history of Israel, for he mentions an actual procession in verse 24, which may be identified with the bringing of the ark to Zion (2 Sam 6). J. A. Motyer, "The Psalms," in Gordon W. Wenham, Alec J. Motyer, Donald A. Carson and R. T. France, eds., *New Bible Commentary* (Leicester, Inter-Varsity, 1994). electronic ed., ad loc.

[37] See Motyer's structure of this psalm, "The Psalms," ad loc.

[38] Kidner, *Psalms 73–150*, 343.

[39] See also VanGemerem, "Psalms," 919; Kidner, *Psalms 73–150*, 429–30; and Broyles, *Psalms*, 445.

[40] Given the fact that these two passages are nearly identical, we treat them together here.

[41] For information how the content of this prophecy parallels the Canaanite conception of the cosmic mountain with a god dwelling on it, see John T. Strong, "Zion: Theology of," in *NIDOTTE* 4, 1317; John N. Oswalt, *Isaiah*, NIVAC (Grand Rapids: Zondervan, 2003), 89.

ship God"[42] seems strange to us. Nevertheless, this incongruity "is intentional; a supernatural magnetism is at work."[43] The LORD is going to bring about an *international* pilgrimage to Zion.[44] But we read also about another global movement with a *centrifugal* focus: "The law will go out from Zion, the word of the LORD from Jerusalem" (Isa 2:3; cf. Mic 4:2).[45] Apparently, this outward progression of God's word from Zion is the very reason for the incoming flow of the nations: the former causes the latter.

In *Isa 11:10–16* we read about God reaching out his hand a "second time" (v. 11). This is the so-called "second exodus," which causes a new and greater pilgrimage.

In *Isa 60* we find another prophecy about the nations' eschatological pilgrimage.[46]

In *Isa 63:11* we read about the people of Israel asking for their God, who led them "through the sea, with the shepherd of his flock." The image is that of God shepherding and leading Israel out of Egypt into the desert wanderings.

We conclude, therefore, that for Isaiah the exodus of Israel out of Egypt was not a one-time event but it was a pattern. It will certainly be repeated in the last days when Yahweh will come to visit his people once again.

In *Hos 2:14–23* we find an echo of Israel's past wilderness experience, which is used by God as the pattern of his future dealings with Israel. Interestingly, every aspect of the wilderness motif in this text is positive: it is the language of love that dominates the whole episode.

The eschatological pilgrimage of the Jews and Gentiles to Zion is touched upon by *Zechariah* as well (Zech 8:20–23; 14:16–19). Here the *purpose* of the Gentile pilgrims in going up to Jerusalem is to seek and entreat the LORD (8:21). The *reason* these nations will give for their desire to accompany the Jews is "because we have heard that God is with you" (8:23).

The Pilgrimage Motif in the Book of Hebrews

Keeping in mind the strong roots of pilgrimage in the OT, we can examine Hebrews 3:1–4:16; 5:11–6:12; 10:19–39; 11:8–16; 12:1–3; and 12:4–13:21 in particular. It is not our purpose to offer a whole-range commentary on these texts, but only to point out their major contribution to the motif of pilgrimage.

Pilgrimage in Hebrews 3:1–4:16

Heb 3:1–4:16 is one of the most influential texts in the whole epistle as far as pilgrimage is concerned.

In 3:1–6 the author of Hebrews identifies his readers as *"holy brothers, who share in the heavenly calling"* (3:1). On the basis of the author's arguments in this chapter, we know that the readers of Hebrews are compared here with the Israelite pilgrims in the wilderness. We can recognize in these words an important characteristic of the godly pilgrims: the heavenly *calling* (e.g. Abraham and Isra-

---

[42] Raymond C. Ortlund, Jr. *Isaiah: God Saves Sinners*, Preaching the Word (Wheaton: Crossway, 2005), 51.

[43] J. Alec Motyer, *The Prophecy of Isaiah: An Introduction and Commentary* (Downers Grove: InterVarsity Press, 1993), 54.

[44] This prophecy is probably based on "the imagery of the pilgrimage feasts under the Mosaic law." See the commentary of Allan Harman, *Isaiah: A covenant to be kept for the sake of the church* (Fearn, Ross-shire: Christian Focus, 2005), 48.

[45] That this is universal as well is implied in the text. See especially the domain and sphere of the LORD's word (Isa 2:4).

[46] Oswalt, *Isaiah*, 642.

el). Thus, the recipients of this epistle are none other than genuine pilgrims,[47] who were invited "into the presence of God where they enjoy privileged access to him."[48]

But the issue at stake – similarly to the case of Israel in the wilderness – is their *faithfulness* to the divine calling. Therefore, the author *exhorts* them to press on in their journey of faith: *"fix your thoughts on Jesus, the apostle and high priest whom we confess"* (3:1). Peterson comments: "Such teaching is designed to encourage the weary, to challenge the sluggish and the disobedient, and to reassure those who are doubting and drifting."[49] The *basis* of his exhortation to faithfulness is none other than the faithfulness of Jesus, as Son over God's house. The writer compares and contrasts Moses with Jesus.[50] He[51] says that just as Moses was faithful, so was Jesus faithful (3:2). Nevertheless, the author emphasizes that Jesus is worthy of greater honour than Moses because *"Moses was faithful as a servant in all God's house"* (5; cf. Num 12:7),[52] while Jesus is *"faithful as a son over God's house"* (3:6). "Faithfulness on the part of a servant is required; faithfulness in a Son is an expression of pure love."[53] Thus the faithfulness of Jesus as *Son* becomes the greatest motivation to the readers' faithfulness as pilgrims to their heavenly calling.

Heb 3:7–19 and the next paragraph are full of warnings.[54] The author draws from Psalm 95 to support his argument. His method of reasoning is to quote first the primary text (3:7–11), then, secondly, to offer his own explanation of it (3:12–19) and thirdly, to exhort his readers on the basis of the given explanation. The explanation serves mainly to support the author's exhortation,[55] which in turn consists of strong encouragement and stern warning.[56] But the *explanation* is often interwoven with the *exhortation*, and together they highlight the urgency of paying close attention to God's voice. Regarding these three aspects of the text (i.e. quotation, explanation and exhortation), we may note: *First*, the introductory formula of the quotation ("as the Holy Spirit says") reveals the contemporary relevance of the psalm: "through the quotation of Scripture the Holy Spirit *is speaking* now…"[57]

Second, reminds the readers of the unfaithfulness of the people of God and stresses the importance of listening to the God's voice. The psalmist and the author of Hebrews speak about the events of Num 13–14, which was the crucial point in Israel's pilgrimage: the LORD interpreted their hardness of heart as consisting in a deliberate refusal on the part of Israel to believe his promises regarding the land of rest (Num 14:10–11).[58]

Third, by applying this Psalm to the readers, the author makes a strong connection between the Israelites in the wilderness, the Israelites in the time of David,[59] and the Christians of the letter to the Hebrews. The author of Hebrews uses the "today" of Psalm 95 as still applicable to his readers in the

---

[47] David Peterson, "Hebrews," in Gordon W. Wenham, Alec J. Motyer, Donald A. Carson and R. T. France, eds., *New Bible Commentary* (Leicester, Inter-Varsity, 1994). electronic ed., ad loc.

[48] Lane, *Hebrews 1–8*, 74.

[49] Peterson, "Hebrews," ad loc.

[50] Donald A. Hagner, *Encountering the Book of Hebrews: An Exposition* (Grand Rapids: Baker Academic, 2002), 64–5.

[51] On the basis of the use of masculine pronoun in alluding to himself, I concur with others that the author was probably male (Heb 11:32). See Attridge, *Hebrews*, 5; Lane, *Hebrews 1–8*, xlix; F. F. Bruce, *The Epistle to the Hebrews*, NICNT, revised (Grand Rapids: Eerdmans, 1990), 18, n. 77.

[52] For the view that this verse may well have reference not only to Num 12:7 but to 1 Sam 1 2:35 and 1 Chron 17:14 as well, see Lane, *Hebrews 1–8*, 76; Kiwoong Son, *Zion Symbolism in Hebrews: Hebrews 12:18–24 as a Hermeneutical Key to the Epistle* (Milton Keynes: Paternoster, 2005), 128–33.

[53] William L. Lane, *Hebrews: A Call to Commitment* (Vancouver: Regent College Publishing, 1985), 60.

[54] In fact, the whole of Hebrews can be called an epistle of warning, because it abounds in exhortations, warnings and admonitions.

[55] That this is the method of the author is supposed by W. L. Lane, *Hebrews 1–8*, c.

[56] In fact, this is the purpose of Hebrews. See Lane, *Hebrews 1–8*, xcviii-ci; and ibid., *Hebrews 9–13*, 568.

[57] Lane, *Hebrews 1–8*, 85. Emphasis included. See also Simon J. Kistemaker, *Exposition of the Epistle to the Hebrews*, New Testament Commentary (Grand Rapids: Baker, 1984), 90–1.

[58] For an excellent but short explanation of what hardness of heart means, see Lane, *Call to Commitment*, 63–4.

[59] The author of Hebrews identifies David as the author of the psalm. See Heb 4:7.

first century CE, while the psalmist speaks of "you" in Ps 95:8 as though his congregation were present in the wilderness![60]

Fourth, the writer expresses strong warnings concerning a hardened heart. We find that the solidarity of these Christians with the Jews in the OT may turn out to be a sad one. For even if the recipients of Hebrews did not yet exhibit the very hardened heart the Israelites displayed during their pilgrimage in the wilderness,[61] they are in great danger of following their bad example.[62] Consequently, they are also facing the same punishment the Israelites were in the desert: to be excluded from the rest of God, a rest which is far more superior to the rest of the Promised Land.

Fifth, the addressees are urged to "encourage one another daily, as long as it is called Today, so that none of you may be hardened by sin's deceitfulness" (v. 13). This admonition shows that "for this community struggling with the problem of spiritual drifting, hardening of the heart was … avoidable."[63] To avoid apostasy, the individual members of the congregation must take care of each other daily (v. 13).

Sixth, the way v. 14 is formulated is similar to what we encountered in v. 6. It contains the same conditional clause: "We have come to share in Christ *if* we hold firmly till the end the confidence we had at first."[64] The first part of the verse shows that the Christians in the congregation have experienced a relationship with Christ: they already have come to share in him. In the light of 3:1–6 this can be understood as being part of his house. However, the conditional clause tells us that this experience is true only if those who have the confidence of being sharers in Christ will hold firmly till the end this confidence.

In Heb 4:1–16 the author continues to put forward his explanation of Psalm 95 and to offer the appropriate exhortation.

One of his most important contributions to the foregoing argument is his teaching about *the remaining promise of rest*: "the promise of entering his rest still stands" (4:1a). But what kind of rest is he speaking about? (1) In the case of Israel, the primary – though not the final – meaning of "rest" was the settlement of Canaan (cf. Deut. 12:9–10). (2) In the case of God, to rest meant to cease from his creating work (4:4).[65] (3) In the case of Christians, the "rest" the author is talking about cannot mean the literal rest of Canaan,[66] for the very Israelites who already entered Canaan under the leadership of Joshua were later urged by David to enter the rest! "For if Joshua had given them rest, God would not have spoken later about another day" (4:8). Consequently, the author must mean the other rest: "For anyone who enters *God's* rest also rests from his own work, just as God did from his" (4:10).[67] It seems that the author is speaking both about the Sabbath rest into which God entered following the works of the first creation (Gen 1–2), and about the believers' entering into that rest following the new creation in Christ.

The good news is that *God's rest is still available*:[68] "It still remains that some will enter that rest… There remains, then, a Sabbath-rest for the people of God; for anyone who enters God's rest also rests from his own work, just as God did from his" (4:6, 9–10). From this we gather that *the reasons*

[60] For similar alternation of pronouns see, for example, Deut 26:5–10 and Ps 81:6–7.
[61] See George H. Guthrie, *Hebrews*, NIVAC (Grand Rapids: Zondervan, 1998), 129.
[62] Although there is no evidence that any of them have ever committed apostasy.
[63] Guthrie, *Hebrews*, 130.
[64] Emphasis added.
[65] See Bruce, *Hebrews*, 106.
[66] Contra G. W. Buchanan, *To the Hebrews*, Anchor Bible 36 (Garden City, NY: Doubleday, 1972), 72–74. Buchanan actually thinks that the author of Hebrews is interested in the occupation of Canaan and in anti-Roman liberation movements of his own time.
[67] Emphasis added.
[68] A. T. Lincoln, "From Sabbath Rest to Lord's Day: A Biblical and Theological Perspective," in *From Sabbath to Lord's Day: a Biblical, Historical and Theological Investigation* ed. D. A. Carson. (Eugen, OR: Wipf and Stock, 1999), 378.

why the promise of entering God's rest is still open today are: (1) because God's rest continues ever since the creation of the world, and (2) because Israel did not enter that rest in the time of Joshua. Therefore it is to be entered by a later people, by the obedient church, of which the readers believe they are part: "Let us, therefore, make every effort to enter that rest, so that no-one will fall by following their example of disobedience" (4:11).

As we focus now on Heb 4:14–16, there are two important hortatory subjunctives in these verses which are representations of two different forms of exhortations that are characteristic of Hebrews.[69] They are: "let us hold firmly" and "let us then approach." These subjunctives are also connected to the motif of pilgrimage. The use of these two exhortations throughout the epistle encourages us to suppose that one of the best ways to understand them is to view them against the background of Israel's different forms of pilgrimage in the OT. We can gather from the Old Testament examples that there are two main forms of pilgrimages: The *first* is journeying *from* a previous country – whether from Mesopotamia, Egypt or Babylon – *to the Promised Land*. Because this journey required the pilgrims in the desert to hold firm to the hope set before them, the present requirement was that the readers of Hebrews did the same (cf. 3:6, 14; 4:14). Thus the original pilgrimage and the exhortation given was the type of which the situation addressed by the letter was the antitype. The *second* is Israel's journeying *in* the Promised Land *to the chosen place*, i.e. to the temple in Zion. Because this pilgrimage implied the privilege and responsibility of approaching the divine presence, it can be perceived as an OT antitype of that exhortation which the author is using in Heb 4:16 and elsewhere.

Of the two kinds of pilgrimage, the first (the pilgrimage from Egypt) focuses on the land and the second (the pilgrimage during the three national festivals, and later the pilgrimage from Babylon) focuses on the temple, yet they are strongly interrelated and each one implies the other. The purpose of the former journey is to find rest, while the goal of the second is to worship God. The former is *unique*, being a one-off pilgrimage, and is not only *progressive* in its nature but also *static*[70] in the sense that the pilgrims are exhorted to hold firmly to the faith they profess and never draw back from their inheritance. By contrast, the second is *recurrent* and is more *dynamic* for it demands frequent approach into God's presence.[71] The lesson the author of Hebrews wants to communicate is that – unlike Israel – the pilgrims of Hebrews must *hold on firmly* to their hope about the goal of their journey (3:6, 14; 4:14) and also *approach with confidence* the presence of God into which they are continuously called (4:16).

Pilgrimage in Hebrews 5:11–6:12

According to Lane, it is generally recognized that this passage forms a separate literary unit within Hebrews,[72] where the author presents the third of his five main warnings (cf. also 2:1–4; 3:1–4:14; 10:19–39; 12:14–29). It can be divided into two major sections: 5:11–6:12 and 6:13–20.[73]

The first major section (Heb 5:11–6:12), is bracketed with the same word *nōthroi*, which is translated "slow to learn" (5:11) and "lazy" (6:12)[74] in the NIV. Because of this the author has to feed them with milk (the elementary truths of God's word), as if they are still infants,[75] and not with solid food (teachings about righteousness, the high priestly office of Christ, etc.), which is for the "mature" or "perfect" believers (*teleios* in Greek). Therefore, he encourages them to move beyond the "elemen-

---

[69] Attridge, *Hebrews*, ibid.

[70] This is denied by such theologians as Paul J. Achtemeier, Joel B. Green and Marianne Meye Thompson. See *Introducing the New Testament: Its Literature and Theology* (Grand Rapids: Eerdmans, 2001), 484.

[71] See: Attridge, *Hebrews*, 21–2. Whether he is indebted or not in any way to Käsemann, *Wandering*, 22–3, is not clear. In either case their thoughts are similar.

[72] Lane, *Hebrews 1–8*, 133.

[73] For the possibility of different divisions and substructures, see Lane, *Hebrews 1–8*, 133–5.

[74] See Lane, *Hebrews 1–8*, 134.

[75] For the view that the author uses only irony here, and does not really think that the readers are still infants in faith, see Lane, *Hebrews 1–8*, 136–7, 139.

tary teachings about Christ and go on to maturity" or "perfection" (*teleiotēta*). Then, (in Heb 6:4–8) the author pronounces one of his most stern warnings, but later (in Heb 6:9–12) he expresses his hope regarding the congregation by saying that even if he uses such a severe language, he is still convinced about the readers' salvation. Therefore, they are told to be faithful: "show diligence to the very end, in order to make your hope sure. We do not want you to become lazy, but to imitate those who through faith and patience inherit what has been promised" (6:11–12).

In the second major section (Heb 6:13–20) the author gives a detailed exposition of the nature of God's promises, which in turn encourages the readers to rely confidently on the certainty of, and wait hopefully for the fulfilment of, these promises. It is the truthfulness of God's promise and its confirmation with a divine oath – exemplified in the case of Abraham – that gives reason for the author's optimism concerning the congregation that is in peril of spiritual immaturity.

Käsemann introduces Gnostic concepts here, as he did with Hebrews 3–4, trying to establish his view on an alleged parallel found in the *Epistle of Barnabas* (1:5; 5:4) and in the *Epistle of Polycarp to the Philippians* (3:3),[76] arguing that the material found in Heb 5:22–6:12 actually corresponds to the examination that the Gnostics practised preliminary to a candidate's initiation. However, as Lane pointed out, there are several problems with Käsemann's arguments:

> The decisive technical vocabulary of Gnosticism … is absent from Hebrews, and even the expression *logos teleios* was coined by Käsemann himself. Moreover, the idea of growth or progressive initiation into perfection through successive stages of enlightenment is not present in 5:11–6:12. … In 5:11–14 "milk" designates elementary instruction; in Gnosticism it is the food of "the perfect" who have been initiated into the word of knowledge.[77]

Therefore, we deduce that there is no basis for Käsemann's discovery of the presence of a Gnostic tradition in Hebrews. The most that can be said, is that far from indicating the presence of Gnostic tradition or vertical dualism in the text, the way how the author uses such words as *teleiōn* ("mature" or "perfect") in Heb 5:14, or *teleiotēta* ("maturity" or "perfection") in Heb 6:1 point to a different direction. For these words, just as the word *epouraniou* ("heavenly") in Heb 3:1, 6:4, 11:16 and 12:22 are used to refer "to the fulfilment of eschatological realities, the historical foreshadowing of which pale by comparison."[78]

Pilgrimage in Hebrews 10:19–39

This section consists of a long exhortation, which is based on the argument developed in 8:1–10:18. The opening and close of the section contain the same word *parrēsian*, which not only emphasizes the factor of faith but also functions as an *inclusio*[79] that frames the whole passage: "Therefore, since we have the confidence" (10:19) and "So do not throw away your confidence" (10:35).

The exhortations are organized around three important cohortatives[80] or hortatory subjunctives (vv. 22–25): "let us draw near" (v. 22), "let us hold unswervingly" (v. 23), and "let us consider" (v. 24). The expression "let us approach" is using the OT picture of the Israelites' individual/personal or corporate/national pilgrimage to the temple in Zion in order to draw near to God and we can recognize in these verses our motif of pilgrimage. The expressions "let us draw near," "let us hold unswerving-

---

[76] Ibid. 189, 192.
[77] Lane, *Hebrews 1–8*, 135.
[78] Hagner, *Encountering Hebrews*, 65. Although Hagner speaks about dualistic Platonism, the same vertical dualism is present in Gnosticism, for which see Hurst, *The Epistle to the Hebrews*, 70. Although the language of Hebrews is similar to the language of Greek dualism, the author in fact did not mean the same thing by the words he used as was meant by Greek philosophy. See Hagner, *Encountering Hebrews*, 112.
[79] An *inclusio* is a literary device that uses similar words or phrases to bracket a unitary text.
[80] "Cohortatives" are grammatical constructions which tend or serve to exhort.

ly," and "let us consider" fit well into the image of pilgrimage, as each one of them applies properly to different elements of it.

Pilgrimage in Hebrews 11:8–16 and 12:1–3

Hebrews 11:8–16 has its own internal structure, which can be put like this: in vv. 8–10 the author presents the triumph of perseverance in the faith of Abraham the pilgrim;[81] in vv. 11–12 we read about Sarah as another example of faith in being able to conceive seed;[82] and in vv. 13–16 the author offers his own commentary on the biblical record of faithful believers introduced so far by him. There is an emphasis upon Abraham's faithful and obedient pilgrimage,[83] which is exemplified: (1) in his immediate departure from the city of Ur with an obedient and forward-looking faith to a land to which God had called him and would lead him;[84] and (2) in his life as a resident alien in the promised land, where he continued his wandering until the time of his death.[85]

We may also observe the contrast that the author highlights between the patriarchs' sojourning in *tents* and their anticipation of "the *city* with foundations, whose architect and builder is God" (v. 10).[86] The tents of Abraham, Isaac and Jacob signifies an ongoing pilgrimage and nomadic sojourning,[87] while life in a city signifies settlement, security and endurance.[88] The city with foundations is an eschatological expectation here. *Hebrews 11:13–16* shows us that the journey of the patriarchs or of Israel in the OT is not the final pilgrimage of the people of God but only a type of it. It speaks about another pilgrimage, which leads through the wilderness of this present world to the heavenly Jerusalem, the city with foundations. For "even in possession of Canaan, Israel remained a wandering people (11:39–40)."[89]

Pilgrimage in Hebrews 12:4–13:21

In this section there are three aspects of pilgrimage: the discipline of the pilgrims (12:4–13), the goal of the pilgrims (12:14–29), and some mandates for pilgrims (13:1–21).

First, Hebrews 12:4–13 speaks about the fact that pilgrimage calls for a disciplined life. God wants his people to be trained, so he uses various disciplinary sufferings which serve as means for leading his people to spiritual maturity and participation in his holiness. If these sufferings are part of the readers' experience, then they can know that God recognizes them as his own children, for he disciplines his true sons.[90]

Second, Hebrews 12:14–29 describes the true goal of the NT pilgrims (vv. 18–28) with some ethical directives along the way (vv. 14–17). As far as the directions are concerned, the author reminds his

---

[81] Donald A. Hagner, *Hebrews*, New International Biblical Commentary (Peabody: Hendrickson, 1990), 189–90.

[82] There is no consensus among commentators or Bible translations about the grammatical subject of Heb 11:11. Apparently it can refer either to Abraham or Sarah. For a brief summary of the possibilities see Hagner, *Encountering Hebrews*, 148.

[83] See Stedman, *Hebrews*, 123.

[84] However, if we are right to take v. 8 as referring to God's *call* of Abraham to journey to the place of his inheritance, then the view of T. R. Hatina must be mistaken, when Abraham's journey from the city of Ur is actually interpreted as his *exile*. See T. R. Hatina, "Exile," Pages 248–251 in *Dictonary of New Testament Background*, edited by C. A. Evans and S. E. Porter (Downers Grove, IL: InterVarsity, 2000), electronic edition.

[85] Hagner, *Encountering Hebrews*, 146.

[86] Emphasis added.

[87] See Ellingworth, *The Epistle to the Hebrews*, 583, who remarks: "Here the tents are simply nomadic dwellings, as in Gen 12:8; 13:3, 18; 18:1, 6, 9f. of Abraham; 26:25 of Isaac; 33:19; 35:21 (LXX 16) of Jacob." See also Lane, *Hebrews 9–13*, 350.

[88] This may also provide an indirect support to our interpretation above that the point of David's concern in 2 Sam 7 lies in the contrast between the ark of the LORD being kept in a tent (and thereby signifying lack of rest), and his peaceful settlement in a house without being pursued by enemies (which points to the enjoyment of rest).

[89] Ellingworth, *The Epistle to the Hebrews*, 254.

[90] Ibid. 650.

readers that they must have a peaceful disposition toward others (v. 14a), live a holy life (v. 14b), display an active sense of God's grace (v. 15) and live in a morally responsible way (vv. 16–17). The fact that these verses are not connected to the previous section[91] and that they are followed by vv. 18–24 suggests that the challenges set forth in vv. 14–17 have been structured with commitment to pilgrimage in mind. Consequently, they can also be viewed as important ethical priorities for the readers on their pilgrimage through the secular world to the City of God.

Third, Hebrews 13:1–19 contains some ethical mandates for pilgrims.[92] Although we could argue that in some sense nearly all aspects of this chapter have some relationship with the motif of pilgrimage, we must restrict ourselves to the following: in 13 the readers are urged to "go to him [i.e. to Jesus] outside the camp." Here the author probably refers to the readers' responsibility to leave the old camp of Judaism[93] and commit themselves wholly to follow Jesus outside that group, which recalls Abraham's deliberate abandonment of his past. Why should this be so? "For here we do not have an enduring city, but we are looking for the city that is to come" (v. 14). Thus we see that the readers are urged to look forward to the coming eschatological city of God, the true goal of their pilgrimage, of which the earthly Jerusalem was only a type.[94]

Conclusion

Having investigated the rich origins of the motif of pilgrimage in the OT and its pervasive presence in Hebrews, we may draw some conclusions concerning its theological and pastoral significance.

(1) The rich material concerning the goal of pilgrimage in Hebrews enables us to say something about the contribution of Hebrews to the biblical *theology of rest*, especially as it is found in chapters 3 and 4. It seems that "rest" in Hebrews has both present and future aspects: in one sense the NT Christians have *already* entered into it, through Christ, and in another sense they *will* enter into it at the consummation. Rest is both the present spiritual *state* of Christians and the future heavenly *place* of their eschatological destination.[95]

(2) We may also observe, that the way the author handles the motif of pilgrimage "enables us to explore *the hermeneutical assumptions of first-century Christians* so as better to learn how to read the Old Testament."[96]

(3) Moreover, the way the author treats pilgrimage in Hebrews can provide us with many of the basic principles and "*working elements for developing a sound biblical theology*."[97]

(4) This raises the question about the nature of the relationship *between biblical and systematic theology*. Because systematic theology is by its very nature a cumulative discipline it must take into account the findings of all the other theological disciplines, most notably exegetical and biblical theology. Learning from the way the author of Hebrews treats the motif of pilgrimage, we should interpret the Bible first of all diachronically and comparatively (the nature of biblical theology) and only then metaphysically and epistemologically (the nature of systematic theology).

(5) Another implication of the way in which the author treats the motif of pilgrimage in Hebrews concerns *the nature of the perseverance of the saints* and the problem of apostasy, which, again, is

---

[91] Ibid. 661.

[92] See Robert Jewett, *Letter to Pilgrims: A Commentary on the Epistle to the Hebrews* (New York: Pilgrim, 1981), 229ff.

[93] See Philip Edgecumbe Hughes, *A Commentary on the Epistle to the Hebrews* (Grand Rapids: Eerdmans, 1977), 579–80.

[94] Donald E. Gowan, *Eschatology in the Old Testament*, 2nd ed. (Edinburgh: T&T Clark, 2000), 17.

[95] See Attridge, *Hebrews*, 126. We may also note with Son, that although the word "heavenly" is not used directly in connection to "rest," "the idea of heaven as the destination of Sabbath-rest is clearly reflected in the expression, *klēseōs epouraniou metochoi* (3:1)." See Son, *Zion Symbolism*, 139. Transliterations of Greek words are mine.

[96] Carson and Moo, *Introduction to the New Testament*, 615. Emphasis added.

[97] Ibid.

bound up with the doctrine of assurance of salvation. Regarding the issues of perseverance, apostasy and assurance, we may point out: *(a)* Whatever standpoint one may adopt about the stern words of the warning passages, it must be in full harmony with those (at least) equally strong texts that speak about the final preservation of the saints by God and Christ,[98] or the full confidence of the Christians about their own salvation and perseverance;[99] *(b)* We must try to distil the relevant theological lessons from the words of the author in Heb 3:14: "We have come to share in Christ if we hold firmly till the end the confidence we had at first" (cf. also 3:6; 4:14; 6:11; etc.). Apparently this verse teaches us that perseverance is a criterion of genuine faith: if one does not persevere in his Christian profession, then he does not possess a truly saving faith,[100] for true believers will hold firmly to the end the confidence they had at the beginning. *(c)* We must admit that, even if we believe in God's omniscience (Heb 4:13) and trust that he knows who is genuinely born again, we are capable of being deceived by pretenders. *(d)* We must also wrestle with the so-called compatibilist view of God's sovereignty and human responsibility, according to which we must keep the proper balance and biblical tension between the two doctrines. As Carson put it:

1.   God is absolutely sovereign, but his sovereignty never functions in such a way that human responsibility is curtailed, minimized or mitigated.

2.   Human beings are morally responsible creatures – they significantly choose, rebel, obey, believe, defy, make decisions, and so forth, and they are rightly held accountable for such actions; but this characteristic never functions so as to make God absolutely contingent.[101]

(6) The motif of pilgrimage in Hebrews has also something to offer on the NT *understanding of eschatology*. It shows that for the author the eschatology to which Israel was looking forward in the OT is already a *realized* or inaugurated one in the NT, but nevertheless, one which still awaits its consummation and therefore *futurist*. For example, in Heb 12:22 the Christians are told that they already have come to the heavenly Jerusalem, while in Heb 13:14 they are still looking forward "to the city that is to come."

(7) The author's teaching has also something to say about the question of *the national-political restoration of Israel*.[102] If the idea of rest in Hebrews is primarily a spiritual reality, as it seems to be, and if that rest is already enjoyed in some measure by the Jewish believers of Hebrews, then "to interpret this rest in terms of national-political restoration is to miss the author's dramatic shift away from earlier limited perspectives toward an understanding of Christ as the fulfilment of the promises and the inauguration of *eschatology*."[103]

(8) It should be also noted, that pilgrimage in Hebrews has both *corporate* (e.g. Israel in Heb 3–4) and *individual* (e.g. Abraham in Heb 11) aspects. However, it seems that the corporate aspect is more dominant (Heb 10:19, 22, 25; etc.).

(9) It is argued by Andreas Köstenberger and Peter O'Brien[104] that the OT prophecies concerning the centripetal movement of the eschatological pilgrimage of the nations to Jerusalem is reversed in the NT by the Great Commission of Jesus, where the emphasis falls on the "centrifugal focus on the

---

[98] This is Carson's observation regarding Howard Marshall's theology of assurance of salvation. See D. A. Carson, "Reflections on Christian Assurance," in *WTJ* 54 (1992), 21. For such texts in Hebrews see 2:10, 16; 5:9; 9:12, 8:10; 15; 10:14, 13:5, etc.
[99] Hebrews 2:16; 4:14, 16; 6:9; 10:39, etc.
[100] As the apostle John implies, genuine faith, *by definition*, perseveres. See 1 John 2:19.
[101] D. A. Carson, *How Long, O, Lord? Reflections on Suffering and Evil* (Grand Rapids: Baker, 1990), 201. See also *idem*, "Reflections on Christian Assurance," 22.
[102] Gowan, *Eschatology*, 29.
[103] Hagner, *Encountering Hebrews*, 72. Emphasis his. And whether or not one believes that Israel as a nation will yet experience a *spiritual* restoration, is entirely a different question.
[104] Andreas J. Köstenberger and Peter T. O'Brien, *Salvation to the Ends of the Earth: A Biblical Theology of Mission* (Leicester: Apollos, 2001).

word of the Lord going forth from Jerusalem."[105] However, it seems to us, that this is not the case. The prophecies concerning the centripetal orientation of the Gentiles' worldwide movement (Isa 2:2) are neither reversed, nor changed: they are *fulfilled*.

(10) Seeing that the motif of pilgrimage is such an important part of Hebrews, we conclude with some recent theologians that it can be regarded as one of the leading themes of the letter, even though we would not regard it as *the* theme of Hebrews. Therefore, Käsemann's view that the motif of wandering forms *the* basic religious pattern of Hebrews must be qualified, to say the least, especially in the light of the traditional view about the central theme of Hebrews, which cannot be so easily set aside. As it is known, the older approach tends to see the topic of Christ's supremacy as the predominant theme,[106] which should still be regarded as the best proposal.

Bibliography

Achtemeier, Paul J., Joel B. Green and Marianne Meye Thompson. *Introducing the New Testament: Its Literature and Theology*. Grand Rapids: Eerdmans, 2001.

Allen, Leslie C. *Psalms 101–150*. Word Biblical Commentary. Volume 21. Dallas: Word: 1998. Electronic edition.

Anderson, A. A. *2 Samuel*. Word Biblical Commentary. Volume 11. Dallas: Word: 1998. Electronic edition.

Attridge, H. W. *The Epistle to the Hebrews*. Hermeneia. Philadelphia: Fortress, 1989.

Borzási, Pál-Zoltán, *An Examination of the Motif of Pilgrimage in the Epistle to the Hebrews with Reference to its Origins and Significance*, 2006. Unpub. Manuscript.

Broyles, Craig C. *Psalms*. New International Biblical Commentary. Peabody: Hendrickson, 1999.

Bruce, F.F. *The Epistle to the Hebrews*. Rev. ed. New International Commentary on the New Testament. Grand Rapids: Eerdmans, 1990.

Buchanan, G. W. *To the Hebrews*. Anchor Bible 36. Garden City, NY: Doubleday, 1972.

Carson, D. A. "Reflections on Christian Assurance." *Westminster Theological Journal* 54 (1992): 1–29.

Carson, D. A. *How Long, O, Lord? Reflections on Suffering and Evil*. Grand Rapids: Baker, 1990.

Carson, D. A. and Douglas J. Moo. *An Introduction to the New Testament*. 2nd ed. Leicester: Inter-Varsity Press, 2005.

Cole, Alan. *Exodus: An Introduction and Commentary*. London: Inter-Varsity Press, 1973.

Craigie, Peter C. *Psalms 1–50*. WBC. Volume 19. Dallas: Word: 1998. Electronic edition.

Dever, Mark. *The Message of the Old Testament: Promises Made*. Wheaton, IL: Crossway, 2006.

Ellingworth, Paul. *The Epistle to the Hebrews: A Commentary on the Greek Text*. NIGTC. Grand Rapids: Eerdmans Publishing Company, 1993.

Gowan, Donald E. *Eschatology in the Old Testament*. 2nd ed. Edinburgh: T&T Clark, 2000.

---

[105] Ibid., 136.
[106] See, among others, Hughes, *A Commentary on the Epistle to the Hebrews*, 2.

Guthrie, Donald. *New Testament Introduction: Hebrews to Revelation.* 2nd ed. London: Tyndale, 1964.

Hagner, Donald A. *Encountering the Book of Hebrews: An Exposition.* Grand Rapids: Baker Academic, 2002.

Hagner, Donald A. *Hebrews.* New International Biblical Commentary. Peabody: Hendrickson, 1990.

Harman, Allan. *Isaiah: A Covenant to be Kept for the Sake of the Church.* Fearn: Christian Focus, 2005.

Hill, Andrew E. *1 & 2 Chronicles.* NIV Application Commentary. Grand Rapids: Zondervan, 2003.

Hughes, Philip Edgecumbe. *A Commentary on the Epistle to the Hebrews.* Grand Rapids: Eerdmans, 1977.

Hurst, Lincoln D. *The Epistle to the Hebrews: Its Background of Thought,* Society for New Testament Studies Monograph Series 65. Cambridge: Cambridge University Press, 1990.

Hatina T. R. "Exile." Pages 248–251 in *Dictionary of New Testament Background* edited by C. A Evans and S. E. Porter. Downers Grove, IL: InterVarsity, 2000 Electronic edition.

Jewett, Robert. *Letter to Pilgrims: A Commentary on the Epistle to the Hebrews.* New York: Pilgrim, 1981.

Kaiser, Walter C, Jr. "Exodus." Pages 64–125 in *Expositor's Bible Commentary. Edited by* Tremper Longman III and David E. Garland. Grand Rapids, MI: Zondervan, 2008.

Käsemann, Ernst. *The Wandering People of God: An Investigation of the Letter to the Hebrews.* Translated by Roy A. Harrisville and Irving L. Sandberg. 2nd ed. Minneapolis: Augsburg Fortress, 1984.

Kidner, Derek. *Psalms 1–72: An Introduction and Commentary on Books I and II of the Psalms.* TOTC. London: Inter-Varsity Press, 1973.

Kidner, Derek. *Psalms 73–150: An Introduction and Commentary on Books III, IV and V of the Psalms.* TOTC. London: Inter-Varsity Press, 1975.

Kistemaker, Simon. *Exposition of the Epistle to the Hebrews.* New Testament Commentary. Grand Rapids: Baker, 1984.

Klein, Ralph W. *1 Samuel.* WBC. Volume 10. Dallas: Word: 1998. Electronic edition.

Konkel, A. H. "דרש" in *New International Dictionary of Old Testament Theology and Exegesis* 1.836–9. Edited by Willem A. VanGemeren. Grand Rapids, MI: Zondervan, 2008.

Köstenberger Andreas J. and Peter T. O'Brien. *Salvation to the Ends of the Earth: A Biblical Theology of Mission.* Leicester: Apollos, 2001.

Lane, W. *Hebrews 1–8.* Word Biblical Commentary. Volume 47a. Dallas: Word Books, 1991.

Lane, W. *Hebrews: A Call to Commitment.* Vancouver: Regent College Publishing, 1985.

Lincoln, A. T. "From Sabbath to Lord's Day: A Biblical and Theological Perspective." Pages 343–412 in *From Sabbath to Lord's Day: a Biblical, Historical and Theological Investigation*. Edited by D. A. Carson. Eugene, OR: Wipf and Stock, 1999.

Merill, Eugene. "גּוּר" in *New International Dictionary of Old Testament Theology and Exegesis* 1.989–93. Edited by Willem A. VanGemeren. Grand Rapids, MI: Zondervan, 2008.

Mitchell, T. C. "Nod." Page 827 in D. R. W. Wood, ed. *New Bible Dictionary*. 3rd ed. Downers Grove: InterVarsity Press, 1996.

Motyer, J. Alec. *The Message of Exodus*: The Days of Our Pilgrimage. Leicester: Inter-Varsity Press, 2005.

Motyer, J. Alec. *The Prophecy of Isaiah*: An Introduction and Commentary. Downers Grove: Inter-Varsity Press, 1993.

Motyer, J. Alec. *"The Psalms."* In Gordon W. Wenham, Alec J. Motyer, Donald A. Carson and R. T. France, eds. *New Bible Commentary*. Leicester, Inter-Varsity, 1994. Electronic edition.

Ortlund, Raymond C., Jr. *Isaiah: God Saves Sinners*. Preaching the Word. Wheaton: Crossway, 2005.

Oswalt, John N. *Isaiah*. NIV Application Commentary. Grand Rapids: Zondervan, 2003.

Peterson, David. *"Hebrews."* In Gordon W. Wenham, Alec J. Motyer, Donald A. Carson and R. T. France, eds. *New Bible Commentary*. Leicester, Inter-Varsity, 1994. Electronic edition.

Sailhamer, John H. "Genesis." Pages 1–63 in *Expositor's Bible Commentary. Edited by* Tremper Longman III and David E. Garland. Grand Rapids, MI: Zondervan, 2008.

Son, Kiwoong. *Zion Symbolism in Hebrews: Hebrews 12:18–24 as a Hermeneutical Key to the Epistle*. Carlisle: Paternoster, 2005.

Stedman, Ray C. *Hebrews*. IVP New Testament Commentary. Downers Grove: InterVarsity Press, 1992.

Strong, John T. "Zion: Theology of." Pages 1314–21 in *New International Dictionary of Old Testament Theology and Exegesis* 4. Edited by Willem A. VanGemeren. Grand Rapids, MI: Zondervan, 2008.

Van Gemeren, W. A. "Feasts and Festivals, Old Testament." Pages 409–12 in W. A. Elwell, ed. *Evangelical Dictionary of Theology,* 2nd ed. Grand Rapids: Baker Academic, 2001.

Waltke, Bruce K. *Genesis: A Commentary*. Grand Rapids: Zondervan, 2001.

Waltke, Bruce K. "The Book of Joshua." Donald A. Carson, et al., eds. NBC21. 4th ed. Grand Rapids, MI: Eerdmans, 1970; Downers Grove, IL: InterVarsity Press, 1994.

Walton, John H. *Genesis*. NIV Application Commentary. Grand Rapids: Zondervan, 2001.

Wenham, G. J. "Cain and Seth." Pages 454–6 in *New International Dictionary of Old Testament Theology and Exegesis* 4. Edited by Willem A. VanGemeren. Grand Rapids, MI: Zondervan, 2008.

Wilson, Gerald H. *Psalms*. Volume 1. NIV Application Commentary. Grand Rapids: Zondervan, 2002.

Wilson, Ian. "Pillar of the Cloud and of Fire." Pages 1052–5 in *New International Dictionary of Old Testament Theology and Exegesis* 4. Edited by Willem A. VanGemeren. Grand Rapids, MI: Zondervan, 2012.

PHILO OF ALEXANDRIA AND THE EPISTLE TO THE HEBREWS ON THE CONCEPT OF THE SPIRITUALIZATION OF THE CULT

AURELIAN BOTICA[*]

Emanuel University

ABSTRACT: Hebrews contains one of the most unique Greek lexicology and syntax of all the New Testament writings. Behind the syntax, however, there lies a very profound theological vision on topics such as Christ, Temple, holiness, perseverance and salvation. Studying Hebrews against the background of Graeco-Roman culture, the source that most contemporary scholars mention as being closest to the world of Hebrews in this context is Philo of Alexandria. Not only on philological grounds, but also in matters of methods of interpreting the Old Testament cult and in theology, Hebrews and Philo share a very common background. Analyzing Hebrews comparatively, we are bound to ask whether or not comparisons such as these are warranted. In the following study we will outline the state of the problem and then will examine the two sources that seem to have served as a means of inspiration for the author of Hebrews: the Old Testament and Philo of Alexandria. We will focus exclusively on the issues of the method of allegory and the spiritualization/reinterpretation of Old Testament cultic entities, since both Philo and Hebrews are characterized by these concerns. In essence, we will want to know who or what served as the most plausible source of inspiration for the author of Hebrews in the particular area of the reinterpretation of the Old Testament cult.

KEY WORDS: Hebrews, Philo, Old Testament, cult, spiritualization, allegory.

Introduction: the State of the Problem and the Background to Hebrews

The title *The Epistle to the Hebrews* has been associated with one of the more controversial debates in the area of the New Testament. It clearly points, on the one hand, to an audience that must have shared in the Jewish culture of the first century church. This assumption makes sense in light of the emphasis that the author laid on Old Testament characters (Abraham and Moses), institutions (Temple ritual and priesthood) and theological concerns, the most important of which is the "forgiveness of sins."

On the other hand, perhaps unlike any other writing in the New Testament, Hebrews contains some of the most Platonic and allegorical features that one can find in the entire Bible. The difference between outward and inward purification from sin, the notion of cleansing the conscience and the superiority of the spiritual equivalents over their earthly incarnation (9:14; 10:22) – these are some of the conceptual innovations that make the letter to the Hebrews a unique document.

It is then not surprising that the majority of commentators have pointed out the similarities between the worldview of Hebrews and that of Platonic, Intermediate Platonic and Gnostic thought.[1] In Hebrews one can hear the echoes of both Jewish and Hellenistic preaching. While we can surmise that the audience of Hebrews knew the Temple in Jerusalem was fully operational and regarded it as vital for their faith experience, we feel the uneasiness of the author with the efficacy of Mosaic enactments. That is why, given his vision, the richness of the vocabulary and the rhetorical complexities that he employed, a number of scholars have identified first century Alexandria as the most natural

---

[*] DAN AURELIAN BOTICA, PhD Hebrew Union College. Dr. Botica is currently teaching Hebrew and Old Testament Exegesis in the Emanuel University of Oradea.
[1] Thus G. Sterling, "Ontology versus Eschatology: Tensions between Author and Community in Hebrews," *StPhAnn* 13 (2001): 210, who argues that "the author of Hebrews combined Platonic ontology with a Christian understanding of salvation history."

environment in which such an author was educated.[2] According to Siegert, however, it is possible that the author of Hebrews was a Jewish Christian from Rome who may have met Philo there.[3]

In order to re-evaluate the topic of the spiritualization of the cult in Hebrews and Philo, we will deal with this phenomenon as it appears in Philo, in the Old Testament, in the New Testament and then in Hebrews.

The Process of Spiritualizing the Cult in Philo of Alexandria

That Philo applied the method of allegory when interpreting the laws of Moses has been recognized as one of the hallmarks of his hermeneutics. To understand better this phenomenon, we list here a sample of the texts which show the transition from the cultic entities of the Law to the spiritual/rational/psychological significance that one may obtain through the method of allegorization.

The reinterpretation/spiritualization of the physical cult

OT Cultic entities	The spiritual/rational/ psychological significance attained through the method of allegory	Textual reference
Tabernacle and altar	Ideas (ἰδέας) and rational spirit (πνεῦμα λογικὸν)	*Ebr.* 134 *Spec.* 1.273–7
The sanctuary	Mental (νοητὸς), invisible order	*Rer.* 75; *QE* 2.51, 83
Holy of holies in Temple	Realm of the mind (νοητός)	*Mos.* 2.81
Temple	The human soul (ψυχή)	*Spec.* 1. 12, 66ff.; *Cher.* 29, 99–100;
Offering incense	Offering the whole mind (ὅλον τὸν νοῦν)	*Leg.* 2.56; *QE* 2.71
Whole burnt offering	The perfect disposition (διάθεσιν) a man seeks to attain	*Spec.* 1.253
Body parts of priestly offerings	Inward virtues, reason	*Spec.* 1.145–50;

[2] Note W. Lane, *Hebrews 1–8*, Word Biblical Commentary (Dallas: Word, 1991), 1; F. F. Bruce, *The Epistle to the Hebrews* (Grand Rapids: Eerdmans, 1990), 12; P. Ellingworth, *The Epistle to the Hebrews. A Commentary on the Greek Text* (Grand Rapids: Eerdmans, 1993), 28.
[3] F. Siegert, "Philo and the New Testament," in A. Kamesar, ed., *The Cambridge Companion to Philo* (Cambridge, MA: Cambridge University Press, 2009), 175–209.

		1.206–08, 216
High priest as mediator	the λόγος	*Mig.* 102; *Som.* 1.215;
Sacrificing perfect victim	Purification of the soul (ψυχή) from passion	*Spec.* 1.259–60
Worship through sacrifice	A soul (ψυχή) bringing simple reality as its only sacrifice	*Det.* 21
Passover	Purification of soul (ψυχῆς κάθαρσιν)	*Spec.* 2.147
Special festivals	Life of the soul (ψυχή), thoughts (logi,smoi), and virtues	*Spec.* 2.42
Circumcision	Excision of pleasures which bewitch the mind (διάνοια), the malady of conceit	*Spec.* 1.6, 8ff., 305; 3.46ff.; *QG* 3.46; *QE* 2.2
Sacrificing the sheep	Purging the mind (διανοίας)	*Mut.* 245–57
Clean beasts and birds	The senses and the mind (νοῦς λογισμοί)	*QG* 2.52
Pouring libation of blood	The blood of the soul (τὸ ψυχικόν αἶμα)	*Leg.* 2.56; *QE* 2.14

As is evident, Philo interpreted the Levitical system of the Temple by employing the method of allegory. He acknowledged the historical reality and the usefulness of the Mosaic system, and yet sought the "higher significance" of its elements. More important, however, is the question about the sources that influenced his method. To answer this question we will examine several possible streams of influence to Philo's thought, namely, the Greek and Hellenistic, the Qumranic, and the Rabbinic sources.

The Greek and Hellenistic background to Philo

To understand the worldview of Philo and of Hellenistic Judaism better, we must remember that the process of re-evaluating the material cult to the point of finding in it higher spiritual, moral or rational meanings, started much earlier in Palestine, and in the Greek world for that matter. In a sense, it is natural that with the passing of time worshipers of a given religion will question or re-evaluate from within the basic assumptions of that religious system. Both Judaism and the Greek religion had to deal with this challenge. As we will argue shortly, the premises on which Judaism started and the methodology it applied in this process differed radically from Greek religion.

In one of our earlier studies and noted that "cult criticism" essentially involved two basic responses: *criticizing* the cult – at times to the point of rejecting its usefulness – and *reinterpreting* the cult, focusing on its spiritual and/or metaphysical significance. In the case of ancient Greek religion (thus centuries before Philo), we noted that one of the reasons for the rise of "allegory" as a critical tool for Greek philosophers was their dissatisfaction with the Homeric worldview of the gods.[4] Xenophanes, the Eleatic school, and subsequent efforts on the part of the sophists – all these reacted against the "anthropomorphistic" manner in which Homer portrayed the violent, promiscuous, and deceiving gods of the Greek tradition.[5]

Evidently other factors beyond the anthropomorphistic vision of Homer were at play. As Burkert argued, in seeking to base their systems on a "rational" explanation of nature, the first "*sophoi* or *sophistai*" drew conclusions from the study of natural philosophy (the topic of "*ta onta*") that indirectly collided with the traditional understanding of the divine world.[6] In time, the critical attitude against the cult took on various forms, from the "theological" argument that the gods need no sacrifices, to the "philosophical" concern that the gods may not be bribed by sacrifices.[7]

Nevertheless, in Greece cult criticism did not radically affect the fundamental beliefs and practices of traditional religion. Even critical philosophers such as Socrates and Epicurus would not repudiate the cult per se.[8] So the majority of the populace continued to fulfill the obligations that Greek religion demanded of them, even during the heyday of Stoicism, Epicureanism and Skepticism. In time, however, under the impact of historical, sociological and cultural (philosophical and religious) factors, Greek traditional religion gradually made room for more transcendent aspirations of some of its worshipers, especially those who had access to philosophical and gnostic sources. The "reinterpretation" and/or "spiritualization" of the cult must be understood in the context of the inability of traditional religion to accommodate satisfactorily the quest for spiritual intimacy on the part of the worshiper. Nevertheless, the material cult continued to play an essential role in the life of the Graeco-Roman worshiper. After all, it was only during the reign of Constantine that the practices of offering sacrifices to the gods were abolished.

Returning to our discussion of Philo, it must be acknowledged that he never sought "allegorical" meanings in the laws of Moses because he considered the laws inadequate for his time. He did not repudiate the laws, even though during his lifetime the Jews in Alexandria were being subject not only to ridiculing, but also to persecution, as was the case with the pogrom of 38 CE. Philo preferred the method of allegory because on Hellenistic philosophical and literary grounds it was a powerful tool with which to interpret ancient writings. Seeking the higher significance of the cultic texts, Philo

---

[4] Reale, *From the Origins to Socrates—A History of Ancient Philosophy*, trans. by J. Catan (New York: State University of NY Press, 1987), esp. 78–81.

[5] Note Botica, *The Concept of Intention* (Piskataway, NJ: Gorgias Press, 2011), 251ff., Pulleyn, *Prayer in Greek Religion* (Oxford: Clarendon, 1997), 196ff., Burkert, *Greek Religion*, esp. 305–37, Tate, "On the History of Allegorism," *Classical Quarterly*, no. 28 (1934): 105–06,

[6] Botica, *The Concept of Intention*, 252, on Burkert, *Greek Religion* (Harvard, MA: Harvard University Press, 1987), 306ff., for his distinction among the early philosophers (Anaximandros, Anaximenes of Miletus, Heraclitus of Ephesus (2nd half of the 6th century), later ones (5th century) Anaxagoras, Empedocles, Leukippos, and Democrit, followed by Socrates) and the later sophists.

[7] Thus Young, "The Idea of Sacrifice in Neoplatonic and Patristic Texts," *Studia Patristica*, no. XI (1972): 279ff., and also Nordern, *Agnostos Theos* (Berlin: B.G. Teubner, 1913), 38ff., for criticism against the priests from Athens who believed the gods depended on humans for their sacrifices.

[8] Thus J. Fergusson, *The Religions of the Roman Empire* (Ithaca, NY: Cornell University Press, 1970), 196, for the recommendation of Epictetus "to pour libations and offer sacrifice according to the customs of our fathers," and Wenschkewitz, *Die Spiritualisierung der Kultusbegriffe* (Leipzig: Eduard Pfeiffer, 1932), 51ff., and Burkert, *Greek Religion*, 334, for Plato's support for Greek traditional religion.

reveals his belief that the purity of mind and soul takes precedence over the material relevance of Temple entities.

It is at this juncture that scholars found in Philo plausible Pythagorean, Orphic, Platonic metaphysics and Stoic influences. As Raasch argued, Philo accepted "purification not simply as a cultic metaphor, but as a spiritual and philosophical process." In this sense Philo may have been among the first to combine in one vision the Platonic "*catharsis*, the Stoics' ideal of *apatheia*..., and the Judaic conception of the thoughts of the heart as determining a man's basic moral orientation."[9] In addition, a number of scholars linked some texts in Philo with Oriental and mystic sources that existed in Alexandria at the time and in the larger context of Egypt.[10] This is not surprising, since Alexandria – with its syncretism of mystic Oriental and rational Greek sources – had replaced Athens as the new cultural capital of the civilized world. Sources like these are evident in Philo when we realize how much he was preoccupied with the realm of the soul.[11]

The Judaic Background

As is evident from the table above, Philo dealt almost exclusively with Old Testament content. Is it feasible to assume that another stream of thought – possibly coming from Palestinian or other sources within Judaism – might have influenced him as well?

First, one may point out that re-interpreting the Jewish material cult was a process that took place not only in Hellenistic Judaism, but in Palestinian Judaism as well. And not necessarily in Jerusalem. This was the case at Qumran, a community that did not seem to be bound theologically or practically to the Temple of Jerusalem. On the contrary, Dead Sea texts show that many at Qumran viewed the Temple in Jerusalem to be too corrupt to be considered authoritative any longer. That is why the Qumranites developed their own interpretation and practice of Jewish sacrificial and purity laws.[12] Still, while one may not want to rule out *a priori* any relationship between Philo and the Qumran community, it is evident that for Philo the Temple – even when pushed for its spiritual significance – had a unique place.

Second, we must state that some Philonic scholars doubt the direct relationship between Palestine and Philo on the grounds that Philo may have not been able to read the Old Testament or Rabbinic Judaism in the original languages. His writings do show that he seemed to have known at least the significance of the Hebrew names. Yet working with the etymology of names does not prove by itself an in depth knowledge of Hebrew or Aramaic. As Kamesar argued, it is entirely plausible to assume that lists with the etymology of Hebrew names were circulating in Alexandria and that Philo had access to them.[13] But the fact remains that some of Philo's treaties resemble – at least in the

---

[9] See Botica, *The Concept of Intention*, 271–72 and Raasch, "The Monastic Concept of Purity and its Sources: III, Philo of Alexandria and Origen," *St. Mon.*, no. 10 (1968): 1–55, for the notion of "moral purification" in Philo (i.e. purification from *evil thoughts*, passions, etc.).

[10] Note Brehier, E. *Les idées philosophiques et religieuses de Philon d'Alexandrie* (Paris: Librairie Alphonse Picard, 1908), 237ff. for the possible influence of Hermetic traditions.

[11] For the theme of "inwardness" and Hellenistic "mysticism" in Philo see Haussleiter, *Reallexikon für Antike und Christentum III* (Stuttgart: Anton Hiersemann, 1957), 815–18; B. L. Mack, "Philo Judaeus and Exegetical Traditions in Alexandria." *ANRW*, no. II.21.1 (1984): 233ff.; E. R. Goodenough, *An Introduction to Philo Judaeus*, 2nd ed. (London: University Press of America, 1962, 1986), 134–60; Pepin, "Theorie de l'exegese allegorique chez Philon," *Philon d'Alexandrie* (Paris: CNRS, 1967), 134ff.; Amir, Y. *Die hellenistische Gestalt des Judentums bei Philon von Alexandrien* (Berlin, Neukirchener Verlag, 1983), 30, and R. Daly, *Christian Sacrifice* (Washington: Catholic University of America, 1978), 403–05, for the "Gnostic intention" in Philo.

[12] Botica, *The Concept of Intention*, 249, and J. Brown, *Temple and Sacrifice in Rabbinic Judaism* (Evanston, IL: Seabury-Western Seminary, 1963), 12ff.; F. M. Young, "Temple Cult and Law in Early Christianity," *NTS*, no. 19 (1973): 325–28; E. S. Fiorenza, "Cultic Language in Qumran and in the New Testament," *CBQ*, no. 38 (1976): 159–77; Daly, *Christian Sacrifice*, 160ff.

[13] Thus Kamesar, "Biblical Interpretation in Philo," in Kamesar, *The Cambridge Companion to Philo*, 65–91, and D. Winston, *Philo of Alexandria: the Contemplative Life, Giants and Selections* (Mahwah, NJ: Paulist Press, 1981), 334–35.

larger thematic context – the Palestinian concerns with the relevance of Old Testament laws to the legal challenges of first century Judaism.

This observation has led various scholars to ask whether or not, or to what degree did Rabbinic thought influence Philo? For example Wolfson, Kasher and others pointed out possible links between Philo and Rabbinic oral (and possibly written) traditions from Palestine.[14] Given the significant number of Jews living in Egypt, it is conceivable that Rabbinic institutions did function in Alexandria and that there existed at least a minimal relationship to those in Palestine. For example, Modrzejewski and Mennard acknowledge that one can detect a Jewish *halakhah* in Egypt, yet one that was more fluid than the one in Palestine.[15] We know that Philo visited Jerusalem and, though his writings bear insufficient direct evidence in this aspect, he should have been familiar with halakhic traditions. Still, as Tcherikower noted, one cannot discuss the similarity between Philo and the Talmudic law till:

> we have discarded the numerous cases where Philo's law, while similar to the rabbinic, may be accounted for (1) by Hellenistic or Roman influence; (2) by an almost unavoidable evolution of ideas; (3) by what must have been familiar to any Jew anywhere; (4) by a naïve interpretation of Scripture.[16]

To these criteria Tcherikower adds a fifth one, namely, "Philo's own moral and philosophical ideas." Similarly, Amir argued that in *De Specialibus Legibus* Philo "did not seek to produce an overview of contemporary Jewish law," but to prove the superiority of Moses over all other law systems and philosophies in the world, by "throwing light on the meaning and intention of the Law."[17] We may conclude that, overall, the consensus falls on the side of Hellenistic Alexandria, not Palestine, as the culture that exerted the most profound influence on Philo.[18] Although parallels between Philo and Palestinian law have been produced, a consensus among scholars seems to have emerged that, unlike Philo, Palestinian law emphasized the *physical*, rather than the *mental* aspect of a crime, and was generally less libertine with the death penalty.[19]

---

[14] See Botica, *The Concept of Intention*, 190, and S. Belkin, *The Alexandrian Halakah* (Philadelphia: Press of Jewish Rabbinic Society, 1936) and *Philo and the Oral Law* (Cambridge, MA: Harvard University Press, 1940); G. Alon, "On Philo's Halakhah," *Jews, Judaism and the Classical World* (Jerusalem: Central Press, 1977), 89–137, esp. 102–24. A. Kasher, *The Jews in Hellenistic and Roman Egypt* (Tubingen: J.C.B. Mohr, 1985), 231–61, 346–57. In particular, see A. Mendelson, *Philo's Jewish Identity* (Georgia: Scholars Press, 1988), 51–75, for Philo's defence of circumcision, Sabbath, sacrifice, and dietary laws. However this picture is complicated by the obvious relationship between Philo and Graeco-Roman thought, as even Belkin, Wolfson, and Alon have shown.

[15] Notice Botica, *The Concept of Intention*, 192, with references to M. Modrzejewski, *The Jews of Egypt* (Jerusalem: Jewish Publication Society, 1995); N. S. Hecht ed. et al, "Jewish Law and Hellenistic Legal Practice in the Light of Greek Papyri from Egypt," *Jewish Law and Hellenistic Legal Practice in the Light of the Greek Papyri from Egypt* (Oxford: Oxford University Press, 1996), 75–99; and J. W. Cairns, ed., "The Septuagint as Nomos," *Critical Studies in Ancient Law, Comparative Law and Legal History* (Portland, OR: Hart Publishing, 2001), 198, and Wolff, "Plurality of Laws in Ptolemaic Egypt," *Revue internationale des droits de l'Antiquite*, 3rd ser., no. 7 (1960): 20–57.

[16] Botica, *The Concept of Intention*, 191, and A. Tcherikower, "Prolegomena," *Corpus Papyrorum Judaicarum* (Cambridge, MA: Harvard Press, 1957), 1:1–111, 32–33, with his reference to Daube (*Biblioteca Orientalis*, 1948), 64.

[17] Y. Amir, *Die hellenistische Gestalt des Judentums bei Philon von Alexandrien* (Dusseldorf: Neukirchener Verlag, 1983), esp. 17ff., 44ff., and also Brehier, *Les idees philosophiques,* esp. 30–32, 61; J. Danielou, *Philon d'Alexandrie* (Paris: Librairie Artheme Fayard, 1955), 88; Tcherikower, "Prolegomena," 1:1–111, esp. 32–36; Sandmel "Philo: the Man, His Writings, His Significance," *ANRW* II, no. 21.1, W. Haase, ed. (Berlin: Walter de Gruyter, 1984), esp. 31ff.

[18] For a stronger position in this matter see Heinemann, *Philons Bildung* and *Die Werke*, esp. 5ff., who argues for the incompatibility of Philo's law with the rabbinic sources.

[19] Thus Botica, *The Concept of Intention*, 188. For the debate on the problem of external influence on Philo see Heinemann, *Philons griechische und judische Bildung* (Breslau: M&H Marcus, 1932), 5–15, 346–419; Hamerton-Kelly, "Sources and Traditions in Philo Judaeus," *Studia Philonica* 1 (1972), 3–26; Borgen, "Philo of Alexandria. A Critical Survey of Research since World War II," *ANRW* II, no. 21.1, W. Haase ed. (Berlin: Walter de Gruyter, 1984): 124ff.; M. Stone, ed., "Philo of Alexandria," *Jewish Writings of the Second Temple Period* (Assen: Van Gorcum, 1984), 257–59, 281–82; Mack, "Philo Judaeus and Exegetical Traditions of Alexandria," *ANRW* II, no. 21.1, 236ff.; Sandmel "Philo: the Man, His Writings, His Significance" *ANRW* II, no. 21.1, esp. 31ff.; Hecht, "Philo's Interpretation of Circumcision," *Nourished With Peace*, ed. F. Greenspahn (Chico, CA: Scholars Press, 1984), 53–61; Reinhartz, "Philo's Exposition of

In the final consideration, we must not forget that Philo was simply a man of his time and place, that is, first century Alexandria. That is why one must avoid obsessively drawing parallels between Philo and Greek and/or Jewish sources. After all, Philo was a highly educated Jew who grew up in the cultural capital of the world and who lived at some great distance from the Temple in Jerusalem. But the distance that separated Jerusalem from Alexandria was not only a problem of space, but of worldview as well. What may have made Philo unable to experience fully the material relevance of the cult was not only the spatial separation, but the spiritual and the intellectual experience that he lived in Hellenistic Alexandria. Philo never disregarded the physical and religious importance of the Temple. At the same time, however, he was raised and influenced to appreciate even more the "spiritual" and the "rational" experience of worship.[20]

The Process of Spiritualizing the Cult in the Old and the New Testament

Since Hebrews relies almost exclusively on the witness of the Old Testament, one is bound to ask if its author was influenced more by the Old Testament and less by Philo or other Hellenistic sources in the process of "spiritualizing" the cult? Secondly, we must take into account the fact that there exists other New Testament texts that reveal the same tendency, some of which bear a Jewish, rather than Hellenistic, imprint. If that is the case, is it possible that the process of spiritualizing the cult transcended the Greek and Hellenistic (Alexandrinian) boundaries, both spatially and chronologically? Before answering this question it is important to see the data in the Old Testament that show this process at work.

The Phenomenon of Criticism and Spiritualization of the Cult in the Old Testament

OT REINTERPRETATION/SPIRITUALIZATION OF THE PHYSICAL CULT

OT CULTIC ACT/ENTITY	OT SUPERIOR SIGNIFICANCE	REF
Burnt offerings and sacrifices, fat of rams	Obeying the voice of the Lord	1 Sam 15:22
Sacrifice, burnt offering	Broken spirit; a broken and contrite heart	Ps 51:16–17
Ox or a bull with horns and hoofs	Praising the name of God with a song; magnifying him with thanksgiving.	Ps 69:30
Attending/dwelling in the Holy Tent	Walking blamelessly, clean hands, speaking truth in heart, not lifting soul to deceit, not swearing deceitfully	Ps 15:1–2 Ps 24:3–4
Burnt offerings and sacrifices	Obeying God's voice, walking in Law	Jer 7:22

---

the Law and Social History," *SBLSP*, no. 32 (1993): esp. 9–13; Jackson and Piattelli, "Jewish Law During the Second Temple Period," *Introduction to the History and Sources of Jewish Law*, ed. N. Hecht (New York: Oxford University Press, 1996), 34.

[20] Thus Nikiprowetzky, "La spiritualization des sacrifices et le culte sacrificial au temple de Jerusalem chez Philon d'Alexandrie," *Etudes philoniennes* (Paris: Le Editions du Cerf, 1996), 83, and Hecht, "Patterns of Exegesis in Philo's Interpretation of Leviticus." *StPh*, no. 6 (1979–80), 81.

OT PROCESS OF CULT-CRITICISM

CULTIC ACT/ENTITY	GOD'S CRITI-CAL RESPONSE	REASON	REF
	Multitude of sacrifices, burnt offerings of rams, fat of well-fed beasts, blood of bulls, lambs, goats	The Lord does not delight in them	Covenant failure	Isa 1:11
	Frankincense from She-ba, sweet cane from a distant land, burnt offer-ings sacrifices	Not acceptable, nor pleasing to God	Covenant failure	Jer 6:20
	Burnt offerings, grain offerings, peace offer-ings of fattened animals	The Lord will not accept, nor look at them	Covenant failure	Amos 5:22
	Thousands of rams, ten thousands of rivers of oil. Sacrificing human firstborn	The Lord will not be pleased with them	Covenant failure	Mic 6:7
	Sacrifice, offering, burnt offerings, sin offerings	The Lord does not delight in them	Priority of obedi-ence	Ps 40:6
Religious prac-tices/entities (sacrifices, pray-er, assemblies)	The sacrifice of the wicked	Abomination to the Lord	Wickedness, evil intent of wor-shipers	Prov 15:8, 21:27
	Feasts and solemn as-semblies	The Lord despises	Covenant failure	Amos 5:21
	Slaughtering ox, sacri-ficing lamb, presenting grain offering, offering of frankincense	Worse than idol worshipers	Their soul delights in abominations	Isa 66:3
	Prayer	Abomination to the Lord	Covenant failure	Prov 28:9
	Honouring God with mouth and lips	Astonish the wise with wonders	Insincere heart, lack of fear	Isa 29:13

Religious personnel	Priests teach for a price; its prophets practice divination for money	Disaster	Corruption	Mic 3:11
	From prophet to priest, everyone deals falsely	Punishment	Corruption	Jer 6:13
	Both prophet and priest are ungodly	Punishment	Ungodliness	Jer 23:11
	Priests profane what is holy; they do violence to the law.	Divine justice	Profanation Violence to Law	Zeph 3:4
Religious institutions (Temple)	Temple has become a den of robbers	Destruction of Temple	Corruption, idolatry	Jer 7:11
	Prophet sent to prophesy against the Temple	Destruction	Corruption, idolatry	Jer 7:12

To a certain extent, the Old Testament paints a picture in which one finds some of the same challenges that existed in Greek religion with respect to "cult criticism." That is, critical voices appear to have objected either against the material cult itself, or the misuse of the cult by those who were bound to honour its laws. But there exists a fundament difference between the native critics of the Greek cult and the Jewish ones. That is so because in pre-exilic Judaism it was the "traditional" camp, not its critics, that spearheaded the movement against the cult. A simple review of the verses listed in the table shows that most of the critical voices were prophetic. Why is this important?

A prophet was a person responsible with guarding the boundaries of the covenant. The prophet would be sent by God in times of crisis (for the most part) to expose the apostasy of Israel and call the people to repentance when the boundaries of the covenant were transgressed. If and when the message of the prophet contain proleptic and apocalyptic warnings, it was so because the people should know what consequences would follow from the actions. This means that the apparent critics of the cult were in fact the very defenders of the cult, as it was understood within the covenant between God and Israel. As they saw it, most people – priests and worshipers – abused the stipulations of the covenant by keeping the "letter," while rejecting the "spirit," of the Law.[21]

That is why, well before the 6th century Greek *sophoi*, 8th century prophets like Isaiah charged that "this people … honour me with their lips while their hearts are far from me" (29:13). No less accommodating were the words of Amos, through whom God said: "I hate, I despise your religious festivals, and I take no pleasure in your solemn assemblies" (5:21). According to the verses we listed

---

[21] For the wider thematic of "cult-criticism" see H. M. Barstad, "התאונה," *Theological Dictionary of the Old Testament*, G. J. Botterweck ed. (Grand Rapids: Eerdmans, 2004), 13:623; T. V. Lafferty, *The Prophetic Critique of the Priority of the Cult: A Study of Amos 5:21–24 and Isaiah 1:10–17* (Eugene, OR: Wipf and Stock, 2012), 84–88; A. Groenewald, "Psalm 51 and the Criticism of the Cult: Does This Reflect a Divided Religious Leadership?" *OTE* 22 (1) 2009: 47–62; Bibb, B. D. "The Prophetic Critique of Ritual in Old Testament Theology," in L. L. Grabbe, ed., *The Priests in the Prophets*, Journal for the Study of the Old Testament, Suppl Series 408 (London: T&T Clark, 2006), 31–43; L. S. Tiemeyer, *Priestly Rites and Prophetic Rage, Post-exilic Prophetic Critique of the Priesthood*, Forschung zum Alten Testament 2/19 (Tübingen: Mohr Siebeck 2006), esp. 115–26.

above, the Old Testament prophets had nothing against the Mosaic cult per se. The problem for them was not that the cultic institutions in themselves were outdated or corrupt. It was the lifestyle of the people and the manner in which they worshiped that attracted the wrath of God and hence criticism of the cult.

Furthermore, the prophets and the authors of Psalmodic or Sapiental literature never criticized the character of God as being immoral, as was the case with Greek sophoi.[22] Rather, what mattered for them first was the *inward intention* and *the outward, practical* life of the worshipper. The material cult was important, but it never superseded the preoccupation with the attitude and practical life of the worshiper. This leads us to conclude that distinguishing between the spiritual and the material significance of the cult was a process that had begun before Philo of Alexandria. Scholars have recognized the fact that the overall data of the Old Testament – legal, historical, wisdom, poetic and prophetic texts – bear an evident consensus in supporting this vision. Whether cultic or private, for an external act of devotion to be effective in the eyes of God it must meet the *internal criteria* of heart purity.[23]

The process of criticizing, reinterpreting/spiritualizing the cult in the New Testament.[24]

Physical Category	*Moral/Spiritual/Symbolical Interpretation*	*Greek terminology*	Reference
	your body is a *temple* of the Holy Spirit within you	τὸ σῶμα ὑμῶν **ναὸς** τοῦ ἐν ὑμῖν ἁγίου πνεύματός ἐστιν	1 Cor 6:19 (3:16)

---

[22] True, authors such as Job and Ecclesiastes, that raised the issue of "innocent suffering" and the implicit assumption that God was less than just for allowing injustice to go unpunished, show that the Old Testament felt comfortable enough to allow such criticism. Yet there remains a fundamental difference between Greek and Jewish "cult criticism." With their objection against the sexual immorality, violence and deceitful ways of the gods, the Greek sophists aimed at reinterpreting the core theological truths of Homeric religion. The Old Testament critical texts, however, never challenged the fundamental truths of Jewish historical revelation. On the contrary, it was the theological premises about the goodness of God and of His revelation that motivated Job and Ecclesiastes to raise the uncomfortable questions. For a discussion of this aspect see A. Botica, *"Theodicy as Theophany in the Book of Job," Perichoresis*, vol. 2, nr. 2 (2004): 93–108.

[23] For the general issue of "inwardness" in Poetic literature see Clements, "Worship and Ethics," in M. P. Graham, ed., *Worship and the Hebrew Bible* (Sheffield: JSOT, 1999), 81ff. For Poetic literature see Nikiprowetsky, "La spiritualization des sacrifices et le culte sacrificial au temple de Jerusalem chez Philon d'Alexandrie," 199–216; Mowinckel, *The Psalms in Israel's Worship* (Oxford: Blackwell, 1962), 2:21f.; H. J. Krauss, *Psalm 1–59*, translated by G. Buswell (Richmond, VA: J. Knox, 1965), 498–506. For Wisdom literature see R. E. Clements, "The Concept of Abomination in the Book of Proverbs," in M. V. Fox, ed., *Texts, Temples, and Traditions* (Winona Lake, IN: Eisenbraus, 1996), 211–226; B. W. Kovaks, "Is There a Class Ethic in Proverbs?" in L. Cremshaw, ed., *Essays in Old Testament Ethics* (New York: Ktav, 1974), 173–189. For specific passages in Prophetic literature see C. Westermann, *Isaiah 40–66* (Philadelphia: Westminster, 1969), 196–97; B. Childs, *Isaiah* (Louisville, KY: Westminster, 2001) 218–19, Oswalt, *Isaiah 40–66* (Grand Rapids, MI: Eerdmans, 1998), 256ff.

[24] For a more complex version of this table see A. Botica, "A Brief History of the Phenomenon of the 'Reinterpretation' or 'Spiritualization' of the Physical Cult," *Perichoresis* 9.1 (2011): 110–13. Unless otherwise noted, the translation of biblical passages that I have used in this article is that of the English Standard Version, as found in *BibleWorks 8* (Norfolk, VA: BibleWorks, 2010).

	holy temple in the Lord	**ναὸν ἅγιον** ἐν κυρίῳ	Eph 2:21
Temple	In him you also are being built together *into a dwelling place* for God by the Spirit	ἐν ᾧ καὶ ὑμεῖς συνοικοδομεῖσθε εἰς **κατοικητήριον** τοῦ θεοῦ ἐν πνεύματι.	Eph 2:22
	for we are the *temple of the living God*, as God said, "I will make my dwelling among them and walk among them"	ἡμεῖς γὰρ **ναὸς θεοῦ** ἐσμεν ζῶντος καθὼς εἶπεν ὁ θεὸς ὅτι ἐνοικήσω ἐν αὐτοῖς καὶ ἐμπεριπατήσω	2 Cor 6:16
	you yourselves like living stones are being built up as a *spiritual house*	καὶ αὐτοὶ ὡς λίθοι ζῶντες οἰκοδόμεῖσθε **οἶκος πνευματικὸς**	1 Pet 2:5a
Food, Offerings and **Sacrifices**	to offer *spiritual sacrifices* acceptable to God through Jesus Christ	ἀνενέγκαι **πνευματικὰς θυσίας** εὐπροσδέκτους [τῷ] θεῷ διὰ Ἰησοῦ Χριστοῦ.	1 Pet 2:5b
	Let us therefore celebrate the festival, not with the old leaven, the leaven of malice and evil, but with the *unleavened bread of sincerity and truth*	ὥστε ἑορτάζωμεν μὴ ἐν ζύμῃ παλαιᾷ μηδὲ ἐν ζύμῃ κακίας καὶ πονηρίας ἀλλ' ἐν **ἀζύμοις εἰλικρινείας καὶ ἀληθείας.**	1 Cor 5:8
	Even if *I am* to be poured out as a drink offering upon the *sacrificial offering* of your faith	Ἀλλὰ εἰ καὶ σπένδομαι ἐπὶ τῇ **θυσίᾳ** καὶ **λειτουργίᾳ** τῆς πίστεως ὑμῶν	Phil 2:17
	so that the *offering of the Gentiles* may be acceptable	ἵνα γένηται ἡ **προσφορὰ τῶν ἐθνῶν** εὐπρόσδεκτος	Rom 15:16

to present *your bodies as a living sacrifice*, holy and acceptable to God, which is your *spiritual worship*.	παραστῆσαι τὰ σώματα ὑμῶν **θυσίαν ζῶσαν** ἁγίαν εὐάρεστον τῷ θεῷ, **τὴν λογικὴν λατρείαν** ὑμῶν	Rom 12:1

When we refer to the "reinterpretation" of cultic concepts, roles and institutions, what we have in mind is the process by which biblical authors sought spiritual significance in entities that would normally function as a physical act or part of the Jewish cultus.[25] Since the Temple was still standing when Hebrews and other New Testament letters were written, their authors never felt the tension of denying the material impact of the Jewish cult. Evidently, the resurrection of Christ changed radically the perception of the Christian church toward the Temple. But since the need for seeking higher spiritual truths in material entities had already been evident in the Old Testament, we are not surprised to see it at play in the New Testament as well. The "transference" of cultic terms into the realm of spiritual significance is an undeniable New Testament phenomenon.[26]

One representative passage that reflects the vision of New Testament authors to search for the spiritual significance of cultic is 1 Peter 2:5: "You yourselves like living stones are being built up as a spiritual house, to be a holy priesthood, to offer spiritual sacrifices acceptable to God through Jesus." Unlike other passages, 1 Peter 2:5 refers both to the Temple and its sacrifices. As we argued elsewhere, the phrases "spiritual house" (οἶκος πνευματικὸς) and "spiritual sacrifices" (πνευματικὰς θυσίας) were part of a larger group of terms already circulating in the Hellenistic world, including Early Christian texts.[27] The apostle Paul wrote that the Holy Spirit took residence in the body/soul of the believer, which made his or her body a "temple of God" (1 Cor 3:16; 6:19) – the equivalent of the "spiritual house." Paul also anticipated the vision that the Apostle Peter shared in 1 Pet 2:5 ("you are being built up as a spiritual house") when he said that the believers as a group are "the temple of the living God."

We have already noted that the concept of God indwelling the human soul was attested in Greece as early as the Pythagorean School, then in Plato, Aristotle and in the Hellenistic literature.[28] The Stoics in particular brought the concept of "deus internus" to a new level with their doctrine of the Logos – the transcendent, yet immanent presence that dwells in the human soul.[29] When viewed from the perspective of the philosophical texts, the notion of "God indwelling the soul" took on a more rationalistic dimension (particularly in Stoic thought), even though Plato associated it with the gift of poetic and/or musical inspiration. When viewed from a more mystical perspective, the indwelling of God was believed to be responsible for ecstatic trances that would result in prophecy, oracles, and the like.[30]

---

[25] In this sense see Botica, "A Brief History of the Phenomenon of the 'Reinterpretation' or 'Spiritualization' of the Physical Cult," 91–122 and *The Concept of Intention*, 99, 101ff.
[26] F. M. Young, "Temple Cult and Law in Early Christianity," *NTS*, no. 19 (1973): 325–28; E. S. Fiorenza, "Cultic Language in Qumran and in the New Testament," *CBQ*, no. 38 (1976): 159–77; Daly, *Christian Sacrifice*, 160ff.
[27] Elliot, *1 Peter* (New York: Doubleday, 2000), 414ff. Schmithals, *Der Romerbrief* (Gutersloh: Gutersloher Verlashaus, 1988) 429f.; Achtemeier, *1 Peter* (Minneapolis, MN: Augsburg Fortress, 1996), 154–59;
[28] Botica, *The Concept of Intention*, 258, Dodds, *The Bible and the Greeks* (London: Hodder & Stoughton, 1954), 196, and Haussleiter, "*Deus* Internus," 794–96, 799–811, with referrences Pythagoras and the Pythagorean School, Heraclitus (the indwelling Logos; *Frag.* 101), Plato, Aristotle, Xenocrates, Theophrastus, and the Stoa. Haussleiter lists Roman Stoa like Seneca, Epictetus, and M. Aurelius as well.
[29] Hence the λόγος and/or the νοῦς as the immanent deity in Stoicism.
[30] Thus Haussleiter, "*Deus* Internus," 794–842.

The New Testament describes a different experience. As we may surmise from the general tone of Paul and Peter's letters, what made possible the indwelling of God in the human soul was the resurrection of Jesus Christ and the coming of the Holy Spirit. Even though the Gospels did not emphasize explicitly the notion of the spiritualization of the cult, they laid the foundation for this experience when Jesus announced that after his ascent to the Father he would send the Holy Spirit on and within the soul of the believer.[31] In essence, this grounds the innovation of Paul and Peter in the witness of the Gospels and its subsequent development in the book of Acts (1:8; 2:4, etc.). The fact that we can establish parallels at the etymological level between the New Testament and Greek literature should not weaken the argument that the main source of influence for Paul and Peter were the Gospels and the Book of Acts – the least plausible candidates for direct Greek influence.

One could make a similar case on the argument on "spiritual sacrifices" (πνευματικὰς θυσίας), "spiritual worship" (λογικὴν λατρείαν) or "living sacrifices" (θυσίαν ζῶσαν) – expressions reflecting the phenomenon of the spiritualization of the cult.[32] Nevertheless, here too the link between the Old Testament and these authors is very evident. Both Paul and Peter drew inspiration from the Old Testament for virtually all of their most important doctrines (e.g., expiation, ransom/redemption, justification by faith, resurrection, etc.). Why would they not rely on the same source when they sought the "higher meaning" behind the material cult? Especially since we established that reinterpreting the cult was a process already at work in the Psalmodic and Prophetic literature.[33]

In addition, as we have argued in *The Concept of Intention*, the preoccupation with matters of the heart versus external appearances was equally important to the Old Testament authors.[34] This is proven by the wide spectrum of terms that Old Testament authors employed when describing the notion of "inwardness."[35] The same vision holds true for the rest of the New Testament. For example, sampling only the first letter of the apostle Peter, we notice how normal seemed to be the transference of physical terms to the realm of spiritual experiences.

τὰς ὀσφύας τῆς διανοίας (the loins of your minds, 1 Pet 1:13)

τὰς ψυχὰς ὑμῶν ἡγνικότες (purifying your souls, 1 Pet 1:22)

τὸ λογικὸν ἄδολον γάλα (the pure spiritual milk, 1 Pet 2:2)

οἶκος πνευματικὸς (spiritual house, 1 Pet 2:5)

πνευματικὰς θυσίας (spiritual offerings, 1 Pet 2:5)

ὁ κρυπτὸς τῆς καρδίας ἄνθρωπος (the hidden person of the heart, 1 Pet 3:4)

---

[31] Note also Luke 1:15, 41, 67, for examples of the Holy Spirit's filling and indwelling prior to the Pentecost.

[32] For general background see Cranfield, *Romans*, 602; J. Dunn, *Romans 9–16* (Waco, TX: Word, 1988), 711; J. Fitzmeyer, *Romans* (New York: Doubleday, 1993), 640–44; and Schreiner, *Romans*, 646–47, Schmithals, *Der Romerbrief*, 429ff.; Fergusson, "Spiritual Sacrifice," 1154.

[33] Thus Morris, "Sacrifice," *The Dictionary of Paul and His Letters* (Downers Grove: Intervarsity Press, 1993), electronic version, for the argument that Paul "spiritualizes the sacrificial idioms of the OT cultus, just as could other sectors of Second Temple Judaism (e.g., 1QS 9:3–5; 4QFlor 1:6–7)," and Fiorenza, "Cultic Language in Qumran and in the New Testament," 159–77.

[34] See especially chapter 3 and the review of Otto, *Theologische Ethik;* Gemsler, "Moral Judgment in the Old Testament;" Kaiser, *Toward An Old Testament Ethics;* Wolff, *Anthropology;* Nowell, "The Concept of Purity of Heart in the Old Testament;" Hogg, "'Heart and Reins' in the Ancient Literatures of the Near East," *JMOS*, no. 1 (1911): 49–91; Petazzonni, *The All Knowing God, 97–114;* North, "Brain and Nerve in the Biblical Outlook," *Biblica*, no. 74 (1993): 577–97.

[35] Thus the nouns: *heart (*standing for "mind, brain, thoughts"), *kidneys* ("emotion, thought, feeling"), *bosom, inwards* ("the inward life"), *womb* ("inmost soul") *soul* ("inward life"), *spirit, breath* ("inward life"), *inclination, striving, predisposition, intention, thought,* and the verbs of "discernment:" *to plan, intend, devise, purpose, conceive,* or the verbs *to test, search, visit, try, prove, seek, know, perceive* (the heart or the thoughts of the heart).

τὸν Χριστὸν ἁγιάσατε ἐν ταῖς καρδίαις ὑμῶν (sanctify Christ in your hearts, 1 Pet 3:15)[36]

Here too we observe the two characteristics that so far defined the process of spiritualization of cultic (and other physical) entities. First, the New Testament authors continued the process that had already begun in the Old Testament. They knew that for every external act to be received by God, there has to be a proper inward transformation. Second, the authors were familiar with, and used terms and expressions consecrated by Graeco-Roman authors. This was a normal process, as it is expected for a minority group to be influenced at the level of language by the richer and more dominant culture in which they lived.

The Process of Criticizing and/or Spiritualizing the Cult in Hebrews

Arguably, the one particular name that commentators referred to more than any other in the context of placing Hebrews within the worldview of Hellenism was the Philo of Alexandria. The theories have ranged from maximal, direct Philonic influence on Hebrews, to indirect, minimal or no relationship between the two.[37] Whether or not the author of Hebrews had access to the writings of Philo it is impossible to establish with any degree of certainty. Scholars have refrained from asserting either conscious borrowing by the author of Hebrews or direct Philonic influence. Since both sources share similarities on the level of terminology and shared conceptual themes with other Hellenistic texts, it is more likely that we can explain them in light of the shared Hellenistic environment in which they worked. We have already listed some of the reasons why Philo went to so great "allegorical lengths" to prove the superiority of the spiritual over the material significance of the cult.[38] But a theory is only as convincing as the evidence on which it rests. In order to determine the sources that appear to have influenced the author of Hebrews, it is essential that we examine the textual data. In this sense, we have divided the verses that are relevant to this theory in two groups. The first table lists the passages in which the author compares events and entities (cultic and non-cultic) of the Old Testament with the new age inaugurated by God in the person of Jesus Christ.

THE FULFILLMENT OF THE OLD TESTAMENT EVENTS/ENTITIES

OT ACT/ENTITY	NT SUPERIOR SIGNIFICANCE	HEBREWS
The Sinai generation did not enter rest	The church generation will enter rest	4:3–10
Human priest unable to sympathize with weakness	High Priest Jesus able to sympathize with weakness	4:14; 5:1–3
Levitical priests did not attain perfec-	Jesus named priest from order of	7:11, 15

---

[36] Note the verb ἁγιάζω (to make holy, to set apart), an LXX translation of the Hebrew קדשׁ, "which clearly is a cultic term, with the sense to *sanctify/set apart as holy* a cultic entity (Sabbath day, priestly clothes, the altar, the tent, the priest/levite) - see Exod 19:23, 20:11, 29:27." See Botica, "A Brief History of the Phenomenon of the 'Reinterpretation of the Cult,'" 115.

[37] One of the first in depth studies to involve lexical and conceptual comparisons between Philo and Hebrews was R. Williamson, *Philo and the Epistle to the Hebrews* (Leiden: Brill, 1970). See also Sowers, *The Hermeneutics of Philo and Hebrews* (Richmond, VA: John Knox, 1965); J. Dunnill, *Covenant and Sacrifice in the Letter to the Hebrews* (Cambridge: Cambridge University Press, 2005), 228;

[38] Note F. Siegert, "Philo and the New Testament," *The Cambridge Companion to Philo*, Kamesar A. ed. (Cambridge, MA: Cambridge University Press, 2009), 175–209, esp. 182, for the notion that "Hebrews makes just as much of the Jerusalem cult as does Philo."

tion	Melchizedek	
Levitical priests subject to limited office by death	High Priest Jesus guarantor of better covenant because he continues forever	7:23–24
The Law appoints priests in their weakness, who offer sacrifice for their own sins	Jesus is holy, innocent, unstained, separated, perfect, and offered himself as sacrifice	7:26–28
Levitical priests offer sacrifices on earth, in tenth made by human hands	Jesus is priest in high places, not necessary to offer sacrifices	8:1–4
Ministry of priests enacted by Law	Ministry of Jesus more excellent, covenant better since it is enacted on better promises	8:5–6
First covenant was not faultless, made obsolete	New covenant written on people's hearts	8:7–13
Earthly Temple limited by repeated sacrifices and High Priest enters it every year	Heavenly Temple not made by human hands, Jesus sacrificed himself and entered heavenly Temple once for all	9:1–11, 25–26 10:1–3
Animal blood purified the flesh, offers temporal forgiveness, unable to remove sins	Blood of Jesus purifies conscience, offers eternal redemption once for all, perfects those it sanctified	9:13–14 10:4, 10, 14, 22
Earthly Temple is a copy and a shadow	Heavenly Temple is eternal	9:23; 10:1
OT believers received temporary promises	New Testament believers saw promises fulfilled	11:39–40
OT believers could not endure the blazing fire, darkness, gloom and voice at Mount Sinai	NT believers approached the city of the living God, the heavenly Jerusalem	12:18–29

First, it is evident that the source that influenced the author of Hebrews beyond any degree of uncertainty is the Old Testament. Virtually every important feature that defines the ministry of Jesus Christ and of the church has an equivalent in the revelation of Old Testament. This means that Hebrews shares the same vision that is so evident in the rest of the New Testament. Which leads us to the second conclusion, namely, that Jesus Christ fulfils the expectations that were already anticipated in the Old Testament. The one concept that works as a common denominator for these verses is the idea of "superiority." The New Testament generation received a greater blessing than the Sinai generation. The sacrifice of Jesus Christ had a definitive, much greater impact than the sacrifices that were brought by Levitical priests. The list could go on.

As we will conclude later, the leading theme that characterizes Hebrews is "fulfillment." What this means, however, is not that Christ invalidates the history or the institutions of the Old Covenant. As the author of Hebrews sees it, they were temporal and limited symbols to a lasting reality. Even though they were superseded by person of Christ, they played an important role in the history of redemption. The point of the author was not to disprove the utility of the Mosaic system for the historical circumstances in which it functioned. One could not find a greater discrepancy between the Greek criticism of the cult and the approach taken in Hebrews. The argument that Hebrews makes is not an "either-or" case, but a cumulative construct in which the efficacy of the former revelation ("Long ago, at many times and in many ways God spoke") has been fulfilled in the new revelation of Christ ("but in these last days he has spoken to us by his Son").

THE RE-EVALUATION OF OT CULTIC/PHYSICAL ENTITIES

Physical Category	*Spiritual/Symbolical Interpretation*	*Greek terminology*	Reference
Temple	but Christ is faithful over God's house as a son. And *we are his house*	Χριστὸς δὲ ὡς υἱὸς ἐπὶ τὸν οἶκον αὐτοῦ· οὗ **οἶκός** ἐσμεν ἡμεῖς	Heb 3:6
Food, Offerings and *Sacrifices*	offer up a sacrifice of praise to God, that is, *the fruit of lips* that acknowledge his name.	ἀναφέρωμεν θυσίαν αἰνέσεως διὰ παντὸς τῷ θεῷ, τοῦτ' ἔστιν **καρπὸν χειλέων** ὁμολογούντων τῷ ὀνόματι αὐτοῦ.	Heb 13:15
	Do not neglect *to do good and to share what you have,* for such *sacrifices* are pleasing to God	τῆς δὲ **εὐποιΐας καὶ κοινωνίας** μὴ ἐπιλανθάνεσθε· τοιαύταις γὰρ **θυσίαις** εὐαρεστεῖται ὁ θεός.	Heb 13:16
	blood of Christ will *purify our conscience* from dead works to serve living God	τὸ αἷμα τοῦ Χριστοῦ καθαριεῖ **τὴν συνείδησιν** ἡμῶν ἀπὸ νεκρῶν ἔργων	Heb 9:14

our hearts sprinkled clean (by the blood of Jesus)	ῥεραντισμένοι **τὰς καρδίας** ἀπὸ συνειδήσεως πονηρᾶς	Heb 10:19, 22
our bodies washed with pure water	λελουσμένοι **τὸ σῶμα** ὕδατι καθαρῷ·	Heb 10:22

We believe that the conclusions we drew in the previous section apply to this section as well. When Hebrews 10:22–23 states that the blood of Christ purifies the conscience of the believers, it essentially describes a reality that was already anticipated by the Old Testament. When Ezekiel 36:25–26 refers to the physical process of sprinkling, it uses a verb that appears quite often in the context of Levitical purification (Lev 4). This time, however, the verb קרה ("to sprinkle") describes an operation that affects the spiritual realm of things ("I will sprinkle clean water on you ... and I will give you a new heart."). This confirms what we have been observing so far in our study. Transferring cultic entities into the realm of spiritual processes is a process of "theological germination" in the Old Testament that will flourish in the New. Note, however, that Ezekiel 36 describes an event with ramifications to be observed in the future. What this means for the author of Hebrews is that the transference of cultic entities into the realm of spiritual realities is possible because of the sacrifice of Jesus Christ. For Hebrews, what was anticipated by the Old Testament has been fulfilled in the person of Jesus Christ.

Likewise, when Hebrews 9:23 states that the earthly temple is but a shadow of a heavenly reality, it shows that the cultic entity of the Old Testament served as a symbol – nonetheless, a historical one – for the higher reality to be fulfilled in the person of Christ. The ministry of bringing gifts and sacrifices to the Sanctuary is "a copy and shadow" (ὑποδείγματι καὶ σκιᾷ) of the heavenly things.[39] "For when Moses was about to erect the tent, he was instructed by God, saying, 'See that you make everything according to the pattern that was shown you on the mountain.'"

As we already noted, various authors have suggested that in the distinction between "the material world and the heavenly world" the author of Hebrews might have been influenced by the classical dualism of Plato. According to Lane, it was possible that this worldview was mediated to the author of Hebrews "by Philo or by the influence of an Alexandrian education."[40]

Others argued that, since for the author of Hebrews the "higher" significance is Christ – who after all came in the material world in bodily, not spiritual, form – it is unlikely that Platonism or Philo had a direct influence on Hebrews. In that sense, if there appears to be any resemblance between Hebrews and Plato and/or Philo, it is "merely verbal."[41] In the view of F. F. Bruce, the similarities work more on the level of language than essential thought. The fundamental worldview of the author of Hebrews is too biblically Judaic to have been shaped at the core by classical or "Philonic" Platonism.[42]

If this is the case, one may argue that the tendency to compare the Old Covenant with the New should be understood primarily in the larger context of the "fulfillment" world view of the Gospels.

---

[39] See also 9:23 ("the copies of the heavenly things") and 10:1 ("the law has but a shadow of the good things to come").

[40] Lane, *Hebrews 1–8*, 207.

[41] For the emphasis in Hebrews on the historicity of Christ in Hebrews, including his human weaknesses, see also F. F. Bruce, *The Epistle to the Hebrews*, 28, and P. Ellingworth, *The Epistle to the Hebrews*, 397.

[42] Note D. Hagner, *Encountering the Books of Hebrews: An Exposition* (Ada, MI: Baker Academic, 2002), 30ff., for the "huge difference" that separates the Epistle to the Hebrews from the worldview of Philo.

Virtually all four Gospels contain "fulfillment" passages, either introduced by the narrators of the Gospels themselves, or presented as the very words of Jesus.[43] The superiority of Jesus over the Law as taught and practiced by the Pharisees, over Sabbath, Temple, priests and sacrifices, not to mention his authority over Abraham and Moses – all these indicate that the reasoning of the author of Hebrews fits comfortably in the wider context of the Gospels.

Now, most commentators who have drawn a clear line of distinction between Philo and Hebrews focused on the thematic similarities and/or differences between the two. Typical themes here include Philo vs Hebrews' vision on the High Priest and Christ, Moses, and the heavenly realm. It is from this narrower, historical perspective that one may justifiably conclude that the influence of Philo on Hebrews was at best minimal or for the most part non-existent.

However, when we approach this issue from the perspective of how a Hellenist believer (Jewish or early Christian) would have viewed the Old Testament cult and how, more specifically, he or she appropriated its personal significance, then the relationship between Philo and Hebrews takes on a different dimension. It is at this point that one finds a shared vision between the two authors on the cult of the Old Testament. Namely, that the cult, with all its immediate material benefits, was meant to have an ultimate impact upon the soul more so than on the body. In this sense, both Philo and Hebrews assume the environment of the Hellenistic quest for the ultimate redemption of the soul. For Philo, when the Old Testament cult is interpreted appropriately – that is, allegorically – it will serve as a means for the purification and the ultimate redemption of the soul. For Hebrews, when the Old Testament is understood correctly – that is, from the perspective of the Christ event – it will serve as a proleptic revelation, as a Christological prototype for Jesus Christ. Hence, the evident superiority of the life, death and resurrection of Christ over the material cult of the Old Testament.[44]

Conclusion

Our study has shown that both the author of Hebrews and Philo aimed at transcending the material boundaries of the cult. Yet, they were driven by different motivations and for the most part had radically different reasons for doing so.

First of all, Philo of Alexandria was a man of his times. The cultural streams of Platonism and Hellenism had flown into Alexandria long before Philo was born, so much so that during his life Philo benefited from the most vibrant philosophical environment the world knew at the time. As we already argued, the early Greek allegorists, Stoic thought and Hellenism in general shaped the philosophical mindset of Philo. To this one must add the factor of the spatial and cultural distance between Philo and the material cult in Jerusalem. That is why, when comparing Philo with Hebrews, one must take into consideration the fundamental criterion that differentiates between the two. Both are interpreting the Scriptures. Both are expecting their readers to respond appropriately. Philo passes all content through the filter of allegory in order to present the Scripture as a superior philosophical treatise. Philo preferred the allegorical method because of his formation as an Alexandrian Hellenistic philosopher, as is evident from his mastery of the Greek language and the profound familiarity with Platonic and Hellenistic Philosophy.[45] Consequently, no one and nothing escapes allegorization in Philo: Abel, Abraham, Aaron, Moses, the Temple, sacrifices and offerings and worship. Reading Philo, one has the sense of reading Hellenistic moral and religious philosophy at its best. And as an

---

[43] Note the Matthean formulae "This was to fulfil what the Lord had spoken through the prophet" (e.g. Matt 2:15), or the reasoning behind the cases "You have heard that it was said…, but I say to you."

[44] See Kenneth Schenk, *Understanding the Book of Hebrews: the Story Behind the Sermon* (Louisville, KY: Westminster John Knox, 2003), 33ff., for how this logic applies to the specific concept of the Levitical cult.

[45] See Sowers, *Hermeneutics*, 11–27, 49–63; Dreyer, *Begriff des Gottgeziemenden* SPUDASMATA, no. XXIV (New York: Georg Olms Verlag, 1970), 135–40; similarly Mendelson, *Philo's Jewish Identity*, 54ff.; Y. Amir, *Hellenistische Gestalt* (Dusseldorf: Neukirchener Verlag, 1983), 124–27; J. Pepin, "La theorie de l'exegese allegorique chez Philon," *Philon d'Alexandrie*, esp. 150ff.; B. L. Mack, "Philo and Exegetical Traditions in Alexandria," ANRW, no. II.21.1 (1984): 227–271 (esp. 250ff.).

apologist, Philo makes Moses or other Old Testament characters the ultimate embodiment of the true philosopher.

The author of Hebrews, however, read the Scripture through the lenses of the "fulfillment" promise. Unlike Philo, who brought the art of allegorization to hear perfection, he writes to a church in a time of crisis, exhorting the people to consider Jesus, the author and perfecter of their faith. He too appeals to Old Testament characters like Abel, Noah, Abraham and the patriarchs, Moses and the rest of the heroes of faith. But for him the Old Testament is less a source to be interpreted allegorically, and more a prophecy that anticipated the coming of Christ. That is why reading Hebrews creates the indelible sense that revelation is a process in history that points forward to its fulfillment in Christ. In this sense, Hebrews shares the vision that animated the rest of the authors of the New Testament, who saw in the Law of Moses a precursor that foreshadowed Jesus Christ.[46]

Second, we must remember that before Philo became a philosopher he was a Jew. In spite of being born in a wealthy family and benefiting from the fellowship of a strong Jewish community, Philo felt personally the anti-Semitic polemics that the Greek populace professed against the Jews of Alexandria. Both ancient and contemporary authors attest to deadly pogroms of 38 CE that the Jews suffered at the hands of the Alexandrians during the time of Philo. A witness to the pogroms, Philo narrates in *An Embassy to Gaius* how he headed a Jewish delegation to Rome in order to petition emperor Caligula to intervene on behalf of the Jews, who were being murdered and deprived of their property.[47]

To understand the intensity of the conflict between the Greeks and Jews of Alexandria, one may remember that several decades after Philo, Josephus had to write the powerful treatise *Against Apion* in order to combat Apion, "a Greek grammarian and head of the Alexandrian school" who wrote fantastic stories about the Exodus from Egypt and made all sorts of malicious assertions about the customs of the Alexandrian Jews.[48] The fact that Josephus engaged in this polemic against the students of Apion while living in Rome, proves how intense the tension between Greeks and Jews had been in Alexandria.[49] It is now easier to comprehend the motivation Philo may have had in presenting Judaism to a Greek audience as a system of thought compatible with the best Greek treaties.

Third, as a Jewish thinker Philo must have felt personally the challenge raised by Greek philosophers against the "anthropological character of the myths."[50] In their eyes, the accounts of Moses about God were no less mythological than the Homeric portrayal of the gods. As a Jew, however, Philo shared a different view of the history of Israel. The fact that he applied the allegorical method in interpreting Moses did not mean that he viewed the Jewish Legislator and his laws as mythological.[51] On the contrary, Philo reverted to allegory simply because he aimed at convincing the Alexandrian

---

[46] Cranfield, *Romans*, 602–03; Schmithals, *Romerbrief*, 429; Dunn, *Romans*, 711; Schreiner, *Romans*, 645.

[47] On the historical context and Philo's treatise see Daniel R. Schwartz, "Philo and Josephus On The Violence in Alexandria in 38 CE," in David T. Runia et al, eds., *Studia Philonica Annual XXIV* (2012): 149–66; E. Gruen, Diaspora: *Jews Amidst Greeks and Romans* (Harvard, MA: Harvard University Press, 2004), 54–83.; P. Schaefer, *Judeophobia: Attitudes Toward the Jews in the Ancient World* (Harvard, MA: Harvard University Press, 2009), 136–160.

[48] See A. Botica, "Profiles of History-Makers: Josephus' "Against Apion." *Caesura* vol. 2.1 (2015): 55–68, and Schurer, "The Jewish Philosopher Philo," in G. Vermes, ed., *The History of the Jewish People in the Age of Jesus Christ* (Edinburgh: T&T Clark, 1973), 3: 605, for the contention that Apion wrote "'fantastic stories concerning the exodus of the Jews from Egypt,' as well as malicious assertions in regard to the Alexandrian Jews and the worship and customs of the Jews in general."

[49] Note in this sense our analysis of Kasher, "Polemic and Apologetic Methods of Writing," in L. H. Feldman and J. R. Levison, eds., *Josephus' Contra Apionem* (Leiden: Brill, 1996), 151, and the reference to other anti-Semitic contemporary authors of Josephus like Frontinus, Quintillian, Martial, Democritus, Nicarchus, Epictetus, Plutarch, and Juvenal.

[50] See Botica, *The Concept of Intention*, 259–60, and Bloningen, *Der griechische Ursprung,* 20.

[51] In this sense see the arguments developed by A. Kamesar in "Philo, the Presence of "Paideutic Myth" in the Pentateuch, and the "Principles" or *Kephalia* of Mosaic Discourse," *StPh Annual*, no. 10 (1998): 34–65, esp. 56–65, and "The Literary Genres of the Pentateuch as Seen from the Greek Perspective: The Testimony of Philo of Alexandria," *StPhAn*, no. 9 (1997): 143–89.

Hellenistic audience "of the superiority of the biblical account."[52] For him the Hebrew Scriptures were the highest form of philosophy and Plato was, in fact, a follower of Moses.[53]

In Hebrews we find clues that paint a scenario similar to the situation in Alexandria, the year 38 CE. Hebrews 10:32 describes a church who struggled with public humiliation, loss of property, affliction and imprisonment (13:3). Repeated warnings against apostasy (2:1; 3:12; 4:1; 6:4; 10:23, 26; 12:3) indicate that some of her members began showing signs of weakness. Perhaps others felt that Jerusalem, with all its grandeur, the multiplicity of sacrifices and the promise of forgiveness of sins, was a more convincing alternative to merely believing in Christ.

That is why, unlike Philo, the author of Hebrews did not seek to convince the audience that the Old Testament was superior to pagan philosophy and culture, but that the Old Testament pointed to Christ and that in him the church finds the Author and the Captain of her faith. As we indicated, Hebrews never derided the Temple, but made the irrefutable argument that the entire Old Testament pointed to something better; a reality neither bound by human weakness, nor restricted by time. Hebrews points to Christ. It lacks the philosophical finesse of Philo, but then, it never aimed at winning philosophical arguments. Hebrews emphasizes the urgency of human responsibility in light of the advent of Christ.

Bibliography

Reference Works

BibleWorks 8. Norfolk, VA: BibleWorks, 2010.

Biblia Hebraica Stuttgartensia. Edited by K. Elliger and W. Rudolph. Stuttgart: Deutsche Bibelgesellschaft 1997.

Greek-English Lexicon of the New Testament and Other Early Christian Literature. F. W. Danker. Chicago, IL: Chicago University Press, 2000.

Greek-English Lexicon. Edited by Liddell and Scott. 9th Edition with new supplement. Oxford: Clarendon Press, 1996.

Interpreters Bible Dictionary. Edited by G. Buttrick. 5 vols. New York: Abingdon, 1976.

New International Dictionary of Old Testament Theology and Exegesis. Edited by W. Van Generem. Zondervan Software. Grand Rapids, MI: Zondervan, 2001.

Philo. Works. Loeb Classical Library. Edited by F. H. Colson and G. H. Whitaker. Vols. 1–10. New York, 1929–1933; vols. 6–10, 1935–1942.

Theological Dictionary of the New Testament. Edited by G. Kittel. Grand Rapids, MI: Eerdmans, 1972.

Theological Dictionary of the Old Testament. Edited by J. Botterweck. 16 Vols. Grand Rapids, MI: Eerdmans, 2006.

Books, Articles

Achtemeier P. *1 Peter*. Minneapolis: Augsburg Fortress, 1996.

---

[52] See Wenschkewitz, *Spiritualisierung*, 83–86.
[53] Note M. Leonard, *Socrates and the Jews. Hellenism and Hebraism from Moses Mendelsshon to Sigmund Freud* (Chicago, IL: University of Chicago Press, 2012), 21.

Alon, G. "On Philo's Halakhah." *Jews, Judaism and the Classical World.* Jerusalem: Central Press, 1977.

Amir, Y. *Die hellenistische Gestalt des Judentums bei Philon von Alexandrien.* Berlin, Neukirchener Verlag, 1983.

Beuken, W. A. M. *Isaiah II.* Leuven: Peeters, 2000.

Belkin, S. *The Alexandrian Halakah.* Philadelphia: Press of Jewish Rabbinic Society, 1936.

_____. *Philo and the Oral Law.* Cambridge, MA: Harvard University Press, 1940.

Bibb, B. D. "The Prophetic Critique of Ritual in Old Testament Theology." *The Priests in the Prophets.* Journal for the Study of the Old Testament. Suppl Series 408. Edited by L. L. Grabbe. London: T&T Clark, 2006.

Borgen, P. "Philo of Alexandria. A Critical Survey of Research since World War II." *ANRW* II, no. 21.1. Edited by W. Haase. Berlin: Walter de Gruyter, 1984.

Botica, A. "A Brief History of the Phenomenon of the 'Reinterpretation' or 'Spiritualization' of the Physical Cult." *Perichoresis* 9.1 (2011): 91–122.

_____. *The Concept of Intention* in the Bible. Philo of Alexandria and the Early Rabbinic Literature. Piskataway, NJ: Gorgias Press, 2011.

_____. Profiles of History-Makers: Josephus' "Against Apion." *Caesura* vol. 2.1 (2015): 55–68.

Brehier, E. *Les idées philosophiques et religieuses de Philon d'Alexandrie.* Paris: Librairie Alphonse Picard, 1908.

Brown, J. *Temple and Sacrifice in Rabbinic Judaism.* Evanston: Seabury Western Theological Seminary, 1963.

Bruce, F. F. *The Epistle to the Hebrews.* Grand Rapids, MI: Eerdmans, 1990.

Bruce, W. S. *The Ethics of the Old Testament.* Edinburgh: T&T Clark, 1960.

Buffiere, F. *Les mythes d'Homere et la pensee grecque.* Paris: Societe d'Edition "Les Belles Lettres." 1956.

Burkert, W. *Greek Religion.* Harvard, MA: Harvard University Press, 1987.

Childs, B. *Isaiah.* Louisville, KY: Westminster, 2001.

Clements, R. E. "Worship and Ethics." *Worship and the Hebrew Bible.* Edited by M.P. Graham. Sheffield: JSOT, 1999.

Clements, R. E. "The Concept of Abomination in the Book of Proverbs." Pages 211–226 in *Texts, Temples, and Traditions.* Edited by M. V. Fox. Winona Lake, IN: Eisenbraus, 1996.

Cranfield C. *Romans IX–XVI.* Edinburgh: T&T Clark, 1979.

Daly, R. *Christian Sacrifice.* Washington: Catholic University of America, 1978.

Danielou, J. *Philon d'Alexandrie.* Paris: Librairie Artheme Fayard, 1955.

Dawson D. *Allegorical Readers and Cultural Revision in Ancient Alexandria.* Berkeley: University of California Press, 1992.

Dihle A. *Theory of Will in Classical Antiquity.* Gottingen: Ruprecht, 1985.

Dodds C. *The Bible and the Greeks.* London: Hodder & Stoughton, 1954.

Dreyer, O. *Untersuchungen zum Begriff des Gottgeziemenden in der Antike.* SPUDASMATA no. XXIV. New York: Georg Olms Verlag, 1970.

Dunn J. *Romans 9–16.* Waco, TX: Word, 1988.

Dunnill, J. *Covenant and Sacrifice in the Letter to the Hebrews.* Cambridge: Cambridge University Press, 2005.

Ellingworth, P. *The Epistle to the Hebrews. A Commentary on the Greek Text.* Grand Rapids, MI: Eerdmans, 1993.

Elliot J. *1 Peter.* New York: Doubleday, 2000.

Farmer, K. *Proverbs and Ecclesiastes.* Grand Rapids, MI: Eerdmans, 1991.

Fergusson E. "Spiritual Sacrifices in Early Christianity and its Environment." *ANRW* II.23.2 (1980): 1151–89.

Fergusson, J. *The Religions of the Roman Empire.* Ithaca: Cornell University Press, 1970.

Fiorenza S. "Cultic Language in Qumran and in the New Testament." *CBQ* 38 (1976): 159–177.

Fitzmeyer J. *Romans.* New York: Doubleday, 1993.

Fox, M. *Proverbs 1–9.* Anchor Bible. New York: Doubleday, 2002.

Glasson, T. F. "'Visions of Thy Head'—the Heart and the Head in Bible Psychology." *Expository Times* 81 no. 8 (1970): 247–48.

Glenn, M. "Cornutus and Stoic Allegoresis." *ANWR* II 36.3 (1989): 2019.

Goodenough, E. R. *An Introduction to Philo Judaeus.* 2nd ed. London: University Press of America, 1962, 1986.

Groenewald, A. "Psalm 51 and the Criticism of the Cult: Does This Reflect a Divided Religious Leadership?" *OTE* 22 (1) 2009: 47–62.

Gruen, E. Diaspora: *Jews Amidst Greeks and Romans.* Harvard, MA: Harvard University Press, 2004, 54–83.

Haussleiter J. *Reallexikon fur Antike und Christentum III.* Stuttgart: Anton Hiersemann, 1957.

Hagner, D. *Encountering the Books of Hebrews: An Exposition.* Ada, MI: Baker Academic, 2002.

Hecht, R. "Philo's Interpretation of Circumcision." Pages 53–61 in *Nourished With Peace.* Edited by F. Greenspahn. Chico, CA: Scholars Press, 1984.

_____. "Patterns of Exegesis in Philo's Interpretation of Leviticus." *StPh* no. 6 (1979–80): 77–155.

Heinemann I. *Philons griechische und judische Bildung*. Breslau: M&H Marcus, 1932.

Hogg, H. W. "'Heart and Reins' in the Ancient Literatures of the Near East." *JMOS* no. 1 (1911): 49–91.

Kaiser, W. *Toward an Old Testament Ethics*. Grand Rapids, MI: Zondervan, 1986.

Kamesar, A. "Philo, the Presence of 'Paideutic Myth' in the Pentateuch, and the 'Principles' or *Kephalia* of Mosaic Discourse." *StPh Annual* no. 10 (1998): 34–65.

_____. "The Literary Genres of the Pentateuch as Seen from the Greek Perspective: The Testimony of Philo of Alexandria." *StPhAn* no. 9 (1997): 143–89.

_____. "Biblical Interpretation in Philo." In *The Cambridge Companion to Philo*. Edited by A. Kamesar. Cambridge, MA: Cambridge University Press, 2009.

Kasemann E. *Romans*. Grand Rapids, MI: Eerdmans, 1980.

Kasher, A. *The Jews in Hellenistic and Roman Egypt*. Tubingen: Mohr, 1985.

Kasher, A. "Polemic and Apologetic Methods of Writing." *Josephus' Contra Apionem*. Edited by L. H. Feldman and J. R. Levison. Leiden: E. J. Brill, 1996.

Kovaks, B. W. "Is There a Class Ethic in Proverbs?" Pages 173–189 in *Essays in Old Testament Ethics*. Edited by Crenshaw. New York: Ktav, 1974.

Krauss, H. J. *Psalm 1–59*. Translated by G. Buswell. Richmond, VA: John Knox, 1965.

Lafferty, T. V. *The Prophetic Critique of the Priority of the Cult: A Study of Amos 5:21–24 and Isaiah 1:10–17*. Eugene, OR: Wipf and Stock, 2012.

Lane, W. *Hebrews 1–8*. Word Biblical Commentary. Dallas: Word Books, 1991.

Leonard, M. *Socrates and the Jews. Hellenism and Hebraism from Moses Mendelsshon to Sigmund Freud*. Chicago, IL: University of Chicago Press, 2012.

Leonhardt J. *Jewish Worship in Philo of Alexandria*. Tubingen: Mohr Siebeck, 2001.

Long J. *Hellenistic Philosophy*. Berkeley: University of California Press, 1986.

Long L. *The Hellenistic Philosophers*. Vol. 1. London: Cambridge University Press, 1987.

Mack, B. L. "Philo Judaeus and Exegetical Traditions in Alexandria." *ANRW* no. II.21.1 (1984): 227–271.

Mennard, J. E. "Philon d'Alexandrie ou Philon le juif." Pages 7 :1299–1304 in *Dictionnaire de la Bible. Supplement*. Edited by L. Pirot. Paris: Letouzey & Ane, 1966.

Morris, L. "Sacrifice." In *The Dictionary of Paul and His Letters*. Downers Grove, IL: Intervarsity Press, 1993 (the electronic version).

Mays, *Psalms*. Louisville, KY: John Knox Press, 1944.

Mendelson, M. *Philo's Jewish Identity*. Georgia: Scholars Press, 1988.

Modrzejewski, M. *The Jews of Egypt*. Jerusalem: Jewish Publication Society, 1995.

_____. "Jewish Law and Hellenistic Legal Practice in the Light of Greek Papyri from Egypt." Pages 75–99 in *Jewish Law and Hellenistic Legal Practice in the Light of the Greek Papyri from Egypt*. Edited by N. S. Hecht. Oxford, Oxford University Press, 1996.

_____. "The Septuagint as Nomos." Pages 183–99 in *Critical Studies in Ancient Law, Comparative Law and Legal History*. Edited by J. W. Cairns. Portland, OR: Hart, 2001.

Mowinckel, S. *The Psalms in Israel's Worship*. Oxford: Blackwell, 1962.

Nikiprowetsky V. "La spiritualization des sacrifices et le culte sacrificial au temple de Jerusalem chez Philon d'Alexandrie." Pages 199–216 in *Etudes philoniennes*. Paris, Serf, 1996.

North, R. "Did Ancient Israelites Have a Heart?" *BibRev* no. 11 (1995): 33.

Nordern, E. *Agnostos Theos*. Berlin: Teubner, 1913.

Nowell, I. "The Concept of Purity of Heart in the Old Testament." Pages 17–29 in *Purity of Heart in Early Ascetic and Monastic Literature*. Collegeville, MN: Liturgical Press, 1999.

Oswalt, J. *Isaiah 40–66*. Grand Rapids, MI: Eerdmans, 1998.

Otto, E. *Theologische Ethik des Alten Testaments*. Stuttgart: W. Kohlhammer GmbH, 1994.

Pepin, J. "Theorie de l'exegese allegorique chez Philon." *Philon d'Alexandrie*. Paris: CNRS, 1967.

Pohlenz, M. *Die Stoa: Geschichte einer geistiger Bewegung*, Gottingen: Vandenhoeck & Ruprecht, 1959, 1992.

Pulleyn, S. *Prayer in Greek Religion*. London: Oxford, 1997.

Raasch, J. "The Monastic Concept of Purity and its Sources: III, Philo of Alexandria and Origen." *St. Mon.* no. 10 (1968): 1–55.

Reale, G. *From the Origins to Socrates – A History of Ancient Philosophy*. Translated by J. Catan. New York: State University of New York, 1987.

Reale, G. *Platon and Aristotle*. New York: State University of New York, 1990.

Reinhartz, A. "Philo's Exposition of the Law and Social History." *SBLSP* no. 32 (1993): 6–21.

Reitzeinstein R. *Hellenistic Mystery Religions*. Pittsburgh: Pickwick Press, 1978.

Rowley, J. *Worship in Ancient Israel*. Philadelphia: Fortress, 1967.

Runia, D. "God and Man in Philo of Alexandria." *JTS* 39 (1988): 48–75.

Sandbach, F. *The Stoics*. 2nd ed. London: Gerald Duckworth, 1989.

Sandmel, S. "Philo: the Man, His Writings, His Significance." *ANRW* II no. 21.1. Edited by W. Haase. Berlin: Walter de Gruyter, 1984.

Schaefer, P. *Judeophobia: Attitudes Toward the Jews in the Ancient World*. Harvard, MA: Harvard University Press, 2009.

Schenk, K. *Understanding the Book of Hebrews: the Story Behind the Sermon*. Louisville, KY: Westminster John Knox, 2003.

Schmithals W. *Der Romerbrief.* Gutersloh: Gutersloher,1988.

Schreiner T. *Romans*. Grand Rapids, MI: Baker, 1998.

Schurer, E. "The Jewish Philosopher Philo." Pages 3.2:809–889 in *The History of the Jewish People in the Age of Jesus Christ.* Edited by G. Vermes. Edinburgh: T&T Clark, 1973.

Schwartz, D. R. "Philo and Josephus On The Violence in Alexandria in 38 C.E." *Studia Philonica Annual XXIV* (2012): 149–66.

Siegert, F. "Philo and the New Testament." Pages 175–209 in *The Cambridge Companion to Philo* Edited by A. Kamesar. Cambridge, MA: Cambridge University Press, 2009.

Sowers, S. *The Hermeneutics of Philo and Hebrews*. Richmond: John Knox Press, 1965.

Sterling, G. "Ontology versus Eschatology: Tensions between Author and Community in Hebrews." *StPhAnn* 13 (2001): 190–210.

Tate J. "The Beginning of Greek Allegory." *CR* 41 (1927): 214–15.

Tate J. "On the History of Allegorism." *Classical Quarterly* 28 (1934): 105–06.

Tcherikower, A. "Prolegomena." *Corpus Papyrorum Judaicarum.* Cambridge, MA: Harvard Press, 1957.

Thompson, W. "Hebrews 9 and Hellenistic Concepts of Sacrifice." *JBL* 98/4 (1979): 567–78.

Tiemeyer, L. S. *Priestly Rites and Prophetic Rage. Post-exilic Prophetic Critique of the Priesthood.* Forschung zum Alten Testament 2/19. Tübingen: Mohr Siebeck, 2006.

Travis R. *Allegory and the Tragic Chorus.* Rowman & Littlefield, 1999.

von Rad, G. *Wisdom in Israel.* Nashville, TN: Abingdon, 1972.

Walter B. *Greek Religion.* Translated by J. Raffan. Cambridge, MA: Harvard University Press, 1985.

Watts, J. D. W. *Isaiah 1–33*. Waco, TX: Word, 1985.

Weiser, A. *The Psalms*. Philadelphia, PA: Westminster, 1962.

Wenschkewitz, H. *Die Spiritualisierung der Kultusbegriffe,* Leipzig: Pheiffer, 1932.

Williamson, R. *Philo and the Epistle to the Hebrews*. Leiden: Brill, 1970.

Whitman J. *Allegory – The Dynamics of an Ancient and Medieval Technique,* Cambridge: Replica Books, 1987.

Willis J. T. "Ethics in a Cultic Setting," *Essays in Old Testament Ethics.* Edited by J P. Hyatt, J. L. Crenshaw and J. T Willis. New York: Ktav, 1974.

Winston, D. *Philo of Alexandria: the Contemplative Life, Giants and Selections*. Mahwah, NJ: Paulist Press, 1981.

Westermann, K. *Isaiah 40–66*. Philadelphia: Westminster, 1969.

Wolff, H. J. "Plurality of Laws in Ptolemaic Egypt." *Revue internationale des droits de l'Antiquite.* 3rd ser. no. 7 (1960): 20–57.

Wolff, H. W. *Anthropology of the Old Testament.* London: SCM Press, 1974.

Young F. "The Idea of Sacrifice in Neoplatonic and Patristic Texts." *Studia Patristica* XI (1972): 278–281.

Young F. "Temple Cult and Law in Early Christianity." *NTS* 19 (1973): 325–28.

THE USE OF THE PHRASE "YOU ARE MY SON." A SEMIOTIC APPROACH TO THE PROFILE OF THE SON IN HEBREWS 1:5a

CALIN IOAN TALOS[*]

Emanuel University of Oradea

ABSTRACT: In this article, I would like to grasp the way in which the author of the Hebrews quotes and uses in 1:5 the simple sentence "you are my Son" from Psalm 2. In order to understand both the reason behind the quotation and its use, I will use the method of interpretation belonging to "integrative semiotics."[1] This hermeneutic approach engages three fundamental characteristics of the sign: *referentiality* (any sign refers to its object); *addressivity* (any sign can have the function to address);[2] and *integritivity* (the reader overwhelmed perichoretically by the narration of the text becomes himself a sign of himself). I notice the following things: 1. The author of Hebrews adopts Psalm 2 on the basis of an approach of interpretation where knowing the Psalter text is supplemented by a Christ-centred interpretation, thus having a hermeneutic which pivots around the text *plus* interpretation; 2. Jesus is superior to angels under the ontological aspect, and must be respected accordingly; 3. The author of Hebrews pretends connecting the reading of Jesus's message with the believer's life. Under these last aspects the present paper has certain pastoral propensities.

KEY WORDS: rhetoric, revelational, Son, perchoretic.

Introduction

This approach resides in an integrative hermeneutic semiotic exercise characterized by three basic methodological stages: the quantitative stage of the text, its addressive reception, and integrative appropriation.[3] The semiotic approach of the text in 1:5 makes the act of comprehending the text not merely a literary exercise, but more of a spiritual experience. Through this experience the reader moves on from the stage of "reader" to the one of "respondent." According to the latter, the reader becomes partner in a divine-human dialogue and the text a voice of the transcendental being. Given the fact that the literary is bounded by the spiritual, and the reader becomes a "respondent," makes "integrative semiotics" a suitable hermeneutic approach (as I introduced in my PhD thesis). It can be an interpretive means which facilitates the understanding of a sacred text, but also self-reflection and prayer, thus betraying the fact that this meaning has pastoral aspirations.

The hermeneutic exercise is based on the epistemological substrata of the triadic semiotic initially elaborated by C. S. Peirce.[4] The sign, under the phenomenological aspect, has three modes of being. On the one hand, the sign points out towards its object, for example the word "God," on the other hand, it is a sign in itself, like any word in any text. Also, the sign is a mental effect, a thought, produced either by a previous thought, or by a precedent sign. What is very important to note here is that

---

[*] CALIN-IOAN TALOS PhD King's College London, UK, PhD Babes-Bolyai University, Cluj-Napoca, Romania, BA University of Bucharest, Romania. Dr Talos currently lectures in the field of Apologetics and Philosophy in Emanuel University of Oradea.

[1] This term stands for a semiotics following the junction between semiotics and Oliver Davies' cosmological approach; "integrative semiotics" was thus defined in Calin-Ioan Talos's PhD thesis, "A Semiotic Approach to the Epistle of James: A General Interpretation in Light of its 'Synergic Pairs'" (PhD diss., King's College London, 2015).

[2] These two aspects of the sign have been highlighted by Oliver Davies in Oliver Davies, *The Creativity of God, World, Eucharist, Reason* (Cambridge, UK: Cambridge University Press, 2004), 137–138.

[3] These hermeneutical steps have been amply developed in Calin-Ioan Talos, "A Semiotic Approach to the Epistle of James," 164–199.

[4] In this article I will abbreviate C. S. Peirce's writings "Collected Paper of Charles Sanders Peirce," as follows: CP - The Collected Papers of Charles Sanders Peirce, Electronic edition, 1 June 1994, reproducing vols. I-VI, ed. Charles Hartshorne and Paul Weiss (Cambridge, MA: Harvard University Press, 1931–1935), vols. VII-VIII, ed. Arthur W. Burks (same publisher, 1958).

in our mind, signs are always in a relationship of association with each other, and this association or continuity is determined by the similarity between ideas.

Concretely, the quantitative stage of the hermeneutic exercise regards the text under its quantitative or formal aspect, namely, the exegete is interested in reducing the degree of vagueness of the text by observing the connection between ideas, what is in the text, the proportion of words, their syntax and logic. Under the quantitative aspect, at the beginning of probing the text, this is vague, encompassing an unlimited number of unknown and unclear issues. Once the exegetic research is carried out, the text will be released from a series of these unknown things, without having the unreal pretence of clarifying the text completely, the exegete being satisfied only with reducing its degree of vagueness. The manner of reducing the degree of vagueness consists in adopting the best explanation and its logic sounds like this: "The surprising fact, C, is observed; But if A were true, C would be a matter of course, hence, there is reason to suspect that A is true."[5]

The addressive stage is the one where the text is approached not only under its referential aspect—through which we see the text as making us think of the Son who receives as legacy a name which is more wonderful than the angels—but also under the addressive aspect, namely in the light of the ability to address. This competence of the sign is initially noticed by Mikhail Bakhtin and taken over by Oliver Davies in two of his works[6] through which he outlined transformation theology.[7] The text is therefore regarded under the narrative aspect of the transformation theology, according to which the uplifted Christ is at the core of every mundane event, the exegetic one included, intermediating its transformative evolution from the very inside of the event in which he is. In this case, the text is God's voice-bearer to the reader, and the reader is absorbed perichoretically by the text and it becomes its own object of reflection.

The integrative stage is the one where the text of Hebrews is received by means of the integrative nature of the biblical text. Integritivity is a third competence or mode of being of the text-sign. Beside the referential one, that of pointing out to something, and the addressive one, to be God's voice-bearer, the text as any sign is the constitutive element of a series of signs, series characterized by a certain succession which own meaning. The reader is encompassed perichoretically by the narration of the text ennobled addressively. Under this aspect the reader analyses himself. Thus the reader becomes a sign for himself. Given that any sign has a successive character (he comes after a sign and is followed by another one), the man as a sign is successive (has a transitory character), therefore the reader, captivated by the narration with addressive value, will see himself, and aware of his following important stage in life, will seek to find out with what exactly the reading of the text helps him to reach the anticipated destination under the expected conditions. Otherwise said, the text is read thinking of the next station of the reader. The reader to whom we refer is the reader in general, the reader is determined by finalities common to the entire humankind, not only by particular finalities, finalities of a certain individual (this last perspective being tributary rather to existentialism). Therefore, under the integrative aspect (which means that I integrate myself as a reader in the narration of the text), I ask myself the following question: with what does the text help me to prepare for the next stage I will reach in life? Of course this question I pose taking into account, in a probabilistic or revelational manner, what I anticipate, as reader, that I am going to encounter as a man. Putting the problem of grasping the text as such, this sends me automatically to a prophetic or anticipative hermeneutic. I read the text not only thinking about the past that it evokes for the reader, or about the present where the reader lives, but also the anticipated future, towards which the reader directs inevitably and consciously.

---

[5] CP 5.189.

[6] Oliver Davies, "The Sign Redeemed: A Study in Christian Fundamental Semiotics," Modern Theology 19:2 April (2003), 227–228; Oliver Davies, *The Creativity of God, World, Eucharist, Reason* (Cambridge, UK: Cambridge University Press, 2004), 137–138.

[7] Oliver Davies, Paul D. Janz, Clemens Sedmak, *Transformation Theology, Church in the World* (London; New York: T&T Clark, 2007); Oliver Davies, *Theology of Transformation, Faith, Freedom & the Christian Act* (Oxford: Oxford University Press, 2013).

Given the fact that the reader, characterized himself ontologically by a series of events holding meaning, intersects perichoretically with the text, the former will try to grasp the meaning of the text, God's voice-bearer, for his ontological finality. The reader will interrogate the text regarding its usefulness for himself as a being characterized by successions and directions. What is the role of the text for himself taking into account the fact that his imminent finality is God? What is the direction of myself now that I have come across Hebrews? The purpose of the book, once established, is God's purpose for the self as a community being. Integrative semiotics allows me to make certain predictions based on probability regarding what I will become as soon as I adopt the message of the text by faith.[8]

The Rhetoric of the First Chapter in the Epistle to the Hebrews

Under the quantitative aspect, the text of the first chapter of Hebrews reveals God as speaking to the Jews "through the Son" (ἐν Υἱῷ).[9] God's announcement through the Son is all the more important as he is completely superior over them, even though the angels' announcement is "proved to be reliable, and every transgression or disobedience received a just retribution."[10] Therefore, the author asks rhetorically: "how shall we escape if we neglect such a great salvation?"[11]

In order to show the superiority of the Son over angels and implicitly the prevalence of his announcement above theirs, the author of Hebrews elaborates a whole rhetoric of arguments in favour of the Son's supremacy over the angelic world. This rhetoric makes reference to six psalms: Psalm 2, 45, 97, 102, 104 and 110. In the table below, I will show the themes brought up by the author of the epistle as they are disclosed by his proceeding to reveal the supremacy of the Son, and at the same time I will indicate the quotation in the Psalms reproduced by the author (also the text in Greek) and the text in Psalms to which the author refers.

We have to mention that the observation of these quotations under the syntactic aspect is intermediated by the terms whose root is either λέγω or ἐρεῶ, namely: "did he say" (εἶπέν) in 1:5, "He says" (λέγει) in 1:6, "He says" (λέγει) in 1:7, the short sentence "but unto the Son" (πρὸς δὲ τὸν υἱόν) in 1:8 and "did he say" (εἴρηκέν) in 1:13.

The theme	The quotation in Hebrews	The similar text in the Old Testament
The name of the Son	1:5; "You are my Son, today I have begotten you." (υἱός μου εἶ σύ).	Ps 2:7; "You are my Son; today I have begotten you."
	1:5; "I will be to him a father, and he shall be to me a son."	2 Sam 7:14; "I will be to him a father, and he shall be to me a son."

---

[8] These hermeneutic aspects have been widely discussed in Calin-Ioan Talos, "A Semiotic Approach to the Epistle of James," 164–199.

[9] In this article quotations of the Greek New Testament are taken from Nestle-Aland, Novum Testamentum Graece, 28th Rev ed. Edited by Barbara and Kurt Aland, Johannes Karavidopoulos, Carlo M. Martini, and Bruce M. Metzger in cooperation with the Institute for the New Testament Textual Research (Stuttgart: Deutsche Bibelgesellschaft, 2012).

[10] ESV 2:2 (notes: all the quotations in the Bible belong to the English Standard Version translation and the ESV abbreviations refer to ESV – Crossway, The Holy Bible: English Standard Version, Containing the Old and New Testaments (Wheaton, IL: Crossway, 2001).

[11] ESC 2:3.

(ἐγὼ σήμερον γεγέννηκά σε).

The relationship of reverence between angels and the Son	1:6; "Let all God's angels worship him." (καὶ προσκυνησάτωσαν αὐτῷ πάντες ἄγγελοι θεοῦ).	Ps 97:7; "worship him, all you gods!" Deut 32:43; "bow down to him . . . ."
The comparison between the king status of the Son and that of a created servant of angels	1:7; "He makes his angels winds, and his ministers a flame of fire." (ὁ ποιῶν τοὺς ἀγγέλους αὐτοῦ πνεύματα καὶ τοὺς λειτουργοὺς αὐτοῦ πυρὸς φλόγα)	Ps 104:4; "he makes his messengers winds, his ministers a flaming fire."
	1:8 ... "Your throne, O God, is forever and ever, the sceptre of uprightness is the sceptre of your kingdom;" (τὸν Υἱόν Ὁ θρόνος σου ὁ Θεὸς εἰς τὸν αἰῶνα τοῦ αἰῶνος, καὶ ἡ ῥάβδος τῆς εὐθύτητος ῥάβδος τῆς βασιλείας αὐτοῦ.)	
		Ps 45:6 ... "Your throne, O God, is forever and ever. The sceptre of your kingdom is a sceptre of uprightness;"
The comparison between the eternal spirit of the existence of the Son and the entropic life of his creation	1:10; "You, Lord, laid the foundation of the earth in the beginning, and the heavens are the work of your hands;" (σὺ κατ' ἀρχάς, κύριε, τὴν γῆν ἐθεμελίωσας - καὶ ἔργα τῶν χειρῶν σού εἰσιν οἱ οὐρανοί).	Ps 102:25; "Of old you laid the foundation of the earth, and the heavens are the work of your hands."
	1:11; they will all wear out like a garment," (καὶ πάντες ὡς ἱμάτιον παλαιωθήσονται).	
		Ps 102:26; "they will all wear out like a garment."
The Son, at the right hand of God	1:13; "Sit at my right hand until I make your enemies a footstool for your feet" (κάθου ἐκ δεξιῶν μου, ἕως ἂν θῶ τοὺς ἐχθρούς σου ὑποπόδιον τῶν ποδῶν σου;)	Ps 110:1; "Sit at my right hand, until I make your enemies your footstool."

The epistle compares the Son to the the angels using parallel references from the Psalms. This parallelism is highlighted by the interrogative particle "Τίνι" in 1:5 and 1:13, and the weak addressative particle "δὲ" in 1:8, 11 and 12. First of all, the Son has a more excellent name (διαφορώτερον) than that of angels (1:5). In the second place, there is displayed the relation of reverence of the angels toward the son (1:6): "when he brings the firstborn into the world, he says, 'Let all God's angels worship him.'" Thirdly, one can notice the king status of the Son; the addressative particle "δὲ" invites the reader to compare the angels created and intended to serve with the "Son" who sits on the throne (1:7–9) and who has the authority to lead and judge the world: "He makes his angels winds.... But of the Son he says, 'Your throne, O God, is forever and ever.'" Fourthly, the epistle shows us that "the Lord" is the creator of the earth and heavens and, compared to the transient nature of these created things, the Lord lives forever (1:10–12): "they will perish, but you remain." Fifthly, unlike angels, the Son sits at the right hand of God (1:13), the position that confers uniqueness and supremacy to the Son: "'Sit at my right hand until I make your enemies a footstool for your feet?'"

According to the parallelism between the Son and angels, we can clearly see that the Son is superior to the latter both under the ontological aspect (1:5) and under that of authority and competency (1:6, 8, 9, 10, 11, 13).

Coming back to the initial moment of the section regarding the rhetoric of the first chapter, we can see (according to the hypothetical logic "[t]he surprising fact, C, is observed; But if A were true, C would be a matter of course, hence, there is reason to suspect that A is true.") that the *surprising fact* of the argumentation articulated in an ample manner can be explained by the fact that the author wants to draw the reader's attention in 2:3–4, that the announcing of the Son is not neglected or disregarded. That is to say, since the word of the angels, who, as we have seen, are neither equal nor superior to the Son, on the contrary, "was binding," all the more the announcing (λαλεῖσθαι) of such a great salvation (τηλικαύτης ... σωτηρίας) made by the Son, cannot be neglected at all (ἀμελήσαντες) as it carries serious and inescapable consequences (πῶς ἡμεῖς ἐκφευξόμεθα).[12] And all the more that this salvation announced by the Son, denominated in 2:3 as the "Lord" (2:3), was confirmed by those who heard him speak, and this confirmation (ἐβεβαιώθη) was backed up by God through signs (σημείοις), wonders (τέρασιν), miraculous powers (δυνάμεσιν) and the Holy Spirit (πνεύματος ἁγίου).

Therefore, the announcement made by the "Son" cannot be overlooked at all, since the "Son" is not equal to angels but he is superior to them (τοσούτῳ κρείττων γενόμενος τῶν ἀγγέλων). Another reason why the Son cannot be placed in the class of angels is underlined in 1:3; he is the reflection and imprinting of "his being" (ὑποστάσεως αὐτοῦ), who holds all things by the word of his power (τῷ ῥήματι τῆς δυνάμεως), who performed the cleansing of the sins and who sat at the right of the Highness, whereas, verse 14 is worlds apart and shows that angels are only serving spirits (λειτουργικὰ πνεύματα) intended for a ministry with a soteriological function oriented toward people's eternal benefit.

The Role of Psalm Two in the Rhetoric of the First Chapter of the Epistle

In the attempt to show the supremacy of the Son over angels and, finally, the exceptional value of his announcement, the author strings (like some pearls on a thread of silk) a series of six psalmic references which draw, each one in its own way, five features of the Son which have no equivalent in the angels' world. The first one refers to the filial relationship of the Son with God the Father, and thus to his being (1:5). The second one concerns the degree of his stature (1:6). The third one underscores the sovereignty of the Son (1:7–9). The fourth one underlines his creative competence (1:10), the Son's immutability and eternity. The fifth one evokes his authority (1:13).

---

[12] The Greek terms belong to the text in Hebrews 2:3.

Although both the first and the fourth characteristics make reference to the ontology of the Son, the first actually states the relationship between the Son and God the Father; a relationship that defines the nature of his being. *The surprising fact* that the author begins with his apology for the supremacy of the Son is that he is thus called not necessarily by people but by God Himself, making appeal to Psalm 2. This is otherwise implied by the argument which begins at verse 4 and flows through verses 5–13 by means of the conjunction "γὰρ." Thus, the "Son" (1:2) is superior to angels because God himself acknowledges his divine filiation. He is greater than angels because he has a different nature than theirs. The divine filiation of the "Son," namely his ontology, is the first step, maybe the most convincing one, from the series of proofs laid at the reader's disposal by the author. It is true that, as P. E. Hughes underscores, quoting an impressive number of psalms is a guarantee that "the recipients of the letter acknowledged the authority of the Old Testament and were open to persuasion from its pages."[13] But is their quoting justified?

Understanding Psalm 2

In this section, I would like to point out the dissimilitude between the profile of the "Son" in the first verses of chapter 1 and the profile of the "Son" reflected by Psalm 2. Even so, it is quite obvious that the author of the epistle relates both profiles without feeling uneasy at all. This evident identification betrays, however, the vague character of the text in Hebrews or, more precisely, of the reason why the author considers himself justified to make the association of these profiles. How can the author associate, by quoting, two profiles which do not match wholly? The reader remarks easily that these profiles purely and simply do not match. Apparently, it would be simpler and easier to say that the "Son" in Hebrews is a completely different person from the "Son" in Psalm 2. Nonetheless, what exactly justifies the author of Hebrews to identify the "Son" in the first verses with the "Son" in Psalm 2? If we can answer this specific question, it will be easier for us to form an image about the reason behind the association of other texts in Psalms with the "Son" in the book of Hebrews. As I am going to show, we will be able to diminish the *degree of vagueness* of this issue by turning to the second fundamental consideration of the *integrative semiotics*, namely, the continuity through similarity between ideas and the effective applicability of the formal logic. Appealing to the link through similarity of ideas, we will observe that there is another phrase identical with the one in Hebrews 1:5, which, analyzed in the context, will bring additional data to the equation of understanding the text in 1:5 and the associated profiles. Also, under the aspect of formal logic, if A includes B, and B includes C, then A includes C, we will notice the fact that the author is truly justified to associate his profile of the "Son" with that in Psalm 2. This will not only further diminish the degree of vagueness of the text, but also disclose the author's hermeneutic outlook, according to which his understanding of the "Son" in Psalm 2 is based on the sum of two essential things: text *plus* interpretation. More clearly, we will see that all the endeavour to understand the "Son" in Psalm 2 focuses on the psalmic text *plus* the Christocentric narration. Interestingly, this hermeneutic habit of analyzing the texts in the Old Testament through the lens of the faith that Jesus Christ is typical especially of Paul from Tarsus. Hence, either the author of Hebrews was deeply influenced by the Christocentric hermeneutic, perhaps Paul's own, or Paul himself is the author of this epistle; although answering this question is not the aim of this paper.

The Metaphysic Profile (Spiritualist-Priestly) of the Son in Hebrews 1:1–4

The author of the epistle sketches the profile of the "Son" in Hebrews in the following way: a) He is the final instrument through whom God has spoken (1:2a); b) He has been appointed heir of all things (1:2b); c) God made all things through him (1:2c); d) He is the radiance of God's glory (1:3a); e) the exact representation of God's being (1:3b); f) sustains all things by his powerful word (1:3c); g) He had provided purification for sins (1:3d); h) sat down at the right hand of the Majesty in heaven (1:3e); and i) inherited a name much superior to the angels" (1:4). Therefore, the Son is in relationship with God through filiation, in relationship with the universe through creation and in rela-

---

[13] Philip Edgecumbe Hughes, *A Commentary on the Epistle to the Hebrews* (Grand Rapids, MI: Eerdmans, 1977), 53.

tionship with man through atonement. The filiation, creation and atonement are three aspects of this profile which give the Son a rather metaphysical aura.

The Son's Historical (Historical-Eschatological) Profile in Psalm 2

Psalm 2 is a narrative song. Its message pinpoints the forming of an international coalition made out of "nations," "peoples," "kings," and "rulers," who organize somewhere on the earth their hostilities against the Lord and his Anointed (Messiah), initially in a closed, secret circle. From the heaven though, the Lord laughs (for the Lord this closed-door meeting is not an unknown thing), holds them in derision, and decides to speak to them and terrify them: "I have set my King on Zion, my holy hill." This statement has its own degree of vagueness. We hardly take into account the name Zion, and admit the relation of similarity between the latter and the Zion in 2 Sam 5:7, where David takes hold of Zion fortress. We accept the idea that David, the conqueror, is the same David as the one in 2 Sam 7:16, the beneficiary of God's promise, to whom God promises an eternal kingdom built up for good. So we realize that the sentence "I have set my King on Zion" can refer to king David and his kingdom which, during the time will become unbeatable, thus making this statement be truly challenging and even terrifying for the emperors of the hostile coalition. The second part of the narration depicts the episode where the Anointed One sends forward a divine message meant to be fully revealed, having a universal importance. The Anointed One claims that the Lord called him Son (2:7), he offered him the possibility to ask him the nations and the earth as inheritance (2:8), and he promises him absolute victory over them (2:9). In fact, these are the three features of the Anointed One from Psalm 2: a) he is called Son at a certain time; b) he is going to become heir; and c) he is going to win the victory over his enemies. The fact that God's Anointed One represents the object of some hostilities coordinated by a union of kings proves the historical character of the Anointed One's profile. And the fact that the Anointed One is going to receive the legacy and win victory over the kings in the world denotes the eschatological nature of this profile.

Similitudes and Dissimilarities

There are two elements of *similarity* which could constitute a bridge between Hebrews 1:2 and Psalm 2. The first one is given by the idea of inheritance that we have in 1:2 "heir of all things" (κληρονόμον) and we find in 2:8 "I will make the nations your heritage." The second element of *similarity* is the idea that the Son is the verbal vehicle of God's words. In Hebrews 1:2, God is speaking to us through the Son, whereas in Psalm 2:7–9 the Son, namely the Anointed One, Messiah (מָשִׁיחַ Psalm 2:2), is speaking to us on behalf of God.

Beside these elements of similarity, there are some of definite dissimilarity. There exist nine features of the Son in Hebrews whereas only three in Psalms. Of the nine features in the Son's profile in Hebrews, four cannot be explicitly found in Psalms. These are: 1. The Son as a means of the creation of ages; 2. The Son as a radiance of God; 3. The Son as an exact representation of God's being; and 4. The Son as a divine motive for cleansing sins. We may say that the other characteristics from Hebrews can be found only implicitly or partly in the text of the song in Psalm 2, namely, that of heir, and of sitting at the right hand of God, presupposing, not without the risk to force the text that this involves the status of complete winner. However, the Son's historical-eschatological profile in the Psalm is marked by the historical and punitive coordinates, where the Son's heritage concerns only the governing actors, peoples and earth and the kings' hostile assault is welcome by the Son's repressive and punitive force. Essentially, the Son's profile in Hebrews is surrounded by a priestly and atoning aura whereas the Son's profile in Psalms has a royal and punitive character.

How can, therefore, the Son's spiritualist and metaphysical image from Hebrews, outlined in 1:2–4, be endorsed by the historical and eschatological one in Psalms, quoted in Hebrews 1:5, since there are more elements of dissimilitude than similarity? The difference between the two profiles is like the difference between atonement and punishment. Susan Gillingham notices as well that "[j]ust as it might seem unusual to use Ps 2:7 to demonstrate the resurrection of Jesus, its use in illustrating Jesus's high priesthood might seem somewhat inappropriate."[14]

Given the fact that the author of the epistle does not seem to be uneasy at all by the few resemblances or by the more dissimilitude between profiles, can mean that he would see these profiles as being in a relation of complementarity one toward the other rather than opposition, and the reason why the author claims on psalmic basis the Son's supremacy over angels does not seem to be centred around a purely textual basis but around a viewpoint of interpreting the psalmic text which may make the two profiles match each other like two puzzle pieces. Consequently, the *surprising fact* that the author of the epistle makes reference to the Son's historical-eschatological image in Psalm 2, when he talks about the supremacy of the Son in metaphysical terms, could be explained through the fact that the "Son" in Psalm 2 means something more than what it comes out of the strict analysis of the song. Now, if this trans-analytical or interpretive understanding of Psalm 2 were true, then its quoting would really be a matter of course. But what does this understanding consist in? In the next section I will show that the author of the book of Hebrews refers to the Son's historical-eschatological profile in Psalm 2 since he resorts to a Christocentric hermeneutic of the Psalm.

The Interpretation of Psalm 2 in Light of the Epistle to the Hebrews

In this section I will demonstrate that the author of the book to the Hebrews is justified to found the "Son's" metaphysical profile on the historical-eschatological one since, following the logic of inclusion (if A includes B, and B includes C, then A includes C), the author considers that the "Son" in Psalm 2 is Messiah/Christ, Messiah/Christ is Jesus, and Jesus combines successfully both the metaphysical and atoning profile and the historical eschatological one. So, the "Son" in Psalm 2 is Jesus who has both the prerogatives highlighted by the metaphysical profile of Hebrews 1:2–4 and the historical-eschatological ones featured by Psalm 2.

In order to clarify the meaning of the quotation in Psalms "You are my Son," it is important to see if the epistle contains new approaches of this quotation and by means of the quantitative approach to follow other connections in accord with the basic semiotic principle of continuity through similarity.

It is outstanding the fact that the *same* quotation "You are my Son, today I have begotten you" can be found *identically* and in chapter 5:5b in the same epistle. This sentence is employed with the purpose to show that the transmitter of these words, God respectively, gives glory to their direct receiver, namely to the Son. Only that, in this verse it is not the "Son" but "Christ" (ὁ Χριστὸς), subject in the nominative, singular, who is the only Christ, is the receiver or beneficiary of the glory offered by God. Subsequently, the author of the epistle identifies here the Son from Psalm 2 with Christ. This term is *identical* idiomatically with מָשִׁיחַ in Psalm 2:2. Christ is also the favourite subject of Hebrews. The Son is, therefore, the Christ. The *same* term Χριστὸς is also used by the author in other twelve places in the epistle (3:6, 3:14, 5:5, 6:1, 9:11, 9:14, 9:24, 9:28, 10:10, 11:26, 13:8 and 13:21). In 3:6 the author highlights the identification of Christ with the Son by making great play with the faithfulness of the "Anointed One" as Son (Χριστὸς δὲ ὡς υἱὸς).

But who is Christ or Messiah as person in the epistle? The answer to this question reduces considerably the degree of vagueness of the motivation made by the author of the epistle for associating the Son in Psalm 2 with the Son in Hebrews 1:2–4. Christ is identified by Hebrews as Jesus. The name of Jesus is attached to "Christ" so that the name and appellative "Christ" form together a single name. Jesus Christ is presented three times as such in Hebrews: Jesus Christ sacrificed his body once forever (διὰ τῆς προσφορᾶς τοῦ σώματος Ἰησοῦ Χριστοῦ ἐφάπαξ) in Hebrews 10:10, also, we are told in Hebrews in 13:8, that Jesus Christ is the same yesterday, today and forever, (Ἰησοῦς Χριστὸς ἐχθὲς καὶ σήμερον ὁ αὐτὸς καὶ εἰς τοὺς αἰῶνας.), and, in Hebrews 13:21, God works in the believers

---

[14] Susan Gillingham, *A Journey of Two Psalms, The Reception of Psalm 1 & 2 in Jewish & Christian Tradition* (Oxford: Oxford University Press, 2013), 40.

through Jesus Christ (διὰ Ἰησοῦ Χριστοῦ). Consequently, Christ in Psalm 2, is Jesus, to whom the author of Hebrews confers this title deliberately and exclusively.

In the same order of ideas, the author of the epistle profiles Jesus both as a transcendental-metaphysical being that performs a priestly and atoning function and as a being with prerogatives of supreme authority who must be honoured and obeyed (10:29–31). Jesus's metaphysical and transcendental profile is reflected by verses such as: 2:9, Jesus tasted death for all (ὑπὲρ παντὸς γεύσηται θανάτου); 3:1, 4:14, 6:20 and 7:21, Jesus is the High Priest (ἀρχιερέα); 10:10, Jesus is the sacrifice brought once for all (τῆς προσφορᾶς), 10:19, Jesus as the facilitator for people to be able to reach the Most Holy Place; 12:2, Jesus suffered the cross (ὑπέμεινεν σταυρὸν); Jesus as intercessor (μεσίτῃ Ἰησοῦ). Also, the profile of Jesus's supreme authority, which coincides with that of the "Son's" authority in Psalm 2, is evoked by several verses. In Hebrews 10:26–31 it is displayed the fact that the one who tramples the Son of God, Jesus respectively, will be punished by God: "a fury of fire that will consume the adversaries . . . It is a fearful thing to fall into the hands of the living God." (10:27, 31). Son's revenge, element that does not result from the introductory verses of the epistle, 1:2–4, can be accounted for also by the fact that he "is seated at the right hand of the throne of God" (ἐν δεξιᾷ τε τοῦ θρόνου τοῦ θεοῦ κεκάθικεν), as it comes out of 12:2c. We have to mention here that unlike Psalm 2 where the "Son" gains his authority and supremacy, ("You shall break them with a rod of iron and dash them in pieces like a potter's vessel." Ps 2:9), in Hebrews, the "Son," Jesus respectively, receives authority and supremacy over his enemies. We have to notice here that even if there is a *similitude* between texts, the Psalmic and the one in Hebrews, by the fact that it is shown in both that opponents are punished, nevertheless there is a difference between these as well. Namely, the "Son" in Psalms punishes his enemies himself, in accord with God's will, whereas the "Son" in Hebrews, Jesus, is rather the witness of them being punished by God, but a punishment which is performed because of Jesus.[15] Anyway, in both profiles, psalmic and epistolary, we can find the punishment of the Son's enemies.

Now, if Jesus is the bearer of both profiles, the metaphysical-transcendental and the historical-eschatological, it means that we can rightly affirm that the "Son" in Psalms is the Jesus of the New Testament, who atones for everybody's sins and who represents the reason for the judgment of the disobedient people. If we admit this series of ideas, namely that the "Son" in Psalms is in fact Jesus from the New Testament whose complex profile entails metaphysical-transcendental and historical-eschatological elements, then the quoting of Psalm 2 is justified, being a *matter of course.*

The Features of Interpretation of Psalm 2 Rendered by the Author of the Book of Hebrews

F. F. Bruce is right when he says "[t]he general New Testament use of the Old Testament is a highly important and interesting study, but the use of the Old Testament in Hebrews, while it has its place within that more general study, exhibits a number of features of its own."[16] In this brief section I will enumerate several aspects of interpretation that the book of Hebrews carries out on the text in Psalm 2, in the context of the rhetoric from the first chapter of the epistle.

First of all, the author of Hebrews appears to justify the quotation from a psalmic text related to the Son, God's Anointed One, authorized to rule and punish nations, according to a hermeneutic which does not limit itself strictly to the analysis of the text in Psalms but appeals as well to an interpretive perspective that comes from somewhere outside the text. We have therefore the text from the Old Testament scriptures, *plus* the author's Christocentric interpretation.

Secondly, another aspect that has to be taken into account is that, by extension, all the Psalms cited in the first chapter seem to be approached from the perspective of the same hermeneutic - text *plus* Christocentric interpretation.

---

[15] Heb 10:30–31
[16] F. F. Bruce, *The Epistle to the Hebrews*, Rev. ed. (Grand Rapids: Eerdmans, 1990), 52–53.

Subsequently, the entire rhetoric related to the supremacy of the Son over angels, announced in 1:4 and argued in 1:4–14, is not based exclusively on the quotations from Psalms although, apparently, the rhetoric in the first chapter seems to be established chiefly on the six psalms, but on its own outlook on Messiah or Christ. We have therefore a rhetoric based on the given text and on one's own perspective. Looking at this hermeneutic from a methodological perspective, we could notice as well that there is a *similarity* between the knowing of the text—the biblical text in general—by the text *plus* the interpretation reflected by the rhetoric of chapter 1 in Hebrews and the knowing of the text in the spirit of the orthodox Judaism where we also find text plus traditional interpretation (although the nature of Jewish traditional interpretation is different from the Christian traditional one).

Thus, the rhetoric of the supremacy of Jesus over the angelic world from chapter 1 in Hebrews provides an interpretive paradigm which can be applied to all messianic psalms in the Old Testament. The fact that the hermeneutic of the author of the epistle is passable especially to messianic psalms explains the richness of quotations inserted in the "fabric" of the entire epistle. Subsequently, an approach of the Psalms quoted in the epistle should not exclude the hermeneutical perspective of the author denoted by the manner in which Psalm 2 is quoted.

Semiotic Conclusions on Hebrews 1:5

The text, as sign, has, fundamentally, the function to refer to something especially, in our case to Jesus's supremacy over angels and implicitly to the urgent importance of complying with the news of salvation made by Jesus, with all that it comprises. At the same time, the text, as a sign also, has the function to address as well. Therefore, on the one hand we have the referential function of Heb 1:5 and of the whole rhetoric encompassed by chapter 1 and 2, and on the other hand we have the addressive function of the text.

The addressivity of the text supplements its indexical capacity "to show towards something," with its addressive capacity, to communicate something to the reader on behalf of somebody becoming an effective voice. If the function of the former aspect of the text, the referential one, is that of making the reader become a visitor of the narrative world of the text, the function of the latter aspect, the addressive one, makes out of the reader a respondent of addressing or a dialogue partner.

We also have to show that, under the addressive and then integrative aspect, the hermeneutic proceeding of diminishing the degree of vagueness of the text does not stop but, on the contrary, continues. The addressive character of the text makes the emphases, interrogations and imperatives of the text be brought to light and noticed as such.

What involves such a perspective is the "transformational" New Testament theological narration,[17] of the ascended Christ who fills all things (Eph 4:8–10), who works concretely even after ascension in the very spatiotemporal sphere of the history of mankind (Acts 16:14) and does this thing on the basis of his prophecies, namely that he will be with his disciples until the end of time (Matt 28:20).

Hebrews shows that Jesus holds all things together (φέρων τε τὰ πάντα)[18] by the word of his power (τῷ ῥήματι τῆς δυνάμεως).[19] Now, since the intersection, at all at random, between the message of the epistle and the reader's availability to know it is one of the things that Christ holds "by the word of his power," means that the epistle itself has an addressive role. Jesus communicates something to the reader through the message of this epistle. He becomes the utterer, the epistle becomes the formal means of his communication and the reader is the receiver of this message and the partner of a dialogue which sprouts in the soil of this literary experience.

---

[17] This theological outlook is outlined by Oliver Davies, Paul D. Janz, and Clemens Sedmak, *Transformation Theology, Church in the World* (London; New York: T&T Clark, 2007).

[18] Heb 1:3.

[19] Heb 1:3.

Analysing the text in 1:5, under the addressive aspect, we observe that we, the immediate receivers of the text, are the recipients of a rhetoric interrogation. As Paul Ellingworth notices, "[f]or to which of the angels did God ever say ...?" As "The rhetorical question "To what angel did God ever say...?" is equivalent to an emphatic negative (Beekman and Callow, 229–248)."[20] Well, following the author's rhetoric, we will realize that, in fact, God did not say to anyone these words, but to Jesus. Since God addresses by the sacred text at the very moment of its reading, under the semiotic aspect, the reader fixes his attention upon the reference of this interrogation (the referential aspect) and, according to the context, will admit that only Jesus is the addressee of these words, which will lead to acknowledging the superiority of his status over that of angels." Now, if, Jesus is completely superior to angels, then the responsibility of the recipients towards his soteriological ministry emphasized by his message is incommensurable and the consequences of the disobedience to Jesus's message are extremely serious: "how shall we escape if we neglect such a great salvation?" Therefore, questions such as "Are angels equal to Jesus?" and "How are we going to escape if we do not obey Jesus and receive his announcement?" reverberates in the reader's mind all the more that the semiotics of reading (the addressive aspect) foreshadows the reader in the direct "respondent" of the divine address and the text is transformed in God's voice now and here.

As Jesus is "the Son of God" who announced to us "such a great salvation," Jesus must be honoured accordingly and a good proof in order to do this lies in relating without "indifference," an active and passionate relating, to the unequalled priestly and atoning ministry of Jesus Christ. The reader feels compelled, by virtue of the addressivity of the text, to answer God, by self-reflexivity and even prayer, acknowledging Jesus's supremacy and cherishing his salvation. Integrative semiotics, by its spiritual, self-reflexive and dialogic aspirations, matches from the functional viewpoint, the author's expressed desire to remove the Christian Jewish readers from the lethargy of an experienced Christian life. The reader is invited to answer God in the same way as a participant in a conversation is provoked to speak by his interlocutor.

Under the integrative aspect, the reader profiled through addressivity in the "respondent" of a spiritual dialogue and, implicitly, in a self-reflexive subject, confident in the anticipations of the biblical text, cannot overlook the future ineluctable moment of the divine judgment announced by the author in 10:30: "And again, 'The Lord will judge his people.'" Further on, the author's warnings are as serious as they can be: "It is a fearful thing to fall into the hands of the living God." (10:31). The *surprising fact*, that the author's purpose is, as Peter T. O'Brien notices, quoting Guthrie, "to exhort the hearers to endure in their pursuit of the promised reward, in obedience to the word of God" [21] becomes a *matter of course* if we think that God will eventually judge his people.

Therefore, the author's effort to argue in favour of Jesus's superiority and his arduousness to make his recipients obey Jesus, aspects evoked by the rhetoric of the first chapter, can be accounted for by the fact that God's people are going to be judged by God and each one desires to survive it happily.

If we take into consideration the judgment as an anticipated moment with serious consequences then the acknowledging of the Son's superiority and complying with his word are compulsory for sure.

As a consequence of it, the reader will enter the projection of this judgment and will reflect on the necessity of accepting Jesus *as* God's Son and obeying his revealed word. In this respect, the insightful interrogations of the rhetoric of the first chapter and the first part of chapter two have an obvious soteriological value. Therefore, the reader can have it in mind to adopt a reverential behaviour toward Jesus, uniting the acknowledgement of Jesus as the Son of God with the obedience to the word, things that once adopted by the reader will be able to be verified later on in his daily, public or private life. The integration of the "respondent" self in the reading of the text from Heb 1:5 facilitates

---

[20] Paul Ellingworth, *The Epistle to the Hebrews, A Commentary on the Greek Text* (Grand Rapids: Eerdmans; Carlisle: Paternoster, 1993), 110.
[21] Peter T. O'Brien, *The Letter to the Hebrews* (Grand Rapids; Cambridge: Eerdmans, 2010), 36.

the fusion between the act of knowing Jesus and the enthusiasm of obeying him and, at the same time, intermediates the union between the reading of the text and the believer's life or between the literary and the spiritual realm.

Bibliography

Aland, Barbara and Kurt, Johannes Karavidopoulos, Carlo M. Martini, and Bruce M. Metzger, eds. *Greek New Testament are taken from Nestle-Aland, Novum Testamentum Graece.* 28th rev. ed. Stuuttgart: Deutsche Bibelgesellschaft, 2012.

Bruce, F. F. *The Epistle to the Hebrews.* Rev. ed. Grand Rapids: Eerdmans, 1990.

Burks, Arthur W., ed. *The Collected Papers of Charles Sanders Peirce.* Vols. VII–VIII. Cambridge, MA: Harvard University Press, 1958. Electronic edition.

Crossway, *The Holy Bible: English Standard Version, Containing the Old and New Testaments.* Wheaton, IL: Crossway, 2001.

Davies, Oliver. "The Sign Redeemed: A Study in Christian Fundamental Semiotics." Modern Theology 19:2 April (2003): 219–241.

Davies, Oliver. *The Creativity of God, World, Eucharist, Reason.* Cambridge: Cambridge University Press, 2004.

Davies, Oliver, Paul D. Janz and Clemens Sedmak. *Transformation Theology, Church in the World.* London; New York: T&T Clark, 2007.

Davies, Oliver. *Theology of Transformation, Faith, Freedom & the Christian Act.* Oxford: Oxford University Press, 2013.

Ellingworth, Paul. *The Epistle to the Hebrews, A Commentary on the Greek Text.* Grand Rapids: Eerdmans; Carlisle: Paternoster, 1993.

Gillingham, Susan. *A Journey of Two Psalms, The Reception of Psalm 1 & 2 in Jewish & Christian Tradition.* Oxford: Oxford University Press, 2013.

Hartshorne, Charles and Paul Weiss, eds. *The Collected Papers of Charles Sanders Peirce.* Vols. I–VI. Cambridge, MA: Harvard University Press, 1931–1935. Electronic edition.

Hughes, Philip Edgecumbe. *A Commentary on the Epistle to the Hebrews.* Grand Rapids: Eerdmans, 1977.

O'Brien, Peter T. *The Letter to the Hebrews.* Grand Rapids; Cambridge: Eerdmans, 2010.

Talos, Calin-Ioan. "A Semiotic Approach to the Epistle of James: A General Interpretation in Light of its 'Synergic Pairs.'" PhD diss. King's College London, 2015.

WHEN OLD AND NEW COLLIDE: THE PERSPECTIVES OF GEORGE MILLIGAN ON THE RELEVANCE OF THE EPISTLE TO THE HEBREWS

CIPRIAN SIMUȚ [*]

Emanuel University of Oradea

ABSTRACT: Hebrews offers valuable insight into what it means to have faith in Christ, as well as why is he valuable for humanity. There is a constant tendancy in the world to question the divine, and in many cases the questions are legitimate. Some lose faith, some stray from faith, some are simply lost, but to all there is one answer: Christ. Unfortunately, it is not that simple, because such an answer will only open the path for other questions. Hebrews manages to answer in an ordered fashion why faith in Christ is important and how it impacts one's spiritual life. The paper aims at presenting the explanations and arguments of George Milligan with regard to the importance of the epistle for his time, as well as contemporary Christianity. It will also present, as snippets, the thoughts of other scholars, more or less contemporary with Milligan. The purpose of the paper is to show that if the epistle was important for Milligan's time, it is at least just as important today.

KEY WORDS: Christ, atonement, sacrifice, Old Testament.

Introduction

Hebrews presents itself in a multifaceted manner. It is an epistle, but it is also a homily, and some have given it more than one guise. The epistle sets two worlds in contrast: the world of the Old Testament and the world of the New Testament. More precisely, it presents the reasons why faith in Jesus Christ is more important and valuable than stopping at the theological and practical world-view which ends with the last book of the Old Testament. There have been, and still are, a number of Christians and non-Christians who seek to understand how the Old and the New Testaments are related, and how one is continued into the other. Some ask whether the New Testament is the natural continuation and fulfillment of the Old Testament, while others remain anchored only in the New, while renouncing the Old altogether. George Milligan sets up a series of arguments which describe Hebrews in great detail. His research takes the reader on a journey of discovery, where one can and will find a complex, but logical display of arguments and contexts which will enlighten and ease the understanding of a crucial question: why Hebrews was important in Milligan's time, as well as today.

This paper aims at presenting only one chapter of Milligan's book, namely chapter X and present his perspective on why he believed Hebrews is important. The ideas and explanations presented by Milligan are presented together with snippet ideas taken from other scholars and researchers who lived around the time Milligan wrote his arguments. The paper does not intend to give a detailed record of Milligan's work, but will try to present a set of principles that were considered vital by Milligan and which play an important role in understand why the epistle is still valuable for the church today.

A Short History of Theological Importance

At the end of his book on Hebrews, George Milligan reflects on "The Present-Day Significance of the Epistle," which constitutes Chapter X of the book. In order to present what he believes to be valuable for his generation, he divides his argument in several sub-chapters. The first one is about the theological influence that the epistle had on various time periods. He tries valiantly, but realistically,

---

[*] CIPRIAN SIMUȚ, PhD (Babeș-Bolyai University, Cluj), is currently teaching Church History and History of the Baptists in Emanuel University of Oradea.

to present in a nutshell the way the epistle influenced the church throughout the ages. Even if such a task is impossible to accomplish in a few pages, he starts with a conclusion: the epistle had an enduring and multifaceted influence, which carved various doctrines. An interesting perspective from Milligan is that he believes the influence is obvious to all.[1] However, we should be able to doubt such claims, especially if we are to consider the level of Bible knowledge among present-day Christians. The situation could have been different in Milligan's time, though it is also doubtful. Milligan does explain the way the epistle influenced the church and his first example is about the parallel between the sacrificial system of the Old Testament and the redemptive work of Christ. In order to better understand what Christ did, one should address the issues presented in the epistle, and Milligan argues for a better understanding of the sacrificial work of Christ, together with the issues of faith and communion.

Jowett, on the other hand, sees the problem of faith and communion in a different way. He argues that Paul is not the author of Hebrews, so in his two volume work, he constantly presents the writings of Paul and the other gospels, as well as the epistle of Hebrews, which has an unknown author.[2] While Milligan presents a positive perspective on the ideas of the author of Hebrews, Jowett presents the issue in negative terms. Faith in the writings of Paul "is the spiritual principle whereby we go out of ourselves to hold communion with God and Christ."[3] In contrast, the epistle of Hebrews presents faith as being somehow in the shadow of the law. However, this is not necessarily a negative perception, because Jowett does emphasize that faith, even if it is in the shadow of the law, does not negate a moral and spiritual reality.[4]

Milligan argues that, as with other biblical texts, some have chosen to abuse the original message by using various verses to fit the ideology of their respective school of thought. The point he makes is not whether this reading into a text a meaning which it did not have is right or wrong, but that the fact these were used to such an extent, proves that the epistle was highly influential. This influence was first proven on a larger scale in the fourth century, when the church faced the issue of Arianism. The Christology of Hebrews played a crushing role in the trial of orthodoxy versus heresy. It formed the theological material which later was used as foundational apparatus of theological orientation. Back in the beginning, it was claimed to be written by Paul, and it was placed among his other writings. However, centuries later, notes Milligan, there was yet another surge of interest towards this epistle. This time it was the Socinian heresy that turned to Hebrews. The Socinians[5] referred to and interpreted the verses which depict Christ's high-priestly office as an argument against his death as an atoning sacrifice.[6] The value of Hebrews transcends the local temporal sphere of its time. It presents itself as a valuable resource for the ongoing debates in the fields of theology and the connected subjects.

This epistle has much material to pick from. Luther was interested in the Priesthood, namely the universal priesthood of all believers. Milligan points out that in spite of having had this epistle for almost two millennia, it still has much to teach the church. The doctrine of the priesthood has found

[1] George Milligan, *The Theology of the Epistle to the Hebrews: With a Critical Introduction* (Edinburgh: T&T Clark, 1899), 213, http://archive.org/details/theologyofepi-st100mill.

[2] Benjamin Jowett, *The Epistles of St. Paul to the Thessalonians, Galatians, Romans: With Critical Notes and Dissertations*, vol. 1 (London: Murray, 1859), 513, http://archive.org/details/epistlesofstpaul01joweuoft.

[3] Benjamin Jowett, *The Epistles of St. Paul to the Thessalonians, Galatians, Romans, with Critical Notes and Dissertations*, vol. 2 (London: Murray, 1859), 536, http://archive.org/details/epistlesofstpaul02jowe.

[4] Jowett, *The Epistles of St. Paul*, 2:536.

[5] Henry Bagshaw, *Diatribae; or, Discourses upon Select Texts: Wherein Several Weighty Truths Are Handled and Applyed against the Papist and the Socinian.* (London: R. Chiswell, 1680), http://archive.org/details/diatribaeordisco00bags; Charles Leslie, *The Socinian Controversy Discussed: Wherein the Chief of the Socinian Tracts Published of Late* (London: Strahan, 1708), http://archive.org/details/sociniancontrov00leslgoog; For more on early writings about Socinianism, see: Ralph Wardlaw, *Discourses on the Principal Points of the Socinian Controversy* (Andover, MA: Mark Newman, 1815), http://archive.org/details/discoursesonprin00wardrich.

[6] Milligan, *The Theology of the Epistle to the Hebrews*, 213.

various interpretations since the time of Luther, and also from the time of Milligan.[7] Westcott presents a view on the universal priesthood related to Melchizedek, not to Christ. He presents Melchizedek as a non-Jewish, universal priesthood representative. There was no recorded ancestry and no privileged line of descendants. There was, also, no connection to any fleshly descent, or any limitations of time. However, his priesthood was related to the kingly office. Westcott also presents the connection between the Abraham and the covenant, and argues that it the same connection between Melchizedek and his priesthood.[8]

The Epistle as a Mirror

After his very short presentation of the influence that Hebrews had for a couple of doctrines throughout church history, Milligan turns to the specific importance of the epistle for his own time. Of all the benefits, Milligan is well aware he can only choose a couple. Both of these are to be found in a then recent commentary on the epistle. His first remark is that the epistle is important because it is like a mirror to his own times. Regardless whether one lived during Milligan's time or before, the epistle offers insights into the everyday theological issues one might come across. Therefore, reading the epistle is useful because it molds on to the readers historical time frame. There are not only theological issues with which one might identify, but also daily issues that are of a more practical nature.[9] From theory to practice, the epistle offers a practical guide into the times it was written, and the issues with which the Jewish Christians were struggling back in their day might very well be issues for contemporary Christians as well.

One example of the complexity behind the epistle is found in Westcott's book on Hebrews, as he argues that the fullness of Christ's humanity or his triumphant humanity is not to be seen in his incarnation, but rather in his resurrection. The fullness of manhood is shown in the power that Christ had over death. There were no more earthly limitations for him. Humanity was fulfilled in his action of resurrection; thus Christ is the one who fulfils humanity's destiny, not humanity or an individual. At this moment, in the ongoing history of mankind, Christ is not bodily present, as he was during his earthly years. However, there will be a second coming and that is the event where Christ will be once more seen as triumphant (Acts 1:11).[10]

The epistle is not as simple as it might seem. There is hardly any proof that an ordinary believer will look at this writing in any other light, except as a simple epistle. However, Milligan quotes[11] Vaughan and points out that due to the complex writing style, coupled with the subjects that it addresses, it can easily be considered and epistle, a treatise, and a homily.[12] Milligan thus underlines the need each generation has to address the issues it faces, and the best way to do it is by finding valuable texts that can shed some light on the path of ethics and normality. One of the reasons the epistle is considered important is due to the emphasis it puts on the Old Testament. Milligan does mark that the reader will not find any information regarding the way the books of the Old Testament appeared, or when they were written. He believes that the author of the epistle might not have known anything about these issues. However, for the writer and the reader of the epistle the most important aspect is related to the spiritual use of the Old Testament, not the technical aspects.[13]

---

[7] Milligan, *The Theology of the Epistle to the Hebrews*, 213.

[8] Brooke Foss Westcott, *The Epistle to the Hebrews: The Greek Texts with Notes and Essays* (London: Macmillan, 1892), 123, http://archive.org/details/epistletohebrew00westgo-og.

[9] Milligan, *The Theology of the Epistle to the Hebrews*, 214.

[10] Brooke Foss Westcott, *The Epistle to the Hebrews*, 23.

[11] Milligan, *The Theology of the Epistle to the Hebrews*, 214.

[12] Charles John Vaughan, *The Epistle to the Hebrews* (London: Macmillan, 1890), xi, http://archive.org/details/epistleto hebrew00vauggoog.

[13] Milligan, *The Theology of the Epistle to the Hebrews*, 214.

A Meeting of Old and New

Milligan emphasizes the importance of the idea that the Old Testament books are the inspired word of God. This fact is underlined, he argues, to the fullest in Hebrews. The writers of the Old Testament are merely vessels of honour for God's direct action. He also mentions that there was a shift in the expressions used in Hebrews. He points out that the usual "God says" is now rendered "Christ says" or "The Holy Spirit says."[14] The importance of the Old Testament is seen vividly in what the author consider to be gradual and progressive revelation of God, not in particular bits of text, but in the entirety of what was later called the Old Testament. The culmination of the revelation, argues Milligan, was in Jesus Christ, the firstborn Son of God. The value of the Old Testament message is ever valid. It speaks today as it spoke back in that day. In other words, the Old Testament is the inspired word of God, that is living and active, regardless of the age in which it is read.[15]

There is a clear message regarding the Old Testament, but not necessarily found in Hebrews, rather in the entire New Testament, starting from the message of Jesus Christ, who unified its message.[16] The point is made even stronger when Edwards explains how the law was replaced by the Son. Therefore, there is no more need to fulfil the law, because it was already fulfilled perfectly by the Son. Instead, man will turn to Christ, and faith in him will replace the need for the law. This stands on the fact that the God of the New Testament is a Father. The relationship with his Son and humankind is of such depth that it sets up the perfect environment in which man can be liberated from under the burden of the law.[17]

As the ages passed, the interpretative key changed in various ways. Not understanding the context in which the texts were written plagued the conclusions and, ultimately, doctrine. This perilous and pernicious action finds its final expression in the thinking and the deeds of the people who accept these teachings. There are warnings about the method of interpretation and the way in which we must approach the epistle.[18] One severe problem, as Milligan points out, is forcing a different meaning into a text, than the original author intended. In spite of such dangers, Milligan underlines that the author of Hebrews does not fall into such a hermeneutical trap. He argues that he does not play a dangerous exegetical game. To the contrary, he uses the typical method of interpretation, not the allegorical. He does not look for some ancient stories, true, partly true, or false, in order to extract some moral or practical lessons. Instead, he considers the ideas he presents as being of a higher rank, than the institutions, the people, or the rites that have historical reality. The ideas he presents were not innovations or new designs, instead they had been used throughout the ages, and they find their completion only in the work of God.[19]

If the Old Testament is the type, then it follows that it is a mere shadow of what was to come, or what was to be fulfilled in Christ. The Old Testament is therefore imperfect and incomplete, by necessity, in order for the anti-typical element to be shown in its completeness and perfection. There is a pertinent place for the Old Testament in its use by modern Christians. It relates the various aspects of faith and it was understood in the past ages. The emphasis on faith, for example, is to be considered with great care, because the notion is also used in the New Testament.[20] The contrast is between the revelation of God and the final revelation of God, which is in Christ. This concept does not make the Old Testament obsolete or useless, instead it places it in a chronological and axiological hierarchy, with the Christ and the New Testament as the fulfilment of the old. However, Milligan make a

---

[14] Milligan, *The Theology of the Epistle to the Hebrews*, 214.
[15] Milligan, *The Theology of the Epistle to the Hebrews*, 215.
[16] Thomas Charles Edwards, *The Epistle to the Hebrews* (London: Hodder and Stoughton, 1914), 6, https://archive.org/stream/epistletohebrews00ewauoft#page/6/mode/-2up.
[17] Edwards, *The Epistle to the Hebrews*, 23.
[18] Alexander Nairne, *The Epistle to the Hebrews* (Cambridge: Cambridge University Press, 1922), xciv, http://archive.org/details/epistletohebrews00nairrich.
[19] Milligan, *The Theology of the Epistle to the Hebrews*, 215.
[20] Nairne, *The Epistle to the Hebrews*, cxxxv.

controversial methodological observation. He argues that in order to understand the type, or the Old Testament, one must focus on the complete and final fulfilment, which is Christ, and seek to understand the sacrificial system that preceded him.[21] This method is accepted in some Romanian Baptist churches, because it would seem to make more sense, than to consider the opposite way of approaching the two writings. There is a trend of looking back into the Old Testament from the perspective and development of the New Testament. The chronological method of study, namely understanding the Old Testament in its own creation and development, and the New Testament as natural continuation and fulfilment of the Old Testament, is often times neglected. However, if context is important, than chronology should be important too.

There is More to Christ than Meets the Eye

A crucial problem, which Milligan emphasizes, is the ascended and glorified Christ, as Person, not the idea or the concept or the myth of Jesus Christ. He returns to the writer of Hebrews, whom he believes concentrates of the glorified person of Christ, not his earthly time. In order to understand the heavenly Christ,[22] one must understand the earthly Jesus Christ. The author of Hebrews, argues Milligan, does not emphasize the supernatural elements of his earthly life, but merely speaks about his ministry in Palestine.[23] Milligan views the contrast between the earthly and the glorified Christ as fundamental for the understanding of his ministry in any age. He argues that the glorified Christ was the one who managed to change the entire world through the presentation of the gospel through the ministry of the believers. Christ is to be thought as belonging to the present, not as someone who was only in the past. This aspect creates a pressure on the way we, as present day believers, look at who Christ is and what he does, now, in the present age.[24]

He describes an idea that does not appear mentioned in the usual, ordinary church life, namely that the memory about Christ is transformed into faith, on account of the reality of Christ's ascension above time and space. Here he turns again to the idea of understanding the Old Testament through the fulfilment and finality of the New Testament. He applies this concept to the way the believers thought and believed in Christ. They looked back at who and what he did while on earth and because of his exalted person, those thoughts/memories turned into faith.[25] Milligan turns to the actions and the incarnate period of Christ's life and states that they must never be allowed to be the stopping point in one's enquiry on the person of Christ. He does admit that these actions and his incarnate period on Earth have had a toll and had given a permanent result on his person, yet they must be seen as an integral part of the process which turned Christ into the Saviour of man's soul. Even though theologians use technical terms as *saving faith*, this construct was not used by the authors of the New Testament.[26] The result of this process of perfecting is that once Christ has risen from the dead and ascended to the right hand of the Father, he became, ontologically, the Saviour of all humankind. Milligan argues that Christ could not claim such a status while on Earth or during all previous eras before his ascension. He could apply the full benefits of his atoning work only after the ascension event. This proves that the divine plan cannot be short-circuited, but it develops with precision and purpose. To prove his point, Milligan turns to the way the writer of Hebrews made reference to Psalm 102:27 in conjunction with Hebrews 1:12, as well as 13:8.[27]

---

[21] Milligan, *The Theology of the Epistle to the Hebrews*, 216.

[22] J. Edgar Goodspeed, *The Epistle to the Hebrews*, 55, http://archive.org/details/epistletohebrews00edgarich.

[23] Milligan, *The Theology of the Epistle to the Hebrews*, 217.

[24] Milligan, *The Theology of the Epistle to the Hebrews*, 218.

[25] Milligan, *The Theology of the Epistle to the Hebrews*, 219.

[26] Moses Stuart, *Commentary on the Epistle to the Hebrews* (Andover: W. F. Draper, 1854), 478, http://archive.org/details/commentaryonepis1854stua.

[27] Milligan, *The Theology of the Epistle to the Hebrews*, 219.

Milligan points out that the author of Hebrews describes and acknowledges Christ as the eternal and immutable HE. Ages did not change him, but in his being, Christ is the very same Second Person of the Trinity.[28] The important difference is that while on Earth, Christ presented the Father in a manner unknown before. His ministry was fulfilled after the ascension, but that shows that all human greatness is incomparable to the immortality of he who is the eternal and perfect high priest and Lord of life. All matters of life and death, as well as all matters that pertain to value, begins and ends with the person of Christ. Milligan tries to explain that once faith has gotten hold of one's mind, issues of value will have to be separated from the worthless ones.[29] Therefore, Christianity is not about mere faith, but also about living in accordance with values that mark the development of healthy relationships between people.

Christ or Sacraments?

The Sacraments have been an integral part of the Christian church since the beginning. They have been set on various theological foundations, which vary their potential. Milligan is looking at the writer of Hebrews and concludes that he never mentioned the Sacraments as such, but only alludes to them. The reason Milligan believes why this happened was not because the Sacraments were not important, or for fear that the Hebrew Christians might embellish them with a higher importance than they ought to have. The genuine problem was related to the fact that they might have considered the sacraments as various ritual elements that make up the foundation of faith. However, Milligan does not believe that author of Hebrews had any such fears. The person of Christ takes precedence to any other element in the Christian life; therefore the cultivation of a genuine relationship with him is paramount. Any other practice, ritual, or physical element is secondary to this purpose. Milligan argues that the author of Hebrews built the argument in Hebrews in such a way as to persuade the Hebrew Christian to follow a well-defined line of argumentation, and thus come to the understanding of the value of Christ for their lives. Only after he was convinced that this idea was properly explained did the author begin to allude in greater detail to these ordinances. The Sacraments have been integrated into the church/es and they are binding, even though the theologies that explain them are different. On this point, Milligan argues that when one wants to build a doctrine of the Sacraments, the fundamental element is the epistle, not the Jewish dispensation that only hints at these ordinances.[30]

The author of Hebrews writes his theology based on the fact that Christ has risen and he is involved actively in the lives of the believers and, thus, in the church. The emphasis of his argument does not lie with on the past actions of Christ, but on his active involvement in the lives of the believers in any age or time. The fullness of the relationship between Christ and his disciples, who live in any historical age, is based on the one atoning sacrifice of Christ. Milligan explains that the Semitic sacrifice, in its essence, was not about using death as an expiation method for sin, but a method of establishing communion between God and the believer or worshipper. The sacrifice was a participation in a common sacred life.[31] The solemnity of the event was explained not exclusively through death, but through the sacredness of life and the reality of a full communion between man and Creator. For Christ, the relationship between the fallen man and his Creator God is re-established through the perfect atoning death of Christ.[32]

Returning to the argument of the writer of Hebrews, Milligan points out that he does not mention the way the sacrifice works. However, there is an argument that refers to the nature of the one who brings the sacrifice. The author makes a connection between the Old Testament and the sacrifice of Christ, arguing that there is a connection, which has to do with the inner being of the one who brings the sacrifice. In the case of humans, it was necessary to repeat the offerings, due to the character of

---

[28] Harris Lachlan MacNeill, *The Christology of the Epistle to the Hebrews* (Chicago: University of Chicago Press, 1914), 98, http://archive.org/details/christologyepis00macngoog.

[29] Milligan, *The Theology of the Epistle to the Hebrews*, 219.

[30] Milligan, *The Theology of the Epistle to the Hebrews*, 220.

[31] See also MacNeill, *The Christology of the Epistle to the Hebrews*, 114.

[32] Milligan, *The Theology of the Epistle to the Hebrews*, 220–21.

man. Man sins repeatedly, thus one needs to bring an offering. The offering is not powerful enough, because it is also a created thing, thus inferior to God. In comparison to human beings, Christ is God, therefore superior to man. The nature of Christ is divine *and* human, thus he can atone with a power infinitely greater than that of man. In comparison, human nature is found wanting, while that of Christ is perfect. No matter what the level of holiness humans might have, the divine nature of Christ is revealed to the only one capable of atoning once and for all for humanity's sins.[33]

There is, however, a difference between the offerings in the Old Testament, the theoretical offering of the man himself and the offering of Christ on the Cross. Any sacrifice which had life would lose it and die when it was brought as an atoning offering. Christ's sacrifice was perfect and it moved into the realm of the spiritual.[34] A man will lose his own life if one brings oneself as a sacrifice. In spite of the fact that Christ died on the cross, he rose from the dead and the New Testament presents him as being alive and sitting at the right hand of God. The difference lies in the result. Any offering that comes from creation is an offering of death or in death, due to the fact that the actual offering loses its life. On the other hand, Christ's sacrifice is only apparently identical with that of a created being, but due to the resurrection it transforms the essence of the offering into one of life. Christ is an offering of life, capable of offering such life to those who have faith in him. This issue places Christ above creation as a creator/giver of life. The purpose of the resurrection was to offer life to man, as a result of becoming man.[35]

Willingness and Death: The Love Dilemma

The argument is taken one step further and Milligan presents the idea that it was not the death itself that was of value to God, nor was the offering of himself, but the free-will offering. It means that had Christ gone to death by force or by any other reason, his death would not have mattered. The only element which makes his death valuable and acceptable to God is his free-will act of accepting and presenting himself as willing to undergo the trial of the death on the cross. Christ accepted his death because of his love for mankind. Milligan concludes that God accepted both the will and the love of Christ. These two elements made the offering and death of Christ foundational elements in the work of salvation.[36] This was the aspect that referred to the relationship between God and Christ, regarding the Son's offering before the Father (Heb 10:8–9).

There is another side of the atonement relationship, but it refers to the connection between Christ and man. Milligan's first point is that we cannot look at Christ as a replacer, but rather as a representative. The proof Milligan brings is that both the Authorized and the Revised versions of the English translation of the Bible use "by" when it should read "in" in chapter 10, verse 10. Therefore, argues Milligan, Christ is our Representative[37] not *by* his will, but *in* his will. Even if the above argument presents spiritual realities, Milligan does mention the need to acknowledge the practical aspects of faith in Christ. In the life of the Christian, there is a radical shift for the source of one's life and provision for both earthly and spiritual life, namely the source of one's faith, the person of Jesus Christ. The fundamental switch is not in an abstract idea of Christ, or in his mere teachings. The change, the life and faith is in a living being, one who is both man and God. Since this God, argues Milligan, has passed through "change and death,"[38] he is qualified to stand before God as a representative for man. The difference between man and God is that Christ, as God and man, has gone through death triumphantly, while man can only die and has no inner power to intervene in his own death and resurrection. By becoming the representative of man, God became man and at the moment of his death he

[33] Milligan, *The Theology of the Epistle to the Hebrews*, 221.
[34] MacNeill, *The Christology of the Epistle to the Hebrews*, 47.
[35] Milligan, *The Theology of the Epistle to the Hebrews*, 221.
[36] Milligan, *The Theology of the Epistle to the Hebrews*, 221.
[37] E. C. Wickham, *The Epistle to the Hebrews, with Introduction and Notes* (London: Methuen, 1910), xxxiv, http://archive.org/details/cu3192402929-4745.
[38] Milligan, *The Theology of the Epistle to the Hebrews*, 222.

made the essential action, by which he returned to life.[39] This was and still is untenable for man, for which reason he requires the intervention of God. Christ's atoning sacrifice assures an everlasting entrance into the presence of God, which was, as noted, untenable for man.[40]

When Christ rose from the dead and offered faith to man, the latter realizes that with eternal life one is "already ideally invested with all spiritual and heavenly graces."[41] This ideal state is not without consequences. Man cannot simply be at the receiving end of these graces[42] and remain unmoved. In a most practical sense, the graces work in man, so that man might bring them to full realization. When Christ intervenes in man's spiritual existence, he brings about a change which is manifested in practical terms, or in one's everyday interactions with fellow men and with God. In this process, the graces are in his task "fully to realize."[43] Milligan does make a case in favor of following the example of Christ, but this can only be achieved by imitating through faith or as a result of one's conviction. He turns to Heb 2:10 underlining that imitating, even in faith, is done in an unpleasant and unattractive way, namely, through suffering and self-sacrifice. Milligan sees man's life in faith as a collaboration with Christ, by which he works one's salvation until the time of one's death. Works and faith go together, but the salvation Milligan is talking about is already secured by Christ through his sacrifice, even though man and Christ are united, they are one.[44]

Milligan returns to the argument regarding the sacrifice of Christ as primarily a liberator from the need of earthly sacrifices, as those from the Old Testament, and presents his act as a "supreme example."[45] Even if his argument removes a fundamental idea, which is much heavier in meaning than the mere example theory, he argues that in an ongoing collaboration with God until one's death, man, now being in the full graces of Christ, will receive a cleansing from the false perception about works, and one will also receive the active involvement of God (Heb 9:14).[46]

The arguments presented afore do not avoid the connection between faith and practice. They are complementary and can only go together. Faith has an intrinsic connection to immortality, as well as the practical aspects of life.[47] Milligan believes that the author of Hebrews was convinced of the same connection. However, he does not mention faith and practice, but rather doctrine and practice. The author of Hebrews is named as being both visionary and the most practical of all New Testament writers. Milligan points out that the use of the emphatic *therefore* argues in favour of uniting doctrine/teaching with works. As the author of Hebrews wrote that if God has showed man what entering in his rest means, together with a series of blessings (4:1; 4:16; 10:19, 22), *therefore* the believer should draw near Christ in full assurance of faith. The drawing near takes place also by practice,[48] namely uniting what one believes with what one does. Being in constant interaction with other people, as well as with God, the believer cannot remain without works or praxis.[49]

---

[39] Milligan, *The Theology of the Epistle to the Hebrews*, 222.
[40] Frederic William Farrar, *The Epistle of Paul the Apostle to the Hebrews* (Cambridge: Cambridge University Press, 1893), 111, http://archive.org/details/epistlepaulapos02farrgoog.
[41] Milligan, *The Theology of the Epistle to the Hebrews*, 222.
[42] Henry Wilkinson Williams, *An Exposition of the Epistle to the Hebrews*, 188, http://archive.org/details/ anexpositionepi03unkngoog.
[43] Milligan, *The Theology of the Epistle to the Hebrews*, 223.
[44] Milligan, *The Theology of the Epistle to the Hebrews*, 223.
[45] Milligan, *The Theology of the Epistle to the Hebrews*, 223.
[46] Milligan, *The Theology of the Epistle to the Hebrews*, 223.
[47] August Tholuck, James Hamilton, and J. E. Ryland, *A Commentary on the Epistle to the Hebrews* (Edinburgh: T&T Clark, 1842), 94, http://archi-ve.org/details/acommentaryonep2rylagoog.
[48] Johannes Heinrich August Ebrard and John Fulton, *Biblical Commentary on the Epistle to the Hebrews* (Edinburgh: T&T Clark; 1853), 105, http://archive.org/details/-biblicalcomment00ebragoog.
[49] Milligan, *The Theology of the Epistle to the Hebrews*, 224.

Conclusions

Milligan presumes that the author of Hebrews believes that the Jewish Christians to whom he writes have already slipped into a different theological perspective than the one he refers to. The reason for their fall is a wrong interpretation of the Christian message. The efforts of the writer of Hebrews are oriented towards properly explaining who Christ truly is and what he has done. Milligan assumes that only a correct understanding of Christ will enable those who slipped into heresy or who are about to do so, to turn back to the correct path.[50]

Milligan's conclusion is addressed to the church of his time. He believes that the church can "rise to the full conception of her Divine Head and Lord"[51] only by understanding both the human activity and the spiritual reality of Jesus Christ. His human activity is important on the one hand, and it has a specific meaning in a set context, but his glorified status as the "apostle and high-priest" of the church's confession and identity, means that it is the only way it can accomplish and fulfil the divine calling.[52] Regardless of the age, the church needs to return to the basics of Scripture, as found in both Old and New Testaments. The specific issues with which the church deals in every age lay a heavy burden on the clergy and the ministry. There is no time of peace. The church will interact with society constantly, mainly because the believers do not separate from the world, but live in it. The scriptures and the church, together with the believers, are in a constant dialogue. The purpose is simple: find biblical teachings that will show the world, without a shadow of a doubt, that God is love, that he is just, and that he is worth at least one's attentions.

Being involved in the world takes a toll on the individual believer, as well as on the church. The reason the author of Hebrews argues in favour of Christ is because the believers he was writing to were wondering whether Christ was really whom they thought he was. The same dilemma is present in modern day churches. People will ask who is Christ and why should they believe. It is up to the church members to present valuable ideas which prove consistency and weight. Superficial arguments are worthless and do no justice either to God or to the believers. Hebrews is an excellent presentation of arguments in favour of Christ and his humanity, as well as his divinity. It acts as a catalogue of arguments that aim at strengthening one's faith, as well as offering a valuable insight into the Christian mind and faith.

Bibliography

Bagshaw, Henry. *Diatribae; Or, Discourses upon Select Texts: Wherein Several Weighty Truths Are Handled and Applyed against the Papist and the Socinian.* London: Chiswell, 1680. http://archive.org/details/diatribaeordisco00bags.

Brooke Foss Westcott. *The Epistle to the Hebrews: The Greek Texts with Notes and Essays.* London: Macmillan, 1892. http://archive.org/details/epistletohebrew00westgoog.

Charles John Vaughan. *The Epistle to the Hebrews.* London: Macmillan, 1890. http://archive.org/details/epistletohebrew00vauggoog.

Ebrard, Johannes Heinrich August, and John Fulton. *Biblical Commentary on the Epistle to the Hebrews.* Edinburgh: T&T Clark, 1853. http://archive.org/details/biblicalcomment00ebragoog.

Edwards, Thomas Charles. *The Epistle to the Hebrews.* London: Hodder and Stoughton, 1914. https://archive.org/stream/epistletohebrews00edwauoft-#page/6/mode/2up.

---

[50] Milligan, *The Theology of the Epistle to the Hebrews,* 224.
[51] Milligan, *The Theology of the Epistle to the Hebrews,* 224.
[52] Milligan, *The Theology of the Epistle to the Hebrews,* 224.

Farrar, Frederic William. *The Epistle of Paul the Apostle to the Hebrews*. Cambridge: Cambridge University Press, 1893. http://archive.org/details/epistlepaulapos02farrgoog.

Goodspeed, J. Edgar. *The Epistle to the Hebrews*. http://archive.org/details/ epistletohebrews00edga rich.

Jowett, Benjamin. *The Epistles of St. Paul to the Thessalonians, Galatians, Romans: With Critical Notes and Dissertations*. Vol. 1. London : Murray, 1859. http://archive.org/details/epistlesofstpaul 01joweuoft.

———. *The Epistles of St. Paul to the Thessalonians, Galatians, Romans, with Critical Notes and Dissertations*. Vol. 2. London, Murray, 1859. http://archive.org/details/epistlesofstpaul02jowe.

Leslie, Charles. *The Socinian Controversy Discuss'd: Wherein the Chief of the Socinian Tracts Publish'd of Late*. London: Strahan, 1708. http://archive.org/details/sociniancontrov00leslgoog.

MacNeill, Harris Lachlan. *The Christology of the Epistle to the Hebrews*. Chicago: University of Chicago Press, 1914. http://archive.org/details/christologyepis00macngoog.

Milligan, George. *The Theology of the Epistle to the Hebrews: With a Critical Introduction*. Edinburgh: T&T Clark, 1899. http://archive.org/details/theologyofepistl00mill.

Nairne, Alexander. *The Epistle to the Hebrews*. Cambridge: Cambridge University Press, 1922. http://archive.org/details/epistletohebrews00nairrich.

Stuart, Moses. *Commentary on the Epistle to the Hebrews*. Andover : Draper, 1854. http://archive. org/details/commentaryonepis1854stua.

Tholuck, August, James Hamilton, and J. E. Ryland. A Commentary on the Epistle to the Hebrews. Edinburgh: T&T Clark, 1842. http://archive.org/details/acommentaryonep02rylagoog.

Wardlaw, Ralph. *Discourses on the Principal Points of the Socinian Controversy*. Andover, MA: Mark Newman, 1815. http://archive.org/details/discoursesonprin00wardrich.

Wickham, E. C. T*he Epistle to the Hebrews, with Introduction and Notes*. London: Methuen, 1910. http://archive.org/details/cu-31924029294745.

Williams, Henry Wilkinson. *An Exposition of the Epistle to the Hebrews*. http://archive.org/de tails/anexpositionepi03unkngoog.

METANOIA IN HEBREWS: EXEGETICAL INSIGHTS

OVIDIU HANC[*]

Emanuel University of Oradea

ABSTRACT: The term *metanoia* appears three times in Hebrews (6:1; 6:6 and 12:17), interestingly with a negative approach in each instance, as a warning against turning away from the Redeemer, not as an exhortation of turning to the Redeemer (cf. Heb 12:25). In Heb 6:1, the author exhorts the audience to continue to grow in faith, otherwise the continual preoccupation with fundamental beliefs will turn vital elements into trivial ones. If a Christian is constantly preoccupied with foundational aspects of the faith (e.g. *metanoia*), that becomes a sign not of his desire to be firm in faith, but a sign of immaturity. Following this exhortation, in Heb 6.6, the repentance is a kind of repentance that does not reflect salvation, but a religious non-salvific experience of God's working power. Similar to those at Kadesh Barnea and similar to thorns and thistles that experience rain from heaven, those described in Heb 6 were informed by God's Spirit, but not transformed by him. Regarding Heb 12:17, the text describes the concept of *changing the mind* with reference to Isaac not Esau. Thus, the passage does not describe the impossibility of repentance of an apostate believer, but warns about God's immutable decision regarding those that live in willful ignorance of divine grace. The author of Hebrews is very emphatic when it comes to the notion of repentance and attaches it to the notion of perseverance. Perseverance becomes a *sine qua non* feature of repentance. The people at Kadesh Barnea, like the ones described in Heb 6, and like Esau's experience in Heb 12, are the type of people that have experienced God's power, but have ignored his redemptive power, and because of this ignorance, repentance becomes an impossible experience.

KEY WORDS: metanoia, repentance, spiritual maturity, regret.

Introduction

The term *metanoia* appears three times in Heb (6:1; 6:6 and 12:17), interestingly in a negative approach in each instance. Similarly, ἀποστρέφω another cognate words that refers to action similar to repentance, appears in its negative form as well, as a warning against turning away from the Redeemer, not as an exhortation of turning to the Redeemer (Heb 12:25).

Apparently, Hebrews seems to challenge the concept of *eternal security*, a theological perspective of salvation in which once the believer is saved, he is considered saved for eternity. Since salvation is one of the most important dogmas in Christian theology, the debate whether salvation can be lost or not is of vital importance. This paper seeks to analyze the term μετάνοια and the way this theological concept integrates within the larger framework of the epistle.

Definition and the Usage of the Term

The noun μετάνοια expresses the idea of regret or repentance from a corrupt spiritual and moral state of being. Although the Greek usage of the term implies a changing of mind/thinking, the term should not to be regarded in an anachronistic psychological sense as a mere intellectual phenomenon. While the modern psychological dichotomy sees the mind as the locus of our intellectual faculty, the ancient understanding of the mind implies a holistic approach in which the mind and the heart represents one's spiritual entity taken as a whole. The term μετάνοια is linguistically a construction of two terms νοῦς – denoting not only intellect but also the spiritual, moral and emotional nature and μετά – denoting change of direction. The term appears 56 times in the New Testament and represents a piv-

---

[*] OVIDIU HANC PhD, MPhil, Queen's University, Belfast, BD Emanuel University of Oradea. Dr. Ovidiu Hanc currently lectures on the New Testament in Emanuel University of Oradea.

otal theological concept in the preaching of John the Baptist (Matt 3:7–10; Luke 3:7–9), Jesus (Matt 4:17; Mark 1:15; Luke 15) and the Early Church.[1]

Howard correctly noted that the term *repentance* is an inadequate translation of *metanoia*, since the Greek term implies far more than a feeling of penitence or contrition; however it is the best that can be used.[2] The term implies a twofold response, namely a complete *turning to God* but also a complete *turning from sin*. While the analysis of the relation between the two aspects and the sequentially of these two actions is beyond the scope of this paper, it is important to note that the epistle to Hebrews uses the term in a way that emphasizes repentance as foundational (6:1) and irreversible (6:6). The term is also used once in reference to Esau who sought for his father's change of mind, but without success (12:17). The verbal form μετανοέω does not appear in the epistle.

There are several other terms that describe the concept of repentance and the action associated to this concept (i.e. regret, transform, turn, remorse, change). One important cognate word that denotes repentance and/or regret is μεταμέλομαι. This word is found only six times in NT (Matt 21:29, 32; 27:3; 2 Cor 7:8 and Heb 7:21) and refers to an attitude of remorse toward sin but does not have soteriological implications.[3] This attitude of remorse is not necessarily describing a turning point toward salvation (e.g. Judas repented in the sense of remorse not salvation – Matt 27:3). The occurrence in Heb 7:21, is a quote from Ps 110:4 and denotes divine immutability regarding the Messianic priestly order. Like in the other New Testament occurrences, in Heb 7:21 the term μεταμέλομαι does not refer to the status of changing the heart toward salvation, but emphasizes God's unchanging character in the sense that he does not "feel sorry" for the covenant that he had established.

Another important cognate words that refers to action similar to repentance is ἀποστρέφω (Heb 12:25). The regular usage of the term in New Testament is that of the returning of the people from sin to God through faith (Acts 3:26; Rom 11:26 quoting Isa 59:20), but in Heb 12:25 refers to the opposite action of returning from God to sin through ignorance.[4]

The term ὑποστρέφω appears once in Heb 7:1 referring to the fact the God will not change his mind, while μεταμορφόω (to be changed in form, to be transformed in Matt 17:2; Mark 9:2; Rom 12:2; 2 Cor 3:18) or στρέφω (to turn, to change) do not occur in the book of Hebrews (see also the constructions that use the same root: e.g. ἀποστρέφω – to return, overturn; ἀποστρέφω – to turn away; ἐπιστρέφω – to convert, turn to; μεταστρέφω – to turn, change).

The purpose of this paper is to evaluate the usages of the term *metanoia* in Hebrews from an exegetical approach. This paper does not intend to reconcile the historical controversy of Calvinists and Armenians, but to give some exegetical insights on the texts, looking at the term *metanoia* and at the way this concept is used in the epistle.

The Foundation of Repentance: A Sign of Firmness or Immaturity? (Heb 6:1)

Chapter 6 can be divided as follows: vv. 1–3 are about sanctification; vv. 4–9 are about salvation; and vv. 10–12 are about inheritance. The author of the epistle to Hebrews challenges his readers to leave the elementary doctrine of Christ and go on to maturity, not laying again the foundation of repentance from dead works and of faith toward God.

---

[1] William Walden Howard, "Is Faith Enough to Save? Part 3," *Bibliotheca Sacra* 99, no. 393 (1942): 97. The Old Testament equivalent for this term is *shûb* and *nāḥam*. See Robert N. Wilkin, "Repentance and Salvation. Part 2: The Doctrine of Repentance in the Old Testament," *Journal of the Grace Evangelical Society* 2, no. 1 (1989): 13–26.

[2] Howard, "Is Faith Enough to Save? Part 3," 95.

[3] O. Michel, "Μεταμέλομαί Ἀμεταμέλητος," Page 589 in Gerhard Kittel, Geoffrey William Bromiley, and Gerhard Friedrich, eds., *Theological Dictionary of the New Testament*, 4 (Grand Rapids: Eerdmans, 1976).

[4] This nuance is present also in Paul's writings (i.e. 2 Tim 4:4; Tit 1:14).

It is important to note that all the verbs (ἀφίημι and καταβάλλω) have a plural form. The author includes himself in this exhortation in which the believers are required to stop gravitating around the elementary truths of the Christian faith. Out of this exhortation it is important to infer a vital truth: repentance is presented as foundational in the process of sanctification. However, the author highlights that the repentance from dead works and of faith toward God, although it is vital, it should not become trivial.

The consequences of spiritual immaturity are presented at length in the larger context. From 5:11 to 6:20, the author explains that this immature state of faith leads to dullness of hearing (5:11), and a return to the infantile condition (5:12). It is important to note that this infantile condition is not due to the milk that is used. The infants need milk in order to grow. If a baby is not growing it is not because the milk is not nourishing enough, but because the baby does not take enough nourishment from the milk in order to grow. If an adult consumes only milk, the problem is not that the milk is not appropriate but is not sufficient and hence it becomes futile. The verb γυμναζω of 5:14 attests the importance of practice that leads to maturity. However, the concern to lay down again the foundation of repentance becomes a sign not of firmness but immaturity.

Furthermore, the danger of immaturity is not that the body becomes stagnant, but atrophied. The urgency of pressing on beyond this fundamental state and grow in maturity is due to the danger of becoming dull of hearing. In a similar way, because of hardness of heart (3:7–19), Israel lost the grace of entering God's rest (4:1–13).

This aspect is described in v. 3 where it is said that the key of advancing in faith is subject to God's work. Apparently, the text seems problematic. The believer is admonished for not growing in faith, but afterwards it is said that the growing in faith is possible if God permits. This verse triggers one important question, namely what is the believer's role in maturity if maturity is an act of divine intervention?

Trying to answer this question, we are led back to the controversy between Augustine and Pelagius. While Augustine considered that the man in not capable of living a moral life, being totally dependent upon the grace of God, Pelagius, looking at the virtuous living of pagans, considered that the man, through the power of his will is capable of living a moral life. The anthropology and soteriology of Hebrews seems to fit the Augustinian categories, rather than pelagian or semi-pelagian ones because the author presents the realization of maturity in the believer's life as God's work (v. 3), while the failure to reach maturity as the guilt of the believer. If the believer gets to maturity, it is because of God, while if the believer remains immature the fault lies with him. This aspect is presented throughout the epistle (e.g. the optative aorist of 13:21: καταρτίσαι, *equip* yourself with everything good that you may do his will). A relevant example of such an instance is that of medicine that heals the body. If a sick person takes some medicine and is healed, his health is due to the medicine. However if a sick person does not take the medicine and dies, he himself is responsible.

The theology of the book of Hebrews integrates very well in the broader theological framework of the Scriptures. In Isa 65:1 God declares that he was ready to be sought by those who did not ask for him; he was ready to be found by those who did not seek him. In Jer 30:21 God asks a rhetorical question: *Who would dare of himself to approach me?* In the New Testament Paul expands in details this notion in Romans 8–11. He underlined Isaiah's boldness regarding the fact that God was found by those who did not seek him. In this way God's will does not nullify our will but governs the process of our maturity. Our will is subject to God's will in repentance and is opposed to God's will in rebellion.

One question that arises here is whether is there a possibility in which the believer might want to grow toward maturity but God not want it? There are instances in the New Testament in which a man does not want to know God, and God allows him to do his will (e.g. Rom 1:28), however later in 12:16–17 the author presents an instance in which God is not willing to change his mind (μετανοίας) in spite of someone's desire. This instance is going to be analyzed later on in this paper. However, at this point, it is important to note that the expression "dead works" (νεκρὰ ἔργα) appears only in this verse and in 9:14. Westcott correctly mentioned that the writer of the epistle is thinking of all the works corresponding to the Levitical system not in their original institution but in their actual relation to the gospel.[5] Thus, the repentance from *dead works* implies the fact that salvation is not obtained by works,[6] however, once the salvation is accomplished, *good works* follow naturally (Heb 6:9). The author of the epistle takes this notion even further not only by going from the concept of "dead works" to "good/mature works," but also by noting that the concept of "good/mature works" follows salvation naturally and necessarily.

Repentance: Between Eternal Salvation and Eternal Condemnation (Heb 6:6)

The following passage in which the term *metanoia* appears is Heb 6.6. This passage is generally regarded as one of the most controversial passages in the epistle, and seems to present a situation in which repentance is impossible. This much debated passage gave rise to a palette of theological paradigms. The main interpretations can be divided into two categories with subsequent possibilities, namely the text refers either to a Christian apostate or to a religious apostate/reprobate unbeliever.[7]

The first interpretation is that in which a believer becomes an apostate and as a consequence it is impossible for such a person to be restored again in repentance since he is crucifying once again the Son of God.[8] The Christian apostate can be one that had lost his salvation, or a Christian apostate that had lost his reward or, a third possibility is that in which the text refers to a Christian believer in a hypothetical apostasy.[9] Compton performed a succinct analysis of each major view with their strong arguments but also their liabilities.[10]

The passage has a strong adjective in v. 4 (ἀδύνατος) and describes a reality in which someone has been: enlightened; tasted the heavenly gift; shared in the Holy Spirit and tasted the goodness of the word of God and the powers of the age to come. The spiritual experiences that are described in vv. 4–5 are indeed impressive; however they are not describing necessarily a conversion experience. Because of this, another possible interpretation is that in which the person in view is that of a religious apostate or a false believer. It is possible for someone to be enlightened (cf. John 1:9), without walking afterwards in the light at all costs (the same verb φωτίζω appears later on in the epistle in Heb 10:32). It is possible for someone to taste the heavenly gift, without feeding himself on a regular basis (cf. Heb 5:13). It is possible for someone to have shared in the Holy Spirit, since there are aspects which Holy Spirit shares with the world (cf. John 16:8–11), however association does not imply necessarily a relation (the adjective μέτοχος in the epistle denotes companion, i.e. Heb 1:9; 3:14; 12:8). It is possible for someone to have tasted the goodness of the word of God (cf. Heb 1:2) and the powers of the age to come,[11] without being converted. According to this interpretation, the text does not say that God does not forgive a person that does not repent, but rather that there are moments in which a person cannot repent anymore. Since faith is a concept that does not have all the time

---

[5] Brooke Foss Westcott, *The Epistle to the Hebrews: The Greek Texts with Notes and Essays*, 3rd ed. (London: Macmillan, 1920), 146.

[6] The concept of "salvation" (σωτηρία) is presented in the book as something that is inherited not merited (e.g. 1:14; 2:3; 2:10; 5:9; 6:9; 9:28). See also Robert N. Wilkin, "Repentance and Salvation. Part 5: New Testament Repentance: Repentance in the Epistles and Revelation," *Journal of the Grace Evangelical Society* 3, no. 2 (1989): 23.

[7] John Calvin, *Institutes of the Christian Religion*, trans. Henry Beveridge, 1845, 3.3.21.

[8] Adam Clarke, *The Holy Bible Containing the Old and New Testaments*, vol. 6 (Nashville: Abingdon, n.d.), 725.

[9] Albert Barnes, *Barnes' Notes on the Bible*, ed. Robert Frew, vol. 13 (Grand Rapids: Baker, 1998), 130.

[10] R. Bruce Compton, "Persevering and Falling Away: A Re-examination of Hebrews 6:4–6," *Detroit Baptist Seminary Journal* 1, no. 1 (1996): 136–45. See also Rodney J. Decker, "The Warning of Hebrews Six," *Journal of Ministry and Theology* 5, no. 2 (1996): 26–48.

[11] The expression δυνάμεις τε μέλλοντος αἰῶνος refers to the messianic age that was inaugurated; cf. Heb 1.2 – the last days are inaugurated; Heb 2:4 – the power of the Holy Spirit is available.

salvific features (e.g. Jas 2:14–20), similarly there are instances in which the concept of repentance does not have necessarily soteriological connotations.[12]

Andy Woods, in a thoughtful proposal, considers that the paradigm of Kadesh Barnea represents the solution to the problem of Heb 6:4–6. According to him, if the Exodus generation was regenerated, believing, and redeemed prior to the events of Kadesh Barnea and its disobedience introduced an irreversible forfeiture of blessings, then, those addressed in Hebrews 6 were also regenerated and on the verge of irreversibly forfeiting blessings.[13]

Woods interpretation falls into the trap of informal fallacy called *secundum quid*, in which he performs a faulty generalization without considering all the variables. To describe the entire Exodus generation as a regenerated, justified and believing one is a gross generalization. Secondly, to reconstruct the "Hall of Faith" by including Moses as a type of regeneration and hence to extrapolate this example to the whole Exodus generation is to create an unbiblical community of faith. To argue that since Moses was saved without entering Canaan as a proof that all those who exited Egypt were saved, is an erroneous reconstruction of the soteriological dimension of the Exodus paradigm. Besides many stipulations in the Levitical covenant concerning offerings for one's personal sin (e.g. Lev 5:7, 11, 15; 6:6, 24:15; Num 9:13), it is important to differentiate between one's rebellion against God and one's personal sin (cf. the request of the daughters of Zelophehad in Num 27:3).

Themes of guidance, redemption, renewal, and inheritance are presented in the Bible as a metanarrative in which the corporate dimension of the believers echoes the experience of the people of God through the desert; however, the corporate aspect of the covenant does not nullify the individual responsibility. The exodus community form together a corporate covenantal reality; however this does not exclude the existence of individuals that are not part of the community of faith. Numbers 11:4 attests this aspect that the mere presence of various individuals or groups, in the midst of the people of God, does not confer the identity of the people of God. This element of physically belonging to the people of God without being in reality part of this community of faith is implied in the preaching of John the Baptist (e.g. Matt 3:9; Luke. 3:8) and Jesus himself (*e.g.* Matt 8:11–12; Luke 13:28; John 8:33–44). Although the verbs of Heb 6 have a plural form, the author addresses in a collective way a group of individual sinful people.

Many scholars argue that the Exodus event becomes a paradigm of salvation, the "New Exodus" being a major theme in both Old and New Testament.[14] However, it is fallacious to extrapolate this paradigm and apply it to all the subsequent events that took place. Taken individually, the exodus experience is not necessarily an experience of faith for every participant. Thus, the issue in Kadesh Barnea is not of a saved generation that falls into unbelief, but of those that were physically delivered out of the bondage without understanding the implications of this freedom. Similarly, in Heb 6, the

---

[12] There are texts in the New Testament where repentance is used to describe a person that is not saved (e.g. Acts 11:8; 2 Cor 7:10). See also Compton, "Persevering and Falling Away: A Re-examination of Hebrews 6:4–6," 159.

[13] Andy M. Woods, "The Paradigm of Kadesh Barnea as a Solution to the Problem of Hebrews 6:4–6," *Chafer Theological Seminary Journal* 12, no. 1 (2006): 44–70.

[14] E.g. Bernard W. Anderson, "Exodus Typology in Second Isaiah," in *Israel's Prophetic Heritage: Essays in Honor of James Muilenburg*, ed. Bernard W. Anderson and Walter Harrleson (Portland, OR: Wipf & Stock, 2010), 177–95; Robin E. Nixon, *The Exodus in the New Testament* (London: Tyndale, 1963); W. D. Davies, "Paul and the New Exodus," in *The Quest for Context and Meaning: Studies in Biblical Intertextuality in Honor of James A. Sanders*, ed. Craig A. Evans and Shemaryahu Talmon (Leiden: Brill, 1997); Sylvia C. Keesmaat, *Paul and His Story: (Re)Interpreting the Exodus Tradition* (Sheffield: Sheffield Academic Press, 1999); N. T. Wright, "New Exodus, New Inheritance: The Narrative Substructure of Romans 3–8," in *Romans and the People of God*, ed. Sven Soderlund and N. T. Wright (Grand Rapids: Eerdmans, 1999); Rikki E. Watts, *Isaiah's New Exodus in Mark* (Grand Rapids: Baker Academic, 1997); David W. Pao, *Acts and the Isaianic New Exodus*, Biblical Studies Series (Tübingen: Mohr Siebeck, 2000); Gary Yates, "New Exodus and No Exodus in Jeremiah 26–45: Promise and Warning to the Exiles in Babylon," *Tyndale Bulletin* 57, no. 1 (2006): 1–22; Matthew Thiessen, "Hebrews and the End of the Exodus," *Novum Testamentum* 49, no. 4 (2007): 353–69; Rodrigo J. Morales, *The Spirit and the Restoration of Israel: New Exodus and New Creation Motifs in Galatians* (Tübingen: Mohr Siebeck, 2010); Tom Holland, *Contours of Pauline Theology: A Radical New Survey of the Influences on Paul's Biblical Writings* (Geanies House: Christian Focus, 2010).

issue is not about saved Christians but of unchanged religious persons. The impossibility of *metanoia* in Heb 6 refers to these religious persons that were nearly saved, but have ignored all the benefits of divine work in their life prior to salvation. Lane correctly noted that stylistically, the aorist participle "fall away" (παραπεσόντας) stands out in contrast to the previous four and indicates a decisive moment of commitment to apostasy.[15] To ignore this divine intervention and to continue a lifestyle that is not consistent with salvation makes repentance impossible.

Although Woods correctly argued for interpreting Heb 6:4–6 not in isolation from the preceding context of Heb 3–4, he made the same error interpreting the passage in isolation from the succeeding context. It is true that in order to perform a valid interpretation, we should be very sensitive to the context of the passage, but not only what comes before the passage but what comes after the passage as well. The immediate context clarifies the passage in a powerful way. Verses 7–8 are illustrating and clarifying the previous verses.[16] The image that is used is that the land that drinks the rain and produces/gives birth to (τίκτω) vegetation (βοτάνη) is blessed, while if it bears or carries (ἐκφέρω) thorns (ἄκανθα) and thistles (τρίβολος) it is cursed and burned.

The example follows the same line of argument as the first part of the chapter. The heavenly gifts (e.g. light, Holy Spirit, rain) should produce new life, however there are situations in which these gifts, even though they are poured out of heaven, the outcome of these blessings is useless. The rain can pour out of heaven constantly, it will not give life to thorns and thistles. Similarly, the heavenly blessings can be poured out upon a religious man, without him being transformed.

The text presents two radically different entities: live vegetation and dead thorns. The two natures of these elements have ontological distinction. The first has life, while the other is dead; in the meantime both are receiving the same rain from heaven.

The context does not present a plant that was watered and produced fruit and afterwards changed its nature and started to produce thorns. The passage presents two different entities in nature and outcome. The same lifeless reality is presented in the concept hardening of the heart (3:8, 13, 15; 4:7: μὴ σκληρύνητε τὰς καρδίας). The apostasy in Hebrews refers not to those that have been transformed by the Holy Spirit and returned to the previous state, but to those that have been informed by the Holy Spirit and remained in their present condition.

Those that have been enlightened, tasted the heavenly gift, shared in the Holy Spirit, and tasted the goodness of the word of God and the powers of the age to come are like those that have seen God's mighty hand in the ten plagues, have eaten the paschal lamb, have crossed the Red Sea, have received the law at God's mountain, have been led by the pillar of cloud and fire, have eaten manna, have drink from the rock, but have hardened their heard, and they died in the dried wilderness.

This interpretation is validated by the exhortation of v. 9. "Though we speak in this way, yet in your case, beloved, we feel sure of better things: things that belong to salvation." The expression "things that belong to salvation" (καὶ ἐχόμενα σωτηρίας) indicate that salvation produces and bears fruit that is evidenced in the work, the love and the serving of the saints (vv. 9–10).

The theology of the book of Hebrews reverberates with the theology of the apostle Paul (e.g. Rom. 8:29–39; Eph 4:30; Phil 1:6); apostle Peter (1 Pet 1:3–5); and apostle John (John 10:27–28; 1 John 2:19).

---

[15] William L. Lane, *Hebrews 1–8*, Word Biblical Commentary 47a (Dallas: Word, 2002), 142.

[16] Paul Ellingworth, *The Epistle to the Hebrews*, The New International Greek Testament Commentary (Grand Rapids: Eerdmans, 1993), 325.

Hebrews 12:17 – God and Repentance

The third place in which the term *metanoia* is found in the book of Hebrews is in 12:17. The immediate context of Heb 12:17 refers to the immorality of Esau, who sold his birthright for a meal. When Esau realized that his twin brother stole his blessing, he pleaded before his father for him to change his mind, but without result.

The term *metanoia* refers to the state of changing one's mind. It is important to note that a careful analysis of the text attests that the passage does not describe Esau's change of mind as some scholars affirm,[17] but refers to Isaac. Thus, the repentance that is presented in chapter 12 is not ascribed to the believer but describes God. As Esau has sold his firstborn right, later on, when his brother took his blessing, he desired to change the mind *of his father*, but he was unable, even thou he sought for it with tears. Therefore the aim of this comparison is to present the fact that as Isaac was not able to change his mind concerning the blessing that he had declared; similarly God will not change his mind (cf. 7:1) to give a second chance to those that neglect the first one.[18]

Jacob understood the spiritual value of the birthright and its blessings and did everything possible to achieve it, even if it implied deceiving. Esau did not understand the spiritual value of the birthright and its blessings and was ignorant about such realities. At the end, when he realized the importance of it, it was too late.

This admonition is a follow-up of the teaching presented before v. 12. The connecting conjunction Διὸ that initiates this paragraph forces us to look more careful to the previous exhortation in order to understand the nature of the later admonition. The author tries to make the readers aware of the fact that Christian living implies determination in spite of discipline (vv. 5–11) and hardships (vv. 12–15). Esau has failed exactly in the lack of determination in the face of problems, and his lack of determination caused his father to refuse to change the blessing. The last part of this chapter (vv. 18–29) functions as a parenetic midrash and reinforces the exhortation not to be ignorant of the inheritance that is available to everyone. As Esau had lost his chance because of his wilful ignorance, and as the generation at Mount Sinai rejected God that spoke from heaven (vv. 18–25), the believers are challenged to persevere and not to be ignorant of the heavenly inheritance that was given to them.

This pericope is a warning not to become like Esau, a serious warning to everyone regarding the ignorance of spiritual elements (see also 12:25). Thus, Heb 12:17 describes the fact that God does not change his mind (*metanoia*) regarding those that have disregarded the first opportunity.

This theological aspect is presented both in the Old Testament (Mal 1:2–3) and New Testament (Rom 9:10–14). Esau's example attests that at the spiritual level, the wilful ignorance of the divine gifts makes later attempts of repentance objectively impossible. Similarly, earlier in the epistle, the author clarified the fact that the nature of apostasy that he has in view is not a passive ignorance of salvation, but a deliberate act of sinning (10.26: ἑκουσίως).

Conclusion

Repentance (*metanoia*) and its diverse derivatives imply a complete changing of the mind. This change of mind is twofold in the sense of a *turning to God* but also a *turning from sin*, and is presented in Hebrews in a unique approach. In Heb 6:1, the author uses the term, admitting that this is fundamental for the Christian faith. However, he exhorts the audience to continue to grow in faith, otherwise the continual preoccupation with things that are fundamental will turn vital elements in

---

[17] Spiros Zodhiates, ed., *The Complete Word Study Dictionary: New Testament* (Chattanooga: AMG, 1994), 971.

[18] Harold W. Attridge and Koester Helmut, *Hebrews: A Commentary on the Epistle to the Hebrews*, Hermeneia (Philadelphia: Fortress Press, 1989), 370.

trivial ones. If a Christian is constantly preoccupied with foundational aspects of the faith (e.g. *metanoia*), that becomes a sign not of his desire to be firm in faith, but a sign of immaturity.

Following this exhortation, the author explains that the danger of ignoring the divine intervention in someone's life will lead to eternal condemnation, without the possibility of repentance (Heb 6:6). Thus, the repentance that is described in this passage is a kind of repentance that does not reflect salvation, but a religious non-salvific experience of God's working power. Similar to those at Kadesh Barnea and similar to thorns and thistles that experience rain from heaven, those described in Heb 6 were informed by God's Spirit, but not transformed by him.

The third passage in which the term *metanoia* appears is Heb 12:17. This text was generally interpreted by the scholars as describing Esau's impossibility to repent. However, a closer look at the text attests the fact that the text describes the concept of *changing the mind* with reference to Isaac not Esau. Thus, it is incorrect to argue using this passage for the impossibility of repentance for an apostate believer, since the texts does not describe such an instance, but warns about God's immutable decision regarding those that live in wilful ignorance of divine grace.

Looking at these instances it must be noted that the author of Hebrews is very emphatic when it comes to the notion of repentance and attaches it to the notion of perseverance.

Perseverance becomes a *sine qua non* feature of repentance, since apostasy after an initial experience of God's divine work makes repentance virtually impossible. The people at Kadesh Barnea described in Heb 3, like the ones described in Heb 6, and like Esau described in Heb 12, are the type of people that have experienced God's power, but they have ignored his redemptive power, and because of this ignorance, repentance becomes an impossible experience.

Bibliography

Anderson, Bernard W. "Exodus Typology in Second Isaiah." Pages 177–95 in *Israel's Prophetic Heritage: Essays in Honor of James Muilenburg*. Edited by Bernard W. Anderson and Walter Harrleson. Portland, OR: Wipf & Stock, 2010.

Attridge, Harold W., and Koester Helmut. *Hebrews: A Commentary on the Epistle to the Hebrews*. Hermeneia. Philadelphia: Fortress Press, 1989.

Barnes, Albert. *Barnes" Notes on the Bible*. Edited by Robert Frew. Vol. 13. 14 vols. Grand Rapids: Baker, 1998.

Calvin, John. *Institutes of the Christian Religion*. Translated by Henry Beveridge, 1845.

Clarke, Adam. *The Holy Bible Containing the Old and New Testaments*. Vol. 6. Nashville: Abingdon, n.d.

Compton, R. Bruce. "Persevering and Falling Away: A Reexamination of Hebrews 6:4–6." *Detroit Baptist Seminary Journal* 1, no. 1 (1996).

Davies, W. D. "Paul and the New Exodus." In *The Quest for Context and Meaning: Studies in Biblical Intertextuality in Honor of James A. Sanders*. Edited by Craig A. Evans and Shemaryahu Talmon. Leiden: Brill, 1997.

Decker, Rodney J. "The Warning of Hebrews Six." *Journal of Ministry and Theology* 5, no. 2 (1996).

Ellingworth, Paul. *The Epistle to the Hebrews*. The New International Greek Testament Commentary. Grand Rapids: Eerdmans, 1993.

Holland, Tom. *Contours of Pauline Theology: A Radical New Survey of the Influences on Paul's Biblical Writings*. Fearn: Christian Focus, 2010.

Howard, William Walden. "Is Faith Enough to Save? Part 3." *Bibliotheca Sacra* 99, no. 393 (1942).

Keesmaat, Sylvia C. *Paul and His Story: (Re)Interpreting the Exodus Tradition*. Sheffield: Sheffield Academic Press, 1999.

Lane, William L. *Hebrews 1–8*. Word Biblical Commentary 47a. Dallas: Word, 2002.

Michel, O. "Metamélomai, Ametamélētos." Edited by Gerhard Kittel, Geoffrey William Bromiley, and Gerhard Friedrich. *Theological Dictionary of the New Testament*. 4. Grand Rapids: Eerdmans, 1976.

Morales, Rodrigo J. *The Spirit and the Restoration of Israel: New Exodus and New Creation Motifs in Galatians*. Tübingen: Mohr Siebeck, 2010.

Nixon, Robin E. *The Exodus in the New Testament*. London: Tyndale Press, 1963.

Pao, David W. *Acts and the Isaianic New Exodus*. Biblical Studies Series. Tübingen: Mohr Siebeck, 2000.

Thiessen, Matthew. "Hebrews and the End of the Exodus." *Novum Testamentum* 49, no. 4 (2007): 353–69.

Watts, Rikki E. *Isaiah's New Exodus in Mark*. Grand Rapids: Baker Academic, 1997.

Westcott, Brooke Foss. *The Epistle to the Hebrews: The Greek Texts with Notes and Essays*. 3d ed. London: Macmillan, 1920.

Wilkin, Robert N. "Repentance and Salvation. Part 2: The Doctrine of Repentance in the Old Testament." *Journal of the Grace Evangelical Society* 2, no. 1 (1989).

_____. "Repentance and Salvation. Part 5: New Testament Repentance: Repentance in the Epistles and Revelation." *Journal of the Grace Evangelical Society* 3, no. 2 (1989).

Woods, Andy M. "The Paradigm of Kadesh Barnea as a Solution to the Problem of Hebrews 6:4–6." *Chafer Theological Seminary Journal* 12, no. 1 (2006).

Wright, N. T. "New Exodus, New Inheritance: The Narrative Substructure of Romans 3–8." In *Romans and the People of God*. Edited by Sven Soderlund and N. T. Wright. Grand Rapids: Eerdmans, 1999.

Yates, Gary. "New Exodus and No Exodus in Jeremiah 26–45: Promise and Warning to the Exiles in Babylon." *Tyndale Bulletin* 57, no. 1 (2006): 1–22.

Zodhiates, Spiros, ed. *The Complete Word Study Dictionary: New Testament*. Chattanooga: AMG, 1994.